Master Betrayal
The Conspiracy to Kill Jane Bashara

ANDREW MORLAN

Acknowledgments

This is the true tale of the Jane Bashara murder-for-hire conspiracy and trial. It is the result of painstaking research and is told from the perspective of those who lived it. Except where noted, all information presented is the product of actual courtroom proceedings, first-hand interviews and realtime media reports.

The impetus of this account was an unlikely conversation in a Puerto Rican bar in old town San Juan in February 2012 when a chance meeting of Detroiters spawned the question: "What's the latest in the Bashara case ...?" What remains is a tragedy worthy of Shakespeare.

My sincere appreciation to George Hunter, Kathy Ryan, Michael Narduzzi and Colin Paolo for their individual contributions and insight. Additionally, to the many others who graciously sat for interviews or otherwise helped push this work to completion.

Also, to my lovely wife for her continued support and patience throughout this seemingly endless project.

CONTENTS

"We do not live an equal life, but one of contrasts and patchwork; now a little joy, then a sorrow, now a sin, then a generous or brave action."

—*Ralph Waldo Emerson*

Introduction...

January 25, 2012

The scene was an alley where Pinewood and Annott Streets intersect in northeast Detroit. The crime was initially believed to be a simple carjacking, an infraction so common as to be routine. But this one was different ...

The vehicle was a black luxury SUV, a *Mercedes* that stuck out like a sore thumb in this vast wasteland, one of countless forsaken parcels of Detroit – a city still gasping for breath after four lost decades caused by *White Flight*, the economic crisis of 2009, and ultimately the largest municipal bankruptcy in American history.

The body was crumpled on the floor. She was white, appeared to be in her mid 50's and dressed in an odd fusion of indoor and outdoor clothing – sweat pants, house shoes and a black down *North Face* jacket – awkwardly shoved on her backwards – it was clearly an afterthought.

Eight hours earlier Jane Bashara, a Grosse Pointe marketing executive and mother of two, was reported missing by her husband Robert, a well known businessman active in the local Rotary club and the owner of an assortment of real estate properties in the surrounding areas.

The Basharas were recognized throughout the community for their fund raising acumen and easygoing friendliness. Robert, or Bob as he preferred to be called, was also known by some as *The Mayor of Middlesex*, an alter ego steeped in hubris, a reflection of the couple's social standing and upscale residence on the fashionable Middlesex Road in Grosse Pointe Park, Michigan.

The grisly discovery, which riveted the tranquil Grosse Pointe community for months, set in motion a tawdry tale that drove a wedge among friends and neighbors and eventually, irretrievably, obliterated a once proud and prosperous family.

Chapter 1

Middlesex

Jane had that rare ability to make people feel they were the center of her world. She'd do anything for anyone and people just plain liked her. "The salt of the earth," was how Jim Wilson described her, one of hundreds who passed through her life.

"When she asked you how your children were, she wanted the 20 minute version," insisted George Sirdenis, a neighbor who's son went to school with Jane's children. "She was heads above in terms of smarts, business sense – everything."

"Beginning when she was five Jane had to be the top of the heap," beamed Lorraine Englebrecht, Jane's mother. "She always wanted to be the leader – she was a born leader."

John Englebrecht (a Korean War Vet) and Lorraine (Naeyaert) were married two years before Jane, their first child, was born on June 22, 1955, the same year as John's discharge. As this new life allowed for more domestication, soon the family expanded to include Janet, John and eventually Julie.

The Englebrechts were a tight knit, typical midwestern middle-class family, living in the small town of Mt. Clemens, Michigan. Originally established by Christian Clemens, the settlement was built to support his distillery near the end of the 18th Century and, by the end of the Civil War when the public library opened, the population swelled past 1,500 (on it's way to just over 20,000 around the time of Jane's birth).

The Englebrecht's home was the one on the block where all the kids wanted to be, where they felt comfortable to be themselves and could expect to find a ready supply of cookies, popcorn and soft drinks.

Growing up Jane was particularly close to her sister Janet, who was only a year behind. "Jane and Janet were tied together," explained Lorraine. "Whatever Jane did, Janet followed." They were good kids, the kind no one ever had problems with. For several years both girls worked at *Miller Brothers Creamery*, a Mt. Clemens institution dating back to the 1920's. "It seems like my kids were always busy," continued Lorraine. "If I wasn't taking one, I was picking up the other one."

Jane quickly developed a voracious appetite for life and a desire to be involved in everything. She was active in *Girl Scouts* and throughout her school years she established herself both academically and in various sports.

"Volleyball was her game," Lorraine said proudly. "She was always a big tennis player too," both of which she pursued beyond her years in school.

As Jane entered her teens the Englebrecht's obtained a cottage in Lewiston, just a stone's throw from Gaylord in northern lower Michigan. Lewiston offered little for teenagers but Jane and her siblings passed the time swimming and water skiing on the Twin Lakes as often as possible.

Jane met her most trusted friend, Patti Matthews, at *Mt. Clemens High School* around 1970. The two were inseparable and remained close throughout their lives. According to a school yearbook, Jane was involved in a number of extra curricular activities including the *French Club, National Honor Society* and the girl's tennis and volleyball teams. She graduated with honors in 1973 before heading north to Mt. Pleasant to attend *Central Michigan University* where she joined the *Alpha Sigma Tau* sorority midway through her freshman year.

In her second year Jane chose to major in business and moved into the *Alpha Sigma Tau* house. Her sister Janet followed, first to *Central Michigan* and then into *Alpha Sigma Tau* as well. According to Lorraine Jane was almost a second mother to Janet despite their minimal age difference. In fact, as Jane ascended into adulthood she became the glue that bound the Englebrecht's together. "Every one of us depended on her," Lorraine said with a sigh.

Jane graduated in 1977 with a BA in Business and Marketing and her first big break came only two weeks later. With the help of a sorority friend she found her way into an internship at *Detroit Edison*, the largest regional power company. *Edison* was in the beginning phase of implementing Affirmative Action policies which made Jane not merely qualified, but also quite attractive to the company. In short order the internship evolved into a full time position and Jane glided with ease into the next phase of her life in the company's new marketing department.

From the beginning Jane's eyes were set on the future. "She started a 401(k) right out of college," recalled Patti Matthews. "She was the type that didn't want to touch it, ever, until she retired."

Jane's lifelong dream was to attend *Harvard Law School*. "A *Harvard* attorney would be the top of the deck," she told anyone who would listen. But despite plenty of encouragement, in a rare show of capitulation she settled for an MBA at the *University of Detroit Mercy*, a decision she deeply regretted. *Detroit Edison*, she explained, kept her far too busy for that kind of commitment.

By mid 1983 Jane accumulated a significant list of accomplishments in her six years at *Detroit Edison*. But as she pushed towards 30 she was keenly aware of her single status, a perceived deficiency she was eager to remedy.

§

Robert Michael Bashara was born December 12, 1957, the son of the Hon. George Bashara, Jr. and Nancy Brinker, who were married earlier the same year. Before too long they added a second child, a daughter named Laura.

Nancy was the daughter of Harold and Grace Brinker, a wealthy and socially connected family in Grosse Pointe, the most prestigious of Detroit's suburbs. Harold made his fortune through a financial firm known as the *Grosse Pointe Research Corporation*, which he established in 1937. It wasn't lost on George, Jr. that the Brinker's social connections and wealth could prove advantageous to his budding legal career.

George Bashara was born the son of Lebanese immigrants in Detroit in 1934. He earned a degree in art from the *University of Michigan* before entering law school at the *Detroit College of Law*, fully bankrolled by the Brinker fortune. Like his father before him George became a widely successful attorney and in the mid

1960s they partnered in the downtown firm *Bashara and Bashara* before George established himself as a prominent Grosse Pointe attorney in his own right.

In the late 1960s George's career quickly took flight, first becoming chairman of the Appeals Board of the *Michigan Employment Security Commission* before his appointment to Probate Court by then-Governor William Milliken. He quickly won election to presiding judge where he became well known for a program that welcomed middle school students into his courtroom on 'Drug Day,' which was geared toward exposing the negative affects of narcotics. The highlight was a tour of the Wayne County Jail. In 1972, at age 38, George became the youngest judge to sit on the bench of the Michigan Court of Appeals.

George and Nancy divorced in 1978, followed two years later by George's second marriage to a secretary in his law firm named Suzanne. He died in 2002.

§

In the early 1960s the Bashara's purchased a home in Grosse Pointe Woods and soon became frequent travelers during young Bob's formative years. According to Bob, the Bashara's occasionally lived beyond their means, a fact he met with approval, saying it afforded him and his sister anything they could possibly want.

Although he didn't really possess the necessary physique, nor the motivation for success, Bob took up sports and achieved modest success in *Little League Baseball*.

This tender young age is when Bob, along with his best friend Bill, claimed to have experienced elements of what he would later recognize as *The Lifestyle*.

"At my house we had a third floor ... with a large room, a bathroom and an attic storage area," Bashara remembered. "One time we were up there I found a magazine about rope bondage. Little did I know this would instill latent curiosity ... Bill and I read it often."

"I found some clothes line," continued Bashara. "We stripped to our underwear. Bill laid on the bench and I bound him tight. We did that for an hour and laughed at our new found adventure ... I enjoyed binding him and had thoughts of doing that to the girls that I knew."

The story goes that Bashara and Bill never spoke of the experience, nor to each other again.

§

Under the auspices of George and Nancy, the Bashara household was strict and proper; breaking protocol would surely garner a strict reprimand or worse. An incident near the end of his days in elementary school, when Bashara allegedly lit his grandmother's mattress on fire, landed him in military school at *Howe Academy* near South Bend, Indiana. It is at *Howe* that urban legends surrounding the antics of Bob Bashara began to emerge. One story alleges that he encountered his first sexual experience when an office secretary seduced and taught him a few things that, up 'till then, he'd only dreamed about.

§

After completing eighth grade Bashara left *Howe* for good in 1973. He enrolled at *Grosse Pointe North High School* in the fall and immediately took up football, dated frequently and gained enough popularity to be elected class president his sophomore and junior years.

While in high school Bashara realized his ambition to become a businessman and he purchased real estate in the form of a small red brick ranch located on Cadieux Rd. in Detroit. The purchase was strictly an investment, a small rental costing him only $1,000. But the experience was infectious and Bashara went on to accumulate several more properties over the next few years.

After graduation in 1976, Bashara headed off to *Albion College*, 50 miles south of Lansing, Michigan. Despite an unremarkable career there, he met Pricilla Langs, whose father was coincidentally also a Grosse Pointe lawyer. The two hit it off immediately and dated throughout their school years and beyond, eventually tying the knot shortly after Langs graduated in July 1981. They were young – he was 23, she 21 – and the union lasted but a single year.

Bachelor life seemed to suit Bashara and the next three years saw him leaping headfirst into the world of business. In late 1983, with his father's financial support, he purchased a restaurant known as the *Wooden Nickel*, or more accurately, a franchise of the original *Wooden Nickel*, which he opened in Grosse Pointe Woods.

Shortly thereafter the father and son team of George and Bob Bashara purchased a strip of properties on Mack Ave. along the Grosse Pointe Park border with Detroit which would soon house *Tom's Oyster Bar*, a popular Grosse Pointe restaurant.

In the mid 1980s Bashara joined the *Rotary Club of Grosse Pointe*, a civic minded group charged with enhancing living environments and relieving poverty. Although initially not particularly active, in later years Bashara steadily increased his involvement, feeding his desire to be seen as a community leader and philanthropist.

§

A party hosted by Patti Matthews in 1983 was the first time Jane Englebrecht laid eyes on Bob Bashara. Despite being two years his senior, Jane thought he was dashing and (as a business owner) he presented himself quite the eligible bachelor. Besides, he was from a Grosse Pointe family with a pedigree, a fact that was instantly appealing to her.

"Bob was a handsome Grosse Pointer," remembered Lorraine, adding that Jane quickly made an impression on Bob's father George.

Bob later described Jane as outgoing and a go-getter. "She was very loving and kind and I was attracted to her right from the beginning," he told Dennis Murphy of *NBC's Dateline*. "We clicked pretty much right away and within two years I asked her to marry me."

The wedding was held on April 26, 1985 at *St. Michael's Church* in Grosse Pointe Woods. Jane's sister Janet was matron of honor and younger sister Julie and Patti Matthews served as bridesmaids. After a quick honeymoon skirting the Mexican Pacific shoreline, the couple set up shop in a St. Clair Shores duplex. Jane got busy advancing her *Edison* career and Bob managed a growing empire of business and rental properties, supplemented by a part time position selling industrial cleaning products for *United Laboratories*.

The Basharas were a busy couple, and Jane was anything but a typical homemaker, always preferring career over mundane household chores. "From the day they got married, Jane never cleaned her house or washed a window," Lorraine boasted, "and Bob never cut grass or cleaned gutters."

Jane wasn't too fond of cooking either, but Bob dabbled in the kitchen and on the grill, specializing in pasta and grilled meat. Once it was affordable they added a housekeeper for the rest.

Three years later, in 1988, the Basharas purchased a 2,500 square foot home on the fashionable Middlesex Rd. in Grosse Pointe Park, known for its large stately homes and spacious grassy median. As if the home wasn't big enough, Bob quickly arranged to build a three season addition overlooking the expansive back yard.

Middlesex was well known for its colorful residents such as the Corrados and Toccos, families long associated with the Detroit mafia, and several older homes are rumored to be connected by escape tunnels, a relic of the Prohibition era. In 2002 *Pulitzer Prize*-winning novelist Jeffry Eugenides published *Middlesex*, named for the street of his youth.

Before long the Basharas had two children: Robert in late 1988, and Jessica, who followed four years later. Bob became increasingly involved in the neighborhood by organizing the annual block party when he'd set up his grill on the median. Eventually his neighbors dubbed him *The Mayor of Middlesex*, a moniker he wore with pride. He was also known for his vanity license plate, a gift from his mother that read *Big Bob*, a clear indication of self-importance and ego.

Steadfast in their determination to climb the Grosse Pointe social ladder, the Basharas began a steady investment in the community. Recognized often for their organizational talent, willingness to volunteer and fund raising skills, they were often called upon to lend a helping hand.

§

Business connections at *Edison* soon led to Jane's developing taste for golf, a sport long known to her husband, who for years knocked around the links with his father. This shared pastime encouraged the Basharas to seek membership in the prestigious and private *Lochmoor Club* in Grosse Pointe Woods, widely recognized as a stepping stone for those pursuing social standing in the Pointes. Bob became increasingly active, golfing three times a week was routine, mixing business and pleasure and still finding time for nine holes with Jane during the summer months. Eventually, he even became president of the Tuesday night golf league.

During this period Bob watched his real-estate acquisitions grow into a sizable empire. One substantial addition came by way of a partnership with local real estate businessmen Jim Saros (who took to calling Bob Barney Rubble after the *Flintstones* character) and Jim McCuish, another golfing friend from *Lochmoor*. The trio purchased a 40-unit complex on Jefferson Ave. in St. Clair Shores eventually known as *Lakeview Apartments*. But soon after McCuish pulled out and Saros walked away, leaving Bashara the sole owner.

§

In 1994 the Bashara's home life hit a rough patch. Jane was involved in a violent auto crash resulting in the loss of four teeth and rendering her unable to eat solid food for months. As a result, improving her smile became an obsession of Jane's for the rest of her life.

"Like any marriage, you have your ups and downs," Bob later told *WDIV (NBC)* reporter Marc Santia. It is rare, however, for troubled times to be as self-inflicted as the storm brewing on Middlesex.

As Jane's relationship with her sister Janet remained close the families spent a great deal of time together. But an incident in 1995 caused an irreparable rift. Following a typical evening at the Bashara's home, Janet's five-year-old daughter reported that on two occasions Bob had caused her to touch his genitals – once while wrestling in his bed, and once while she was being spanked. She even claimed that Bob once tried to convince her that she enjoyed spanking.

On August 1 local police opened an investigation, led by Detective David Hiller of the Grosse Pointe Park police department, which resulted in a threat by Wayne County prosecutors of a charge of second-degree criminal sexual conduct.

"Bob's dad called me, called Janet, called Mark," remembered Lorraine. (Mark Gottsleben was husband to Janet at the time). "He told me Bob could get 15 years."

During the investigation Bob passed two polygraph tests and many years later, under oath, he described the incident:

> "We wrestled on our bed on a number of occasions … It was like king of the hill, and I would get on the bed and put a cover over me and the kids would jump on me and attack me, and I would throw them off the bed, in a nice way. We put pillows on the outside, so when they fell they wouldn't fall on the floor. But my daughter, my son and (niece), we all did this at the same time together … But several times the kids walked in while I was changing and I was naked."

Obviously scandalized, the Englebrechts were caught in a tough spot: what would Jane do if Bob was prosecuted? What would happen to their granddaughter? From that point on, however, one thing was certain: Mark forever hated Bob and Janet became outspoken in her determination that Jane should divorce; and for a time Lorraine felt she had to choose between her daughters.

"Janet wouldn't speak to Jane or Bob," Lorraine said, putting it mildly. "She wouldn't go anywhere Bob would be, like Christmas or family reunions."

Eventually, Janet and Jane mended their relationship, but never again would Janet so much as speak to Bob Bashara. To this day the Englebrechts maintain that George, Jr. used his influence with Wayne County prosecutors and successfully persuaded the Gottslebens against prosecution on the grounds that it would do irreparable harm to the family. Ultimately, charges were not pressed, and life, for Bob at least, returned to normal. But perhaps more importantly, the incident became the first of many red flags for Jane.

§

In the years following her divorce from George, Nancy Bashara's parents died, leaving her the Brinker fortune, which was believed to be several million dollars. She shared a fairly close relationship with Jane and Bob and before long she was doling out $10 thousand annually to each family member. She also foot the bill for several family vacations, usually to exotic destinations such as Cancun and Jamaica. She also occasionally picked up the tab for a quick weekend getaway in Las Vegas with Bob and his sister Laura.

Jane continued to emerge as a fixture in Grosse Pointe, central to her family and friends, a born leader, a confidant and general all around fixer. Her children and family always came first, and the Bashara's home, at 552 Middlesex, was always full of young people, just like the Englebrecht's Mt. Clemens home many years before.

As the children grew older, the Basharas geared their community involvement toward their interests. Bob became active as a *Boy Scout* leader and coached *Little League* where he gained a reputation for being a bit hardcore. One such occasion came during a grueling game played in pouring rain and 40 degree temperatures. Bashara refused to call the game as his team was still behind: "One more inning," he bellowed, "one more inning!"

One baseball season the Basharas were asked to raise funds and organize the league's concession stand behind *Defer* School. Legend has it that food items and even cash occasionally went missing, but no one was ever able to put their finger on where it went.

Robert and Jessica Bashara attended *Trombly Elementary School*, just two blocks down Middlesex. The Bashara's connection to the school ran deep as both Jane and Bob were involved in the PTO, of which Bob eventually became president. One year he was pressed into service by the principal to lead the school Halloween parade in her stead and soon their connection became social as Bob used his membership at *Lochmoor* to sponsor her wedding reception there. A short time later the very same principal bestowed upon Bob the symbolic title *The Mayor of Trombly* and asked him to assume responsibility for organizing the school's 70th Anniversary banquet, which incidentally was to be held at the *Lochmoor Club* in 1997. In 2000 the Grosse Pointe public school district bestowed upon the Basharas its *Golden Apple Award* for their assistance in planning, organizing and soliciting donations, as well as for rounding up volunteers to help the school auction raise $39,000, which they accomplished in a single evening.

Incredibly, *Trombly* is where another urban legend emerges involving Bob Bashara. Allegedly in the mid 1990s a BDSM-styled sex dungeon (bondage, dominance and sadomasochism) was discovered in the basement of the school, conceived by a school custodian and frequented by an office secretary. Although the names of the school's principal and Bashara's were invariably linked, their capacity, and the veracity of the legend itself, remains elusive.

§

Pushing past 40 in the late 1990s, Bob Bashara began to experience symptoms of erectile dysfunction. He is diabetic and has a history of weight problems, both of which are common factors of ED.

Jane, too, experienced issues associated with aging. Most prevalent was an increased sensitivity to normal menopausal symptoms such as night sweats and hot flashes. These issues, coupled with Jane's injuries from her car accident, became major factors in the slow decline of the Bashara's physical relationship, which was eventually rendered nonexistent.

§

In the first few months of 2000 Jane took on a position managing *Edison's* 350-person call center while, at the same time, Bob became increasingly more involved in online gambling, an activity he attributes to his accidental discovery of BDSM related pornography websites.

> "I didn't just seek *'The Lifestyle'* out ... I like to gamble and I went on the Internet to a site called betus.com ... There are popups, and on that site specifically, popups would come on that deal with adult websites. One of them was alt.com, the other was collarme.com. I looked up what it was about and I found it was rather intriguing."

The Lifestyle, as it is sometimes referred, is a polite reference to BDSM (bondage, dominance and sadomasochism) which is often described as a variety of erotic practices or roleplaying, something in which Jane repeatedly expressed no interest whatsoever.

"She described it as weird sex," Bob explained later. "She knew that I viewed pornography on the Internet, but it wasn't like I was a regular ... I am a very outgoing, dominant person (and) it intrigued me for two reasons ... One, because I never was familiar with *The Lifestyle*; and two, because the more I got into it, I would read of women who were submissive, who were seeking a dominant or a master."

(Within BDSM culture, participants usually fall into one of two persuasions: Dominant, known as a Master or Dom; and submissive, often referred to as

slaves. The designation determines the role each would assume in the relationship and/or during BDSM 'play').

"I got into *The Lifestyle* by talking to people," explained Bashara. "I got into it and I started learning and I went to events around town."

These events, known as 'munches', are a sort of informational social gathering for people involved in or interested in learning about BDSM. But as Bashara's viewing and enthusiasm grew, he became increasingly reckless, frequently using the family computer which was located in a common space in the house.

"I found him on pornographic web sites," lamented Jessica. "It upset me a lot, because I was in the same room when it happened."

"Jane was livid and the kids were very upset with him," remembered Patti Matthews.

"Bob has no boundaries," Jane routinely complained to Matthews. His 'weird pornography' viewing continually upset the whole family. Eventually, he took it a step further and hacked into his children's eMail, posing as them while exchanging messages with other *Lifestyle* enthusiasts.

§

Jim Wilson and Bob Bashara met for the first time on the links at *Lochmoor* in the spring of 2000. Wilson was a frequent golfing partner of Bashara's father George, so he introduced himself to Bob and the two instantly hit it off, often partnering during the time Bashara served as president of the Tuesday night men's league. Years later Wilson said the men's league provided much more than just a friendly game, it was the perfect cover for their mutual interest in illegal narcotics, particularly cocaine, which they often ingested on the back nine.

"We would smoke marijuana or do cocaine out on the course ... Just the two of us," Wilson recalled. "It was safer to do it on the golf course than in the clubhouse ... but we never did it around our families."

§

Although he'd been dallying in extramarital affairs for some time, since his discovery of *alt.com* Bashara had been on the lookout for someone he could 'help' and in 2005 he found her in a woman named Venita Porter, with whom he finally began to push further beyond the confines of his domestic life.

Porter was in her early 40s, petite and not unattractive, and perhaps most important, interested in pursuing the life of a submissive within *The Lifestyle*. At the time she was working in the front office of a Grosse Pointe construction company and after a brief period of online communication they decided to meet at a Southgate *Red Robin* near her home.

"She was married and her husband was also in *The Lifestyle*," explained Bashara. "He had his own submissive and she was free to do what she wanted. She taught me a lot because she was in it for years."

"He said he'd been a good man and father for years," recalled Porter, "and that he and Jane were not getting along ... They didn't want the same future, and although he was not free to do what he wanted completely in the open, they had an arrangement, they were planing a divorce when the kids were out of school."

Soon Bashara and Porter became practically inseparable. Oddly, although seemingly unaware of the nature of the relationship, Jane and the rest of the family appear to have been frequently in her presence:

> "I went to church with Jane and Bob every Sunday," Porter said.
> "I went to Rotary with Bob. I went to community projects. I
> went to movies with him and his mother. I went to dinner with
> Rob when he was home from college and Bob at Dylan's. I went
> to volleyball games at Grosse Pointe South to see Jessica play. I
> attended and helped with his birthday party with Jane and
> Jessica ... I was involved in quite a bit of his life."

As Bashara's enthusiasm for *The Lifestyle* intensified he came to the conclusion that he needed his very own BDSM-styled sex dungeon. The opportunity presented itself during a period of remodeling at the *Hard Luck Lounge*, a bar located within his Mack Ave. business property.

Taking the first step, Bashara had the basement partitioned into two separate spaces. "The *Hard Luck* had one basement and the second door was the entrance into Bob's basement," described Porter, who helped in the construction. She painted the interior and then transported the bed, strapped precariously to the top of her car.

"When you came into the basement, first you saw a storage area, then you went through a second door," described Porter, picturing in her mind the dank, musty and windowless fifteen by fifteen foot space.

At various places throughout the room were floor and ceiling hooks used for submissive bindings. On the right hand wall a TV was mounted next to a cabinet with rope and candles. "I kept everything he had kind of in cupboards and put away," explained Porter.

On the left side wall as you entered the room was a medieval candle holder sitting next to a bed with a mirror affixed to the ceiling above it. The other wall sported a mounted dagger sword.

"There were some S&M toys and things in there," added Porter, describing a peculiar looking sex machine on the floor and a rope spider web, another device used as a frame upon which to bind a submissive.

> "When I would get together with Bob … it would be more like a scene that we'd go into … a little spanking and then, with his inability and his impotence, a little head," recounted Porter. "There were a few occasions where it got a little crazier and when we were playing he choked me … I would get very dizzy and unconscious. I didn't particularly like it, and I would mention being uncomfortable. He would back off, that wouldn't happen for months until I'd be a little more comfortable, and then surprise! it would happen again … it was not something I asked for."

In an odd twist, Porter and Bashara began attending church together, but the nature of their interaction was completely misunderstood. Other than Bob, the family always sat together, but Jane's mother Lorraine made the observation that Bob was nearly always late and drove his own car. He explained it away as necessary due to possible emergencies at his rental properties. But then bizarre behavior would ensue:

"He'd leave, then he'd come back and then he'd leave again," explained Lorraine. "I'd whisper to Jane, 'Where's he going?'" Jane always dismissed it with the same line, that he must have left for his rentals.

"But ten minutes later he's in the aisle, going to communion," protested Lorraine. "He didn't have time to go to his rentals and get back to church for communion." Then she noticed he was in the back of the sanctuary with an unfamiliar woman whom she later learned was Venita Porter.

"I asked him about Venita," Lorraine said skeptically. "He said he was helping her because she needed a church … He was in the back row with her," Lorraine said, shaking her head in disgust. "We didn't know her."

But Porter's presence didn't remain unknown for long. Robert (son) remembered her as "a lady we knew through church … We met her before, but very briefly."

At Christmastime Porter gave Bob a gift, one received freely in the open. "It was a shirt and pair of pants," recalled Robert. "It was unusual because it was a gift from someone I didn't know very well, and it was odd, she knew his size."

Porter continued to insert herself into Bashara's world, intermingling with several of his friends from *Rotary* and *Lochmoor*. One in particular was Jim Wilson, Bashara's friend from the back nine.

"We got together a few times … At one point we went to his house," Porter explained, remembering the Wilson's stately Grosse Pointe home. On another occasion Bashara invited them to tag along to a party at the downtown *Leeland Hotel*.

Porter recalled occasionally meeting Wilson and Bashara at the *Hard Luck Lounge*. "They liked to drink, and Jim seemed to have access to cocaine," continued Porter. "I went to the restroom while they were doing those things, and I came back and saw residue … The only time I ever saw Bob around cocaine was when Jim was around."

Wilson's life was soon to take a negative turn and as a result he came to the conclusion it was time to stop doing drugs. "It was affecting my life very negatively … The economic downturn had a very traumatic effect on my business," Wilson explained, referring to 2009. "I went bankrupt." He also suffered a divorce and crucially, his son was imprisoned.

"It was a big wakeup call, and I changed my life."

Wilson's hardship appeared to have temporarily strengthened his friendship with Bashara. "He was always someone I could rely on for a positive word," remembered Wilson. "I would just tell Bob I couldn't believe all this was happening at the same time and he would say 'hang in there, you know, you're a smart guy and you're gonna bounce back.'"

§

As the Bashara children entered their teens, the family again pivoted their attention toward their interests. Jane became involved in school activities, fundraising for the athletic teams and music program before finally serving as head of the *Grosse Pointe South Mothers Club*, a prestigious and influential group charged with raising scholarships and funds for classroom expenses.

Wishing to engage even further with her children, in 2006 Jane accepted a buyout after a 25 year career at *Detroit Edison*. Robert had just graduated and was headed to *Purdue University* while Jessica was preparing for high school. Jane's plan was to run Bob's office and rental business, but she "couldn't make heads or tails about the books," complained Matthews, "he was cheating and hiding money and everything."

One particular mystery was where Bob got the cash for his extracurricular endeavors when his business was chronically in such disarray. What became abundantly clear is that his practice of robbing Peter to pay Paul (the constant cash flow between his accounts) wasn't limited to repairs and general upkeep. Jane discovered a massive amount of cash routinely found its way into Bob's pocket that was otherwise unaccounted for.

As Jane crept deeper into the morass it became abundantly clear that the problems were much bigger than expected. Jane was a co-signer on most of Bob's properties and his continual lack of payment led the Bashara's to lose all lines of credit.

"I knew there was a problem because Jane couldn't get a credit card," remembered Bob's mother Nancy. "I let them have mine and whenever I got my bill I'd take it over and Jane would check off exactly what was hers and she would write me a check."

Sorting out Bob's books proved a massive undertaking and Jane was forced to hire a professional accountant which led to another disturbing discovery: in a desperate move, Bob hacked into Jane's 401(k) using forged papers and withdrew $10,000.

"She told me she was having this guy come in to straighten out the books," explained Patti Matthews. "Evidently that didn't work."

Soon after the Bashara's were forced to borrow $20,000 from Nancy, who eventually also provided financial support for Robert and Jessica's college expenses. These events, combined with the effects of the 2009 economic slump, Bob's business woes and the lack of credit reluctantly pushed Jane back to the work force the following year. She accepted a job at *Frontier3 Advertising* in Grosse Pointe and soon after she assumed a more permanent position as senior marketing manager at *Kema Services*, an energy consulting, testing and certification company closely aligned with *Detroit Edison*.

§

Jim Wilson was hurting in the late summer of 2009. He was bankrupt, freshly divorced and in the process of selling his home in an effort to relocate to Ft. Lauderdale. During a final round of golf at *Lochmoor* with Bashara the two discussed marriage, finances and the many life changes they were experiencing. "Thank God I have Jane," Wilson remembered hearing.

Wilson said throughout his friendship with Bashara he never witnessed any sign of marital discord between Jane and Bob, and he never knowingly met any of Bashara's liaisons, but he did acknowledge awareness of Bob's cheating. In one odd exchange Bashara once asked him if he "liked to spank girls" before lamenting that Jane "didn't like getting spanked."

In their parting conversation Bashara told Wilson he was happy Jane went back to work and that he was "living the dream," but Wilson just wasn't buying it. After Wilson's move the two made sporadic contact but never again saw each other socially.

§

By all appearances Jane was far from oblivious to the steady erosion of her marriage. "Bob always lies," Patti Matthews often heard. "You couldn't count on what he said and you couldn't trust him with money."

Jane also told Matthews that Bashara offered to leave once Jessica entered college. By this time Jane was way past accepting the sexless nature of the union and apparently she wasn't too concerned about Bashara's occasional flirtations with other women either.

"Bob's a big flirt, but it was all just a show," she often told Matthews, "because he couldn't get it up." Jane was anything but a quitter, and wishing to save her marriage she pushed Bob into counseling, established a regular date night and, hoping for lasting reconciliation she even planned a trip to Hawaii. Confident in her success, she later told Jessica the trip saved their marriage.

Jane also tried to help Bashara with his more frequent health issues, particularly concerning his rapid weight gain which likely led to his diabetes. She would make dentist and doctor appointments for him but he would routinely blow them off.

Once second child Jessica was off to college Jane devoted more of her time to *St. Michael's Church,* serving on the vestry and becoming a valuable addition to a campaign to refurbish a rare 1928 *Skinner 705* pipe organ obtained from the now defunct *St. Columba Episcopal Church* in Detroit.

Meanwhile, Bob spent a great deal of time outside the home, his hands always full dealing with his rentals and ever increasing involvement in the *Rotary* club. He made his most positive contribution to the community in July of 2009 by initiating a campaign known as the *Three Million Pound Challenge*, the goal of which was to collect one million pounds of food, one million pounds of clothing and one million pounds of books for the needy. By all accounts it was wildly successful and led directly to his election as club president the following year.

§

Although none of Jane's family or friends realized the magnitude of strain on her marriage, cracks were steadily beginning to show.

"All those years were not like the last two," Lorraine said protectively. "Any time we went over there Bob would get the cards out … But the last year or two he would get the cards and then disappear."

Marriage failure was becoming more common among Jane's inner circle of friends, and she began to display an increasing level of concern. But despite the glaring signs to the contrary, in the viewpoint of those who knew her best, the Basharas appeared to be different, a testament to the sanctity of marriage.

But the end of the beginning, when it all began to unravel for Jane and Bob, came much sooner than anyone realized; and while Bob's interest in *The Lifestyle* became more influential, an alter-ego emerged he called *'Master Bob'*. In a bold move that would forever change his life, he posted a very personal message on *alt.com*, his cyber conduit to *The Lifestyle*:

> *"Welcome to my world … I am Master Bob, a complete trainer*
> *… I will open, train and guide you in this lifestyle … Kneel*
> *and have all your desires and cravings opened to you … Are*
> *you ready for Master Bob … I will make you love and enjoy*
> *the lovely mix of moderate pain and pleasure … Know I am*
> *true and skilled in this lovely life … So I await you … Come to*
> *me … MB."*

Chapter 2

Lifestyles

In August of 2008 Rachel Gillette had been divorced for nearly seven years. The average looking 48 year-old single mother had more than one failed relationship behind her and she was growing tired of being alone.

"A friend told me about this website," Rachel said, referring to *alt.com*, the singles site dedicated to *The Lifestyle*.

Gillette's friend knew her personality and what she liked. "She said I should try to find someone there because the men were more dominant, much more take charge than the men I knew in the regular world."

Gillette was living in Dearborn Heights, a medium-sized suburb west of Detroit. With a population just over 50 thousand, it was the 25th largest community in Michigan and comprised of a roughly equal blend of blue and white-collar workers, a classic sampling of 'vanilla' America, a term frequently used by *Lifestyle* enthusiasts to describe 'plain, old and boring.'

"I first met him on *alt.com* in August," Gillette said of Bashara. "I wrote a long profile; that I was single, a submissive looking for a dominant single man."

Describing himself as a widower, Bashara made initial contact. In the beginning they communicated exclusively online, but that soon evolved into a verbal relationship and Bashara again said he'd been a widower for a few years. He also said he was raising a teenage daughter (it was much later when he admitted to having a son). He never said how his wife died, and for a long time he didn't volunteer any details about her whatsoever.

Communication via eMail, Instant Message (IM) and phone went on for a couple weeks before they finally met in person. Soon they were dating about once a week and within three more weeks the relationship became intimate.

"Sometimes he would come pick me up, we'd go to dinner near my area of town," recalled Gillette. "Sometimes I would drive … closer to where he lived," in Grosse Pointe.

Bashara was, of course, still married to Jane and carrying on a relationship of sorts with Venita Porter, but she was nearing the end of her rope. "I asked Bob for a night of fun," Porter said. "I needed a break. I wanted to go to dinner, I wanted to go dancing."

Bashara embraced the idea and the two agreed to meet at *Dylan's Raw Bar*, which had moved into the space left vacant after the local favorite *Tom's Oyster Bar* closed it doors. It was a convenient spot for Bashara, he owned the entire block of adjoining buildings located on the east side of Mack Ave. between Nottingham and Somerset in Grosse Pointe Park. The complex also included several second floor rental apartments.

"I'd gone in and had a drink," said Porter. "I didn't see him so I tried calling. He said he was over at the *Hard Luck*. He had a few friends he wanted to show 'the room' to and then we'd be off on our evening."

The 'room', of course, was a subtle reference to Bashara's pride and joy, his homemade BDSM sex dungeon that Porter helped build a couple years back by converting a storage room underneath the *Hard Luck Lounge*.

"I finished the drink I was having and went next door to the *Hard Luck*," said Porter. " There was no one there, they told me he'd gone downstairs … I called Bob and he told me to come down to the dungeon. I found him with Rachel."

Porter had never met, nor even heard of Rachel Gillette, and that was a big problem; because one thing was clear as hell: there was going to be sex.

"I went ham," said Porter, describing the incident. "I went absolutely crazy. It was not something I was going to tolerate, not something I put up for. I was set up for a different kind of evening."

"I couldn't believe he was doing this to me," Porter continued. "I just kept lookin' at him and the phrase (he often used) was 'you and me against the world.' This is not you and me against the world."

"They blew me off," complained Porter. "They went into the room and closed the door. I didn't leave because I was upset ... I stayed in the outside room for a couple hours until they were done and then I went crazy on 'em again."

"He stood over me with a look on his face," said Porter. "I don't think I would have recognized him if I didn't know him."

"I humiliated myself," recalled Porter. "I begged him not to do this to me while he and Rachel stood there, arms crossed ... He kicked me out and stole my key."

Porter said Rachel observed the whole debacle until at last she "reached over and put her hand on his arm and told him not to be so mean to me ... But then they kicked me out at 3 o'clock in the morning anyway."

"She was too needy," Bashara recalled later. "She wanted me to raise her kids for her and I wasn't prepared to do that."

With that Venita Porter was finished, so far as Bashara was concerned.

§

Robert Godard was an old business and golfing friend that Bashara knew from *Lochmoor* (and the rare individual who circulated in both realms of Bashara's world). Godard was well acquainted with most of Bashara's women, and he knew all about Rachel and that she was not only one of Bob's slaves, but quickly becoming his favorite.

Early on Rachel learned about Bashara's erectile dysfunction problem, but she said they could achieve intimacy in other ways: "orally with the use of sexual toys". Oddly enough, she began telling people they met on the 'mainstream' online dating site *Plenty of Fish (pof.com)* suggesting she may have had some discomfort with the truth.

A few months later Gillette became 'collared' to Bashara, a formal BDSM process similar to engagement. As regarded by those in *The Lifestyle*, collaring effectively solemnizes the relationship and is similar to formal engagement or marriage, with the collar assuming a similar significance as a ring. It also serves notice to other dominants of that submissive's status within the relationship.

The collar itself is typically made of black leather, occasionally adorned with metal studs and worn around the neck similar to those used for the family dog. They often have metal D-rings allowing for the attachment of a leash, rope or other restraints and some even include an actual padlock.

Even as their relationship intensified Bashara refused to reveal his address. Astonishingly, Gillette doesn't appear to have found this odd and their partnership progressed smoothly for several months. But one constant nagging question continued to dog Gillette, the nature of Bashara's marital status.

"I think there was a series of events, little things said here and there," said Gillette. "I got hunches. At one point I found mail in his vehicle that was addressed to Jane Bashara. At first I thought, well maybe it's just something that, whatever that bill was or whatever that piece of mail was, they hadn't changed the name."

Suspicion is a tricky emotion to tame, and something Gillette was clearly not prone to do, so she *Googled* Bashara. She didn't find much, but she found a great deal on Jane. "There were articles about her volunteering at the school, different things she was doing in the community ... There was one article I read about them hosting a *Rotary* party at their home."

Gillett immediately confronted Bashara saying she knew he was married. "I couldn't believe he'd lied to me. We subsequently broke up," explained Gillette. "He apologized and said he really was separated from his wife, but if he wrote separated on his profile woman wouldn't be as likely to date him because they wanted somebody who was actually, totally divorced."

Gillette walked away for a few weeks. But after a while she decided to reconcile, "to give him another chance, to forgive him."

It was a clear indication of things to come.

§

With their first breakup and reconciliation behind them, the relationship resumed and intensified, but Bashara's story about his marriage remained constantly in flux. "At first it was that she was out of town," said Gillette, "she didn't care anyway."

Eventually Bashara began to share selected details about Jane: she'd recently retired from *Detroit Edison* and was receiving a pension. She also had a sizable 401(k).

"He told me they weren't intimate," said Gillette. "They were not even affectionate, they hadn't been for years. Initially, when I found out they were still married, I thought they were separated and living in separate homes. He subsequently told me they were living in different parts of the house … in different bedrooms."

Bashara described Jane's personality as 'dominant', like his own, and that they were ultimately unable to get along. "He wasn't respected at home," said Gillette. "His decisions were questioned constantly … and he described feelings of emasculation."

Eventually Bashara told Gillette they had finally agreed to a divorce, but were simply waiting until their youngest child graduated from high school. At that time Jessica was in her junior year and due to graduate in 2010, nearly 18 months down the road.

§

As winter set in Bashara apparently wanted to spice things up. "We are looking for a special girl," Gillette posted on *alt.com*, "a third to round out our relationship. My very first requirement is that they have to adore *MB*," (*Master Bob*).

"A woman eMailed me to let me know that Bob had been contacting her," said Gillette, referring to a woman known as 'Lynn', an obvious pseudonym, when interviewed by *Dateline NBC* in 2012.

"She was a friend of ours for several years … her [*sic*] and I had a lot of things in common," explained Gillette. "We started talking (online), and Bob set this up for us, I think as a surprise to finally meet her in person, 'cause we seemed to hit it off."

With Jane off traveling with Jessica to various prospective colleges, Bashara arranged for Gillette and 'Lynn' to meet for dinner before they proceeded to the dungeon for an hour of 'play'.

"He blindfolded us and put us in his van, and said we were going somewhere ... after he led us into the building I realized we were in his home," said Gillette. "When he let us take our blindfolds off I pretty much freaked out ... because I didn't want to be there."

Following a brief come-to-Jesus-moment, Gillette elected to stay and the threesome spent the evening engaging in sexual activities in various parts of the Bashara's home. Once finished Gillette showered and then spent the night on the floor, behavior expected of a submissive, while Bashara and 'Lynn' slept in the bed in the master bedroom. The next morning they went out for breakfast.

"At that point the relationship – the emotions involved – I had fallen in love with him," lamented Gillette, "and every time I brought up issues ... we had a conversation after that about what happened that night ... He always seemed to be able to say exactly the right thing, to suck me back in."

Over time Bashara developed a friendship of sorts with Gillette's co-workers at *Wayne State University* where she worked as a secretary in the development and alumni affairs office. They thought of him as her boyfriend and the two often went to lunch and various post work happy hours and parties.

§

Rachel Gillette was becoming more immersed in *The Lifestyle* and she kept tabs on the various parties and events through *Yahoo* chat groups and *fetlife.com*. She often received invitations via eMail and eventually began chronicling her relationship with Bashara on *Bella's Blog*, which she maintained on *alt.com* under the screen name *B's Bella*. Other fantasy names used by Gillette (common within *The Lifestyle*) includes *Slave*, *Slave R* and even *I Am What I Am* on *Yahoo* chat. Bashara, on the other hand, simply went by *Master Bob*, often signing off his *Lifestyle* related correspondence as *MB*.

In the early spring Bashara and Gillette became acquainted with Patrick Webb, known among *Lifestyle* circles as *Sir Patrick*, who was hosting a *Lifestyle* party on his property in Milan, Michigan (near Ann Arbor). Webb described the facility as a two story "bed and breakfast," but in reality it was merely a residence with five bedrooms and a big open foyer. Gillette referred to it as "a rental house" where they often went to party.

"I had a sex swing," described Webb. "There were 'pain' or 'sex' benches, depending on what type of instrument they were holding in their hands ... There was a big spider web and an eight foot cross, bondage equipment that you could be tied to and laid down in a vertical position."

The gatherings at Webb's 'facility' were numerous and, depending on your perspective, could get pretty wild. But, as Webb pointed out, there was a clear protocol guests were expected to follow in order to keep the peace:

> "If there's a man or a woman sitting with a group of people and he or she is the head of the household, knowing the protocol, you can't just go up and talk to one of them without asking for permission. It's a sign of respect. You violate that, then it's showing the other people that you have no respect for the agreements those people have ... and you will be excluded from their private parties or gatherings."

Webb went on to describe the strict code of conduct within *The Lifestyle*. Participants, he said, "have to 'earn their leathers' ... The power within the relationship lies between the dominant and the submissive person."

> "It's a way that a master or a dominant would conduct himself with his slaves. If you're too rough, don't follow safety precautions ... if you put other people at harm by not controlling your play, you lose respect in the community ... BDSM is not, per se, abusive power. The power lies within the submissive ... they control the scene, and when they say stop, it stops."

Webb's parties sometimes cost as much as $50 per couple, which is forked over like a donation. One particular New Year's Eve party netted Webb over $6,000.

Gillette and Bashara attended six or seven parties in 2009 before Webb's facility burned to the ground April 1. After that Bashara stepped up and hosted a few parties at his Grosse Pointe dungeon below the *Hard Luck Lounge* where his marital status was often a topic of discussion. Webb took note of one particular exchange:

> "We were all joking about strains on life and, as people talked about divorce one night, it was let out (by Bashara) that 'it would be cheaper to kill the bitch. Sometimes I think that it would be cheaper to kill the bitch.' At that point in time I took it just like any other blue collar American would take it, just blowing off some steam."

Seeking a permanent solution for the loss of his facility, Webb hatched a plan to build a new one from scratch. But, lacking the necessary funds, he called upon one of his biggest patrons, *Master Bob*, for a loan.

The plan was formulated around the idea that Bashara would float the necessary funds to cover the concrete foundation while Webb would pay the rest. Ground was broken in July with an intended completion date in September. Supplies were ordered, arrangements were made while parties continued at Bashara's dungeon. But funds from Bashara never materialized.

Eventually, Webb's new facility, now located in Ann Arbor, was finished and dubbed the *A2 Reformatory* and Gillette and Bashara frequented parties there throughout 2011.

"All in all I would say Bob's a nice guy," ventured Webb. "But he can be hard to handle inside the club."

> "Bob would come in, and he's a big guy, and he always liked to dominate the room … I had parties about once a month or every other weekend, depending on what time of year it was. The other parties that I threw were swingers parties. People in the lifestyle don't necessarily trade partners or let other people play with their slaves. The swingers aren't about humiliation or domination. Some like to watch people having sex, some people like being watched having sex. But very little domination or power of control is going on, they like dancing and free consensual sex."

"The club was big," Webb remembered, describing the nearly 8,000 sq. foot space. "Some of the equipment I had in there was bulky ... too big to be put away every week ... I had eight private bedrooms, four were semi-private and an open playroom ... All the equipment was out on the floor (and) ... some of the swingers would want to play around on the equipment, experimenting or whatnot."

"Bob showed up at one of the swingers parties. He had Rachel tied up on the cross and he was going to town on her with a belt. The swingers are more sensual, and it was offending some of the guests. (They) don't understand The Lifestyle and were taking notice of it. I had to go over and (tell) Bob... 'kind of calm it down, this is a swingers party not a BDSM party.' Everything was good for about 10, 15 minutes ... Then I looked over and he's got a two foot dragon slayer sword and he was running around Rachel's body and teasing ... or poking at her with it, and that made some of my guests uncomfortable. I had to tell him to take it to the bedroom."

"Bob likes to be in control," Webb said shaking his head. "At that point in time maybe it was a little embarrassing for him. But I had to maintain the atmosphere of the party and get that stuff off the main floor."

§

As spring eased into summer, Gillette began spending three to four nights a month at Bashara's dungeon. But in August she decided it was time for a permanent move and she rented a space above *Dylan's Raw Bar*, which was owned by Bashara. They began to meet several times a week and often multiple times a day. In fact, after the move, they were in constant contact via phone, text and Instant Message.

A similar relationship pattern continued throughout 2010. "I tried to break up with him," lamented Gillette, despite her move to Grosse Pointe and continually pressuring Bashara over his marital status. But Bashara always seemed to find ways to manipulate her back. "I have this plan," he wrote. "Things will work out."

Apparently Bashara's original plan, to divorce once Jessica graduated from high school, was now delayed until her departure for college in the fall. "I tried to get him to go to counseling," said Gillette. "I thought that would help him and Jane."

Gillette didn't necessarily wish to marry, but she did fully expect him to make a choice. However, there was an incident involving Bashara and Jessica that particularly troubled her: "Jessica saw a text message from another woman," explained Gillette. "A picture she'd sent of herself and some lewd comments."

What Jessica actually found was a text message written to a woman named 'Rose' which read: "Get on your knees and give me head."

"I was pretty disturbed by it," remembered Jessica, who immediately confronted her father. "He asked me to hand him his phone. He looked at it and started pressing buttons and then handed it back to me and said 'look, no message.'"

"I told my mother immediately," continued Jessica. ... "and my dad tried to deny it (but) she basically took my side."

In defense, Bashara did admit he'd frequented pornographic websites, but tried to explain it away as an attempt to better understand his ED. "He wanted to know if the problem was with him or my mother," said Jessica.

In damage control mode, that night Bashara reluctantly cancelled his evening plans with Gillette and agreed to remove text messaging from his phone. But as soon as the issue blew over he reinitiated the service, telling Jane he needed it for work. Jessica simply decided it best to ignore the whole incident.

As the Bashara's home life became increasingly strained, Jane prevailed in her attempt to get Bob to enter marriage counseling. However, little benefit appears to have come of it as Jessica's discovery of Bashara's smutty text messages and how Jane's 401(k) might affect a possible divorce settlement appear to have dominated the sessions.

§

As winter's chill slowly set in, Gillette's desire for a more conventional relationship began to take shape and they started to share a more public social life. But there was one major flaw, she continued to be introduced as merely 'just a friend' or even more degrading, his tenant.

"The very first time I met Rachel," remembered Michael Carmody, a fellow *Rotary* member, "was at Winter Blast in 2010 ... Then shortly thereafter Rachel would show up for work at our receiving center (behind *Grosse Pointe Memorial Church*) for the *Three Million Pound Challenge*, Bashara's *Rotary* initiative that collected a million pounds of food, clothing and books for the needy.

"There was also the time when I went to the *Hard Luck Lounge* to have a drink with Bob and Rachel," explained Carmody. Rachel's son had just returned from Afghanistan and she was living in the apartment on the second floor. "All of these times Bob always said she's just a friend."

§

"In February Bob gave me a ring," said Gillette. "An old diamond ring. It was a promise ring ... that eventually we'd get married." The problem was, this particular ring had a family history.

"It was a diamond ring with a silver white gold band," described Jessica, an heirloom from Bashara's great Aunt Jenny. Upon her death Jenny intended it to be willed to Jane and eventually Jessica, but it went missing sometime in 2009.

"My mother asked me where it was," said Jessica. "I wasn't sure but ... I thought maybe I'd lost it, I didn't know where it went."

According to Jessica, her father later told her he had "kept it in a drawer for a year and (since) no one asked about it, (he thought) no one would miss it ... therefore that made it OK for him to give it to his girlfriend."

Bashara intended that Gillette wear the ring on her left hand but she refused. "I couldn't wear it on that hand ... knowing that he wasn't free. I wouldn't wear it on that hand until he was divorced." However, she gladly displayed it on her right hand.

"As far as he was concerned, we were engaged and he thought I should wear it," said Gillette. "He talked a lot about plans … our life together, the house we would buy. I would help him with his business, things like that."

§

The 2009 economic downturn took a heavy toll on the real-estate business and Bashara was no exception. He owned a rental property at 5935 Cadieux Road on Detroit's east side that was terribly underwater, so in April 2010 he hatched a plan to unload it.

"He was behind on payments," recalled Donald Calcaterra, a mortgage broker with *Town Mortgage* and a 20 year Bashara family friend. *Town* also held the mortgage on the Bashara's Middlesex home.

"He was hoping to sell the house on a short sale to avoid foreclosure," explained Calcaterra. Not uncommon during that period, a short sale allows for a property to be sold for less than what is owed to the bank, which in turn agrees to accept less than full payoff in order to sell the house.

An 'arms-length sale' is what Calcaterra told Bashara was required for this type of transaction. "I told him that we couldn't do a short sale to someone that he had identified and that it would have to be listed with a real estate agent, then … a buyer would be identified and we'd be able to submit a request to the investor to accept the short sale."

But Bashara already had a buyer in mind, and had every intention of pushing the transaction through, and he never revealed the buyer's identity to Calcaterra. The two never spoke of the matter again, and it wasn't until late 2012 that Calcaterra learned the details of the sale.

By all available accounts, Bashara 'sold' the property to Rachel Gillette using borrowed money from his mother Nancy, and Gillette began 'managing' the property the following year.

§

Gillette again attempted a clean break in June of 2010 due to the continual lack of clarity concerning Bashara's marital status. As usual this would bring out Bashara's manipulative and poetic side in the form of an eMail. An intriguing detail common within *The Lifestyle* is the constant reaffirmation of the roles each plays in the relationship in terms of dominance and submissiveness, and in most written communication between them Bashara, being the 'dominate', is indicated, even in pronouns, by capital letters for himself and lower case for his 'submissive'.

> *"Hello and good morning, My slave,*
> *I do not understand how you can love someone, stay with Me and now as we're about to be us you wish to leave … I cannot imagine, and will not do so, a life without you, plain and simple. Know this: what we have and what we will be about is so special. We cannot let it go. It has almost been two years and I'm sorry if you have been tortured. I like to think of us as evolving and growing. I'm ready to make a life-changing event for you and for us, and at the time of this happening you again wish to leave Me … I am here and will not release you. I am your Man, you are my woman. I remain, Master Bob."*

Once again swayed by the irresistible Bashara charm, Gillette elected to stay, but not for long. The two split again before the summer was out, this time prompting Gillette to seek independent accommodations nearly a mile and half away in an upper flat on St. Clair Ave. in Grosse Pointe.

§

"I wasn't aware of his finances," recalled Gillette. "But over the years … I'd overheard … phone conversations or discussions with contractors that he owed money to, or tenants that owed him money … There always seemed to be some extenuating circumstances, somebody didn't complete a job right so he wasn't going to finish paying them. There was a lot of little things that just made me uneasy."

"I knew he spent a lot of money, I knew he always had a lot of cash, I assumed from the rentals," reflected Gillette. "We went out a lot, he always paid for everything. A lot of times he would have a couple hundred dollars."

"There were times with the rentals that he would borrow money from one and pay to get something fixed on another," continued Gillette. "There seemed to be that borrowing money back and fourth from accounts a lot."

Occasionally, Gillette lent a hand by cleaning and painting and Bashara often paid her with checks from different business accounts. Indeed, money, and the lack of it, was an unrelenting motivating factor for Bashara. Everything seemed to hinge on finances. It was always a heated topic when the Bashara's discussed divorce. Jane's sizable 401(k), which she had spent a lifetime building since college, was rumored to be valued at more than half a million dollars.

"In the event of a divorce," said Jessica, "ideally she just hoped that she'd be able to take her 401(k)."

For Jane this was the only non-negotiable item in a possible settlement and Bashara knew it would surely spell financial ruin for him. Jane would keep the 401(k) and he would be forced to live off his paltry rental proceeds and the small income he made from *United Laboratories* sales.

Bank records indicate a wide discrepancy in the Bashara's income. In 2009, Jane netted nearly $80,000 while Bob made less than half. In 2010, Jane made almost six figures while Bob barely made more than $20,000. In 2011 the trend continued and Jane made just over $90,000 while Bob made less than $20,000.

In several October 2010 eMail exchanges with Gillette, Bashara began to lay the groundwork for the kind of lifestyle they might share post divorce:

> *"My lovely slave,*
> *While I have been accustomed to the best in life, and yes I do keep a lot of stuff, for one never knows when one needs stuff. But I could live in a one room house and be happy as long as you are with Me, and fortunately I will never have to do that. As for my mom, she is most generous, but I try not to impose on her money and good nature. Finally, as for the income I will be missing, oh well. Again, I would rather be poor and happy than rich and not so. These are things you should not worry about. And when we are together I will lay out My future, a future with you at my side. And I as well think you are pretty neato kean and most swell, and I am your Master Bob.*

But the breakups mounted and followed a similar pattern, occurring every two to three months, with Bashara reacting with eMails and IMs designed to coax her back into the fold. Some breakups appeared to be more significant than others, at least for Gillette, leading Bashara to seek more extreme measures. One such occasion, coming on the heels of Gillette's move to Saint Clair Ave., found him sitting on a lawn chair outside her door, head in his hands, the scene complete with tears.

"He said he was sorry," said Gillette. "Please take him back, that kind of stuff." As he was effectively blocking her from entering her apartment, she got back in the car and drove away. When she returned an hour later Bashara was still there, begging her to talk. That display was followed by a familiar exchange:

> *"Slave R,*
> *No no no, you are so wrong. Damn it, I love you and do not want to lose you, ever. We are perfect for each other and you know it. I have asked for a year and you need to understand my relationship with her is over… No sex, no feeling. Hell, she said she is not happy and wants to part. So we are working on a plan. I have given you all of Me, is that not enough? … I will not let you go. You are collared to Me and I want you period, MB.*

After repeated overtures and Instant Messages, all rebuffed by Gillette, Bashara called and enlisted her teenaged daughter for help, but Gillette still declined. This continued for several days, but in the end Gillette again decided to return to Bashara. They were rarely apart for more than a few days to a week.

"I truly wanted to break up," Gillette said with a sigh, "but I just never could."

§

When summer arrived Bashara was again pressing for a third wheel in his relationship with Gillette, who began posting their intentions on *Bella's Blog*:

> *"We are looking for one unique individual who can fit with us and our personalities … an attractive female, ages from late 30's to early 50's, must be able to relocate to us … willing to*

obey His directions concerning finances, health issues, and self growth ... gainfully employed."

Scrolling through profiles on *alt.com* Bashara came across Therese Giffon, a 50-something former Chicago police officer who wished to become a BDSM submissive.

"He approached me on *alt.com*," Giffon recalled. "He said he was looking for a third person to join him and his slave," whom she later learned was Rachel Gillette. "I heard she went by *Bella* and he called himself *Master Bob*."

When they first made contact, Bashara's instructions, in no uncertain terms, indicated she had to become friends with Rachel, "read her blog and get to know her," he wrote. He also described himself as divorced and stressed there could be no small children in the mix.

In December Giffon traveled to Detroit and Bashara accompanied her to an unexplained 'dangerous place' before going back to Bashara's dungeon for a play scene.

"At one point he tied me to a cross and flogged me, and on another he had me sit on a chair and used a hand vibrator," said Giffon, describing the encounter as "intimate, but not sexual". She went on to say that their "clothes were off" and Bashara used "nipple clamps" on her.

It appears, however, that Giffon failed to satisfy and this 'interview' for a third proved to be short lived. The two met on only one subsequent occasion the following year when Bashara happened to travel to Chicago for a *Rotary* convention. The dalliance officially ended via Instant Message:

> *"Of course it does not bother Me that you have kids. R and I both have children we are in touch with and love. However, one of My requirements for the third that we seek has always been one without young kids, as we have raised ours already and wish to have an adult-only household. That is not something new and I am sure we have talked of it and it has been on her blog."*

Chapter 3

The Manipulation Game

Expressing Hopes and Dreams:
Excerpts from Jane Bashara's diary, January 5, 2011
"Why we fight: Bob makes plans, doesn't tell me."
"Bob says he says things he doesn't."
"Can't trust what he says."
"Bob says things without talking to me."
"Selling house, going out with guys."

As 2011 began, many of the same old challenges faced Bob Bashara and Rachel Gillette. He remained a representative for *United Laboratories*, made most of his income from rental properties and was still married to Jane. But Gillette was hoping against hope all this would soon shift in her favor.

> "He told me they were living in the same house but sleeping in separate parts," said Gillette. "At one point ... Mrs. Bashara was out of town, we were going somewhere and we stopped by his house to feed the dog ... He showed me his office area and the guest room where he told me he was sleeping. When I looked across the hall into the master bedroom, that's where his sleep apnea machine was, and I could tell that he hadn't been sleeping in the guest room."

When confronted, Bashara told Gillette he'd moved back into the master bedroom because the bed was more comfortable: "But they slept in separate covers and he was totally covered and disconnected from her." Wrapped like a cocoon, he said, their bodies did not touch.

Accepting she had to set a strong contrast from Jane, Gillette chose not to criticize and Bashara, via eMail, kept up the pressure to keep her in the fold:

> "My Slave ... What you say, about you wondering what you were doing, what you are doing and have been doing is building a life with Me. Hello? Have we not built something special? Have we not grown close, very close? My situation is secondary to what we have and yet ending soon ... I feel your frustration with the time frame, and while I understand you feel guilty, you will stop this now. I have chosen you, you are here with Me ... And you can throw all the cliche's around, but that is not Me. I am real, I am here and want you for the rest of My life."

> "I do move at a pace you are not used to, and I will tell you a lot will settle down as I become single and can focus on us. But it is most important for you to keep your head straight and do not let some of My comings and goings mess with you. I will not stand for that. You know that I love you ... Be secure in that and you will deal with My schedule, as we are close to our time coming."

As spring settled in, in a surprise move Bashara declared his divorce was final. "You mentioned you will have to live with the way I am or leave," Bashara wrote to Gillette. "Now that I am divorced the hiding and lying will stop."

In June Gillette discovered Bashara was again corresponding with another woman on *alt.com* and she still hadn't seen any official divorce documents. Several times in the past they talked about bringing in a third to join their 'family' (as the dalliance with 'Lynn' and Therese Griffon, the former Chicago police officer demonstrated). Gillette recognized that Bashara's promiscuous nature dictated this would come to pass, with or without her blessing, so she embraced the idea.

"I actually kind of thought maybe it would help him," explained Gillette, "to stay more faithful."

By July Bashara was walking a dangerous line, redoubling his efforts to keep Gillette in the fold without letting the cat out of the bag publicly.

"That summer he went crazy," remembered Lorraine Englebrecht. One incident in particular was at an annual summer picnic hosted by the *Rotary* club. "He took Rachel when Jane was in Germany with Jessica."

He also made a public scene at *St. Micheal's Church* (which is situated adjacent to *Parcells Middle School,* the site of Grosse Pointe Wood's annual July 4 fireworks). "Our pastor got into it with Bob over parking," recalled Englebrecht. Parking was scarce so the church made their back lot available for $5. Ignoring protocol, Bashara directed Gillette to park in the driveway, effectively blocking others. "That woman can't park there," Englebrecht remembered hearing the pastor tell Bob. "'She's got to follow the crowd' … Bob was planning to let her park there for free."

All along Bashara maintained that he and Jane owned the Middlesex property together and suggested that in the event of divorce they would divide the proceeds. But now in a long drawn out eMail to Gillette, he sounded suspiciously like he alone would benefit.

> *"You and I have been together for almost three years … I doubt that I can find someone as close to what I want in My life, for the rest of My life. We gel in so many ways, yet there has been friction, mostly centered around My situation, now coming to a close. I have made some poor choices, and I have made you feel badly, something I had no intention of doing as I love you and always will … I was up late writing and thinking about this, and have given us and our future a lot of hard, wonderful thought … I said I need to sell Middlesex to buy another, well I am finding out I do not."*

Then Bashara sketched out what appears to be long term plans for their relationship:

> *"I will continue repping United and the rentals. You may ask how this can happen from a money standpoint. Well, with a house in a lower price range and, hence, lower expenses, I and we can make it very nicely with the money I get from Middlesex. I will then have no mortgage, only taxes and health*

insurance. You won't have to work ... You will never have to want for anything."

"You worry about assimilating into Grosse Pointe, well do not. I am a huge figure here and have many friends, but also we and you and I will make new ones. Our friends who know and like us for us. If there are those who choose not to remain my friends, oh well."

"I realize I do not want a life without you. I hope you'll also know that I am not perfect and hiding and lying has been needed to cover us ... I will now stop the lying, and know that it is My hope that I regain your trust ... You have put up with My living situation. Know that our life will be a lot different ... and the need to hide will be a huge rock lifted off us, a rock I am lifting now."

"As for the poly situation, I will leave that up to you. If we find one that is perfect to come to us, great. If not, you are all I want and need. I will not be on any sides, I will not contact anyone ... I have now learned My lesson."

But apparently it only took a day before Bashara broke his promise, something Gillette couldn't help but document on her *Bella's Blog.* This action was met with a similar manipulative eMail plea from Bashara:

"I am sitting here with tears running down My face and in disbelief that you feel so much like you do. I eMailed one girl, I was a fool in how I handled it. I am your Master and did what I did. Not to whore around but to make and find one for us ... All the (blog) comments say how bad it is that you and I cannot work it out ... I know that this waiting has been hard, but the wait is over. The promise of our life, a life for us that you dream of, is at hand."

§

As pressure mounted to come clean on the divorce, Bashara dodged the issue, pivoting the conversation to the possibility of purchasing a home together. Loraine

Muccioli, real estate agent with *Johnstone & Johnstone* recalled one particular showing with Bashara and Gillette in St. Clair Shores (MI) where she overheard them discussing engagement. Bashara, pushing a step further, explained he was recently divorced, but still living with his ex-wife.

House hunting activity intensified in late summer as Bashara and Gillette began a more public existence. "We started going more places openly, and more places in Grosse Pointe," said Gillette. "We started seeing each other a lot more ... pretty much every day at that point."

Late in August Bashara made an offer on a home on Bishop Rd. in Grosse Pointe Park. His original finance plan was to borrow money from his mother Nancy but later reconsidered, preferring an earlier plan to sell the home on Middlesex, only to return to Nancy before the deal ultimately fell through.

After home searching all over Metro Detroit, Bashara decided to narrow the playing field, looking exclusively in Grosse Pointe. Not surprisingly he told Gillette he'd never live anywhere else because of his mother's connections and his father's standing in the community.

"I would've really rather moved far away from Grosse Pointe," lamented Gillette. But Bashara was adamant, adding that his involvement in *Grosse Pointe Rotary* and his recent term as president were also deciding factors.

Increasingly distressing for Gillette was her now routine introduction as a 'tenant' or 'friend' when meeting friends or acquaintances around town. "Even though the divorce was final, a lot of people didn't know it yet," Bashara explained, adding that he and Jane wanted to tell them in their own time, specifically family and close friends.

One such occasion involved Joy Jolly (ex-wife of Bashara's *Lochmoor* friend Jim Wilson) who was in the process of selling the family home after the recent death of her parents: "I was going through a divorce, so I moved there with all my furniture," recalled Jolly. At the time she was also holding an estate sale.

"The doorbell rang. I opened it and there was Bob," Jolly recalled. "I explained it was my parent's home and we were selling it." Jolly noted that Bashara was with a realtor and a third woman. "When she realized Bob knew me she put her head down and walked around him into the house." The unknown woman, Jolly learned later, was Gillette.

Bashara sheepishly passed the woman off as a friend, and made no attempt to introduce her. "She's not from the area and I'm just helping her look for a home," Bashara said finally.

The following morning Jolly left a voice message on the Bashara's home machine: "I don't appreciate you gossiping about me or the house. That would be like me going around town telling everyone you're having an affair with the woman you brought through my house."

Less than two hours later Bashara was knocking on Jolly's door: "I never said anything negative about you or the house," pleaded Bashara, "and I don't know what you're talking about."

But Jolly's lasting impression was Bashara, again and again, repeating that she was just a friend: "She needed my help," he insisted.

§

Bashara's life outside Grosse Pointe was far removed from the one he cultivated with Jane, Jessica and Robert. *Rotary* campaigns, family vacations and community volunteer projects were a far cry from Bashara's otherworld, the center of which was his St. Clair Shores rental property known as *Lakeside Apartments*.

Populated by ex-convicts and drug dealers, this place was frequented by seedy businessmen and small timers who saw Bashara as a kind of low rent mob boss. Here Bashara hired and spent time with those even he would have otherwise considered low life's and losers.

On a warm and hazy late summer afternoon, Bashara held a picnic BBQ in the *Lakeside* courtyard for his tenants. "It was because people cleaned up the yard and paid rent on time," explained William Schatz, a slight man of about 40 who was a tenant and sometimes employee for the odd jobs and handyman work Bashara often needed help with.

Others in attendance included workers Bashara hired to keep the operation afloat including Robert 'Ponytail Bob' Fick, Ralph (pronounced Raif) Lee and a shady plumber named Thomas Ramsey. According to Schatz there were lots of people there and Bashara himself was working the grill. These men (save for Fick, who was previously acquainted with Gillette) all noted the presence of an unknown woman that Bashara was introducing as 'just a friend' to some, and a 'girlfriend' to others.

"I seen her there collecting coins out of the washing machine and dryers," observed Fick, who was also known for doing numerous improvement projects on Bashara's Middlesex home.

"At the time he said she was a friend," remembered Schatz, who'd never seen her before, but later learned her name was Rachel.

"She was introduced as his girlfriend," insisted Lee.

On more than one occasion Fick and Lee were asked to work on Bashara's Cadieux property. "He asked me to do covert and discreet work for him," said Fick, adding that Bashara, not Gillette, was the one he worked for.

"Bob said it was Rachel's house," said Fick, sounding surprised. "Why would Bob Bashara buy Rachel a house?"

§

In the early fall 'Bob and Rachel' sitings were becoming common around Grosse Pointe. Eileen Stratelak, a close friend of Jane's, once spotted them at a restaurant in nearby St. Clair Shores. Stratelak and Jane often attended high school sports together as their daughters both played for the *South* volleyball team.

"I was having dinner with a couple girlfriends at *Cedar Gardens* at 9 mile and Mack," explained Stratelak. "Bob came up and talked to us … told us he was meeting a tenant and they had dinner together. But when they left she went out the back door, he went out the front, and then they met up outside."

"Jane thanked me for accepting Bob because none of her friends liked him," Stratelak said later, shaking her head.

The long tedious process of house hunting finally showed promise when Bashara and Gillette found a suitable home at 1011 Kensington Rd. in Grosse Pointe Park. About 13 blocks from the Bashara's home on Middlesex, it happened to be next door to Bashara's *Rotary* friend Michael Carmody.

Bashara made a lasting impression on another *Johnstone & Johnstone* realtor, Kathy Young, due to his odd behavior. "The basement is a good punishment room," she heard Bashara say, "suitable for a dungeon. How many people can fit in the shower?"

She also remembered rude comments directed toward her: "You seem to be a very submissive person," he'd said. On another occasion Young, running late for a showing, alerted Bashara via text, to which came the reply: "Bitch n p" (no problem).

Michael Carmody was aware of Bashara's intension to downsize, but he never heard Jane speak of it. However, Bashara was obviously excited about the move and he shared as much to his friend Robert Godard (whom he knew from *Lochmoor*) saying he planned to purchase the home and make a life with Gillette.

A few months later, in October, Bashara approached Godard with a question: "He asked if I knew someone who could rough someone up," remembered Godard. "He said he had a difficult tenant that he wanted to send a message to."

The prospect of moving into a home with Bashara fortified Gillette's mounting domestic ambitions. "I wanted the relationship that we established, the relationship side of it," remembered Gillette, "but not the parties and the other parts."

"I envisioned a lot of problems because I knew from things that Bob told me how he wanted our lifestyle to be," continued Gillette. "He wanted to have parties at our home with BDSM people. I didn't want that in our home, and definitely didn't want it in our home next to people he knew."

"My interests weren't the same as his," continued Gillette. "He was more interested in it (*The Lifestyle*) than me. He didn't want to stop."

In early December Bashara and Gillette shared the Kensington decision with Gillette's daughter, which helped solidify their plans for the move.

According to realtor Kathy Young, Bashara again indicated he planned to finance the house "with a mortgage, but then said he was going to get $190,000 from his mother and would have to come up with the balance."

Before the purchase could be finalized there was a legal matter that needed settling. State Dower Rights require the title of the home to specifically state marital status for the purpose of inheritance, meaning that a woman is, by law, entitled to claim the lands and tenements obtained during the marriage upon the death of the husband. In short, realtors needed to know Bashara's legal marital status in order to complete the sale.

Bashara insisted he was divorced and revealed that in their settlement Jane would retain her 401(k) and he would receive all the properties, some of which he intended to sell, to cover the balance on the Kensington purchase. Bashara's offer of $230,000 was eventually accepted and a closing date was set for January 27.

§

Bashara's eye was again wandering, actively seeking spice to add to his relationship with Gillette. "He couldn't have a traditional relationship," insisted Gillette. "One of the things he told me was that if he had two women at home he wouldn't have to be on the websites looking for more ... I believed him."

On November 21, despite his promise to Gillette, Bashara again made first contact, this time with a spunky and attractive single mother living in Oregon named Janet Leehman. She appeared to be just what Bashara was looking for, as she later admitted she "liked it a little rough."

After a few false attempts on more mainstream dating sites, it was Leehman's first time on *alt.com*, and she was only on for a day or two before Bashara contacted her.

"I've been on some of the other (dating sites) and they all sucked," observed Leehman. "They're all dangerous ... There are bad people on all of them."

"But I had a boyfriend that was a little twisted and I liked it," Leehman continued, "so I was dipping my toe. He was twisted and fun ... So then I thought I'd find another. I was looking for a type-A mover and shaker who was kind of dominant and a business man."

"My father was a big-time judge," Bashara bragged via Instant Message, trying to entice. He told Leehman of his local connections and businesses, which impressed her.

"I'm a businessperson," Leehman said later. "I like hanging out with business people. I don't date musicians … I like people that run on a tight watch and run businesses and are smart and funny."

Bashara was one of several who responded to Leehman's post. "He was the only nice one," she said sardonically. Correspondence ensued and soon expanded to phone conversations. At Leehman's request Bashara sent an eMail to a potential rival telling him to buzz off. "Keep your hands off My property," Bashara wrote.

In a familiar tale, Bashara told Leehman he was divorced, and according to Leehman he added very little about his wife. He also said his attorneys advised sharing the current house until the kids were grown and he was planning to move out soon after.

"I asked him where his ex-wife was planning to go," said Leehman, "because he sounded like he would get all the proceeds from the house sale. He said he didn't know … she might get a condo."

Bashara said his wife "wasn't interested in an intimate relationship … and was sickened by giving head," which had ended their sexual relationship more than seven years ago.

"Bob said he was looking for a third," said Leehman. "I didn't want to be a third wheel but Bob said it wouldn't be like that, it would be equal, with *Bella*."

In an Instant Message exchange the following day, Bashara began to lay it on pretty thick: "OK, little one, I've given you a task and you've done well. So tell Me about the distance, you say you do not want to relocate."

"It seems premature," replied Leehman, who was now going by the screen name *Slave J*.

"Like you said," continued Bashara, "we will chat, talk and go from there. My *Bella* will reply and you two can talk. It is important you two hit it off or being together won't work. I am pleased with you."

Bashara told Leehman he was purchasing a home on Kensington in Grosse Pointe with Gillette at the end of January and he wanted her to move in and form a poly three-way relationship with them.

Leehman had once before relocated for a man. It hadn't ended well and she had little desire to do it again. She had deep roots in Oregon, a career, a child and grandchildren, but despite all that she replied: "I won't close the door on it."

Wasting no time, Gillette began to write on *Bella's Blog* of their new plans:

> *"We are a true D/s triad … a group of three. Master Bob is the head of our home, respected and cared for by His two lovely slaves, Bella and J."*

Despite a mountain of nagging doubts, Leehman never said one way or another about the Kensington plan. "I was just listening. If I loved someone and spent three years getting to know them I might move, but I wasn't planning to."

In a December 1 Instant Message with Leehman, Bashara described one of Gillette's favorite recreations. Clinically known as *erotic asphyxiation*, many in *The Lifestyle* like to call it *breath play*. According to *Wikipedia* it is "the intentional restriction of oxygen to the brain for the purposes of sexual arousal."

Not to be confused with *autoerotic asphyxiation*, which occurs when the act is conducted upon oneself (and a leading cause of accidental suicide), *breath play* is performed by a BDSM dominant on his/her submissive as a demonstration of control.

"I did some breath play," wrote Bashara. "I can choke her (Gillette) just enough to make her woozy, and having My large hand on her neck excites her. I will do the same to you."

"Breath play, Sir?" questioned Leehman. "I'm almost a breath play virgin."

"Well you are a virgin in a lot of ways," wrote Bashara. "I will open to you a lot of all I am and you will be like a kid in a candy shop."

In another Instant Message Bashara wrote that he'd "stop by (Gillette's) house at night to tuck her in with breath play."

"Sir, very sweet of *Bella*," replied Leehman. "She's sleeping?"

"Out like a light."

(The practice of erotic asphyxiation has been known since at least the 17th century and, ironically, was first thought to be a treatment for erectile dysfunction. Again, according to Wikipedia, the "idea likely came from subjects who were executed by hanging. Observers noted that male victims developed an erection, sometimes remaining after death and occasionally ejaculating once hanged. However, post-mortem ejaculation occurs in hanging victims after death because of disseminated muscle relaxation, which is a different mechanism.")

§

A few weeks later Bashara sent Leehman a package containing a $25 *Olive Garden* gift certificate and a leather string with instructions to wear it on her wrist. In the enclosed note Bashara wrote "you served Me wonderfully." He also included a T-shirt he'd worn for three straight days.

In an Instant Message dated December 12 Bashara wrote: "Between you and *Bella*, I know I will be taken care of. You both have your time with Me, together and separately."

"I understand, Sir," Leehman replied, amused to play along.

"Good girl," wrote Bashara. "Now I am whipped and I'm glad we have made this point of service clearer, that now you will have a crystal clear view when you come to Me. I'm glad you are mine, I'm in serious like with you."

"How so Sir?" Leehman shot back, "you've not met me."

"Be well and know I'm happy, pleased," parried Bashara. "Know several things … I am a very good judge of character; and … unless you are not being real, which I know you are not, your slave-hood and service to Me is both real and valued. Plus I think you're cute as well."

"Thank you, Sir."

"Sleep well with thoughts of your Master."

§

As 2011 waned, Jane's high school friend Patti Matthews began to notice how unavailable the Basharas had become of late. "Jane would tell me that Bob was gambling on Saturday nights. He would do a sleep over at a place because he would be far away and spend the night."

"We tried to get appointments with them," continued Matthews, "to play cards or something and you know, he was unavailable because he was doing that." Matthews was right that they were increasingly unavailable, but the reason was likely too foreign for her to comprehend.

§

Midway through 2011 Patrick Webb (*Sir Patrick*) was forced to declare bankruptcy and the future of the *A2 Reformatory* was in jeopardy. "I was going to the bank with as much money as I could gather," said Webb, "to see if they would postpone the foreclosing." Webb was in arrears to the tune of $88,000.

"It was in the early part of December," recalled Webb. "I met with Bob and Rachel at the *Hard Luck* ... I told him my situation, and he said he'd like to help me out."

"I was trying to find alternative financing," Webb continued, "to save my home, to save the club. Bob was working on getting me alternative financing."

"He explained he was doing some things for Rachel," Webb persisted. "He couldn't put his name on anything at that point, meaning cosign for a loan. That was the same conversation when he told me in the near future he'd be coming into some money."

"I had one investor that had some money and Bob said he could come up with $20,000," said Webb.

Bashara had a plan: He went to the office of an old golfing acquaintance from *Lochmoor* named Charles Gabel who was in finance (they were also acquainted through *Rotary*).

"He had an investment proposal," Gabel recalled. "He was trying to raise money for a friend." Bashara had never approached him like this before and he already had the scheme written out:

"I have a long time college friend who owns 11.5 acres in Milan (Michigan) and has run into difficulty and needs some short term help. I wish to raise at least $40,000 ASAP and have broken this opportunity into $10,000 increments. You may take part or whole. Here are the numbers: for a $10,000 share, a payment of 110 is based on 9% over 15 year amortization with a balloon after three years. At the end of the three years balances will be paid off and a thank you bonus of $1,200 will be paid. Additionally, there will be an extra $100 principal added to each month. I've invested one $10,000 share and will manage all aspects of the deal including paperwork, leans in your name, proof of taxes being paid, insurance payments made out to each investor as laws payee. I know my friend has recovered to make this a reality but needs our help now. I am confident and will also cosign each loan. Call Bob Bashara to sign up and for more information."

It is unclear how many others Bashara approached with this offer, and it appears he never revealed the true nature of the investment. In the end, however, *Sir Patrick* Webb never received a dime from Bashara.

During the upheaval at the *A2 Reformatory* Bashara continued to host regular *Lifestyle* parties at his dungeon on Mack Ave. underneath the *Hard Luck Lounge*, and Patrick Webb was a regular guest.

"We were sittin' around having a couple'a drinks," Webb recalled. "There was a group of us down there, and he had actually invited me and my wife to come spend the night at his house. I declined because I knew (Jane) wasn't cool with the idea, and I didn't know what story he was telling her."

"There were conversations that his marriage was coming to an end," continued Webb. "He wanted to get away from her and live *The Lifestyle* with Rachel, and she wanted Bob to herself. She was tired of playing second fiddle."

Throughout their friendship it was common for Bashara to share his marriage troubles with Webb. "The last meeting I had with Bob," recalled Webb, "he said he was making a life with Rachel … the divorce was going though – Rachel was happy."

§

As the end of the year rapidly approached Gillette and Bashara were making plans to attend the late December wedding of Gillette's daughter in South Carolina. Bashara wanted to be directly involved, to play the role of the father-figure. "He gave me money as expenses came up," recalled Gillette. "I told her I would pay for half of her wedding dress, so Bob gave me a few hundred dollars for that."

"At one point I think he gave me $300 for flowers," Gillette continued. "He also wanted to provide the alcohol and liquor for the reception."

Plans were progressing smoothly, but there was one snag needing to be dealt with: "He said he told Jane he was going to a wedding," said Gillette. "He just didn't specifically tell her it was his new girlfriend's daughter's wedding."

In actuality, Bashara had a better plan in mind. While out on his daily walk, old golfing buddy Jim Wilson received an odd phone call: "You need to do me a favor," insisted Bashara. "I need you to cover for me this weekend."

"What do you mean?" protested Wilson.

"Cover for me. If anybody asks you, I'm with you."

"No one better call me," Wilson said forcefully, pointing out he had no desire to lie to Jane.

As plans for the trip solidified, Bashara made a surprise declaration to Gillette: Christmas 2011 "would be his last" with the family in the Middlesex home.

§

"On December 23, Jane was going to come over to the house and see my family," Patti Matthews recalled. "The kids were in town for one afternoon and when Bob was leaving I said 'we'll see you New Year's Eve,' because we were having a card party at our house."

"Well, there's a little snag in that," Bashara told her. "Jane is pissed, but I'm going to a Member-Guest golf outing with Jim Wilson down in Florida."

"When Jane came in an hour later she was in a good mood and everything," remembered Matthews. "She was going to pick up her son at the airport so I didn't bring up the subject."

"Jane told me Bob was going to Florida," her mother Lorraine remembered. "They had Christmas in their home and I said to her, 'he's going to fly for New Year's Eve? What are you gonna do?' I mean, that didn't even open her eyes?"

§

The day after Christmas Bashara and Gillette departed for South Carolina. For all practical purposes Bashara, as intended, acted as the father of the bride and picked up several additional expenses, in excess of $4,000 for lodging alone.

On New Year's Eve, Debbie Breen, a member of Jane's closest inner circle of friends, came for dinner; Jane was making frog legs, her son Robert's favorite, in celebration of his last night at home. While cooking Jane received a call from Bob. "He told her he was with Jim (Wilson)," Breen remembered. "They were golfing and he got a hole in one!"

The Breens, like several of Jane's friends, were breaking up, and by all appearances their split weighed particularly heavy on her. She began sharing the dreadful news with her mother, blow-by-blow. "Debbie had to live with her husband 'til they sold the house," Jane lamented, "and they were getting a divorce!"

"Jane's marriage was in big trouble at that point," Lorraine Englebrecht stated matter-of-factly, and yet, "she was so concerned about the Breens."

§

Sandra Ennis and Jane Bashara were friends for more than 20 years, dating back to a time when both worked for *Detroit Edison*. Ennis was still employed there and the two were scheming to arrange a summer internship for Jessica.

Their families were often social and the second week in January they had plans to meet for dinner and a show at *Grosse Pointe Theatre*, but six days out Jane needed a change of plans:

> *"Hi Sandy, I'm really looking forward to Sunday. However, Bob has just found out he needs to go to Portland, Oregon for a sale training this weekend. He was hoping it was going to fall through but it didn't. So I was wondering if one of your girls would like to go to the show with us?"*

"At intermission Jane revealed Bob was training on a new chemical waste product," recalled Ennis. "She was quite excited and thought it was going to be really good for him, help him in his sales."

It was true, Bashara did head out to Portland the pervious Thursday, but his mission had nothing to do with training or *United Laboratories*. In actuality it was about closing the deal on Janet Leehman. Plane tickets were purchased for January 12-15 and Leehman made arrangements to take a few days off work.

Gillette dropped Bashara off at Detroit's *Metro Airport* early on the morning of January 12. "He told me he told Jane he was going to Oregon for business with *United Laboratories*," remembered Gillette.

> **January 12**: *Bella's Blog* at *alt.com*:
> *"Oregon also has one very special girl that I am just dying to meet! And now for this weekend only ... Oregon also has my Master!"*

§

While Bashara was out of town, Jane spent time with several friends. "She was at our house for dinner on Friday night because Bob was out of town," remembered Matthews. "She said he was in Oregon ... something to do with the chemical company he worked with." Sunday was the night at the theatre with the Ennis family.

Bashara called Gillette shortly after arriving in Oregon to report that he liked Leehman, but he wasn't sure if the two women would get along, his sole requirement for the three of them to live together on Kensington.

Bashara arrived carrying "a big wad of money," observed Leehman. On the way to her place they stopped at a hardware store and Bashara bought a cattle whip and a section of rope. "I thought I was getting into some light bondage and a little whipping," remembered Leehman, recalling that her former boyfriend had a little crop he would spank her with. But she'd never been tied up before, and unfortunately, Leehman's past experiences were woefully inadequate to prepare her for her first encounter with *Master Bob*.

"He being the dominant one, it was his responsibility to clear with me what he was doing, and beating me half to death with that thing was not it," said Leehman. "I had no idea (of Bashara's intensions,) I nearly passed out."

"It was awful. I had marks on my body for three months," remembered Leehman. "I had thrash marks, it was painful ... My role as a submissive is to submit to that. But I didn't have a safe word," she added, shaking her head, "because I am an idiot."

Over the course of the weekend they went out to a handful of places: dinner, a ski resort, even a football game. In preparation for the weekend Bashara had texted: *"How you will feel my passion,"* which apparently gave Leehman false expectations. They attempted sex but immediately Leehman noticed something wasn't right.

"His appendage doesn't work," she said, sounding surprised. "The chairman of the board didn't show up for work ... He never said anything about erectile dysfunction. Instead, he brought with him a couple of strap-ons."

Then, without warning, Bashara introduced Leehman to breath play, failing to allow her any time to prepare. "He just did it," recalled Leehman. "He was standing behind me and he wrapped his hands around my neck and then I saw stars."

"You should have told me you were getting bad," Bashara said, excitement building in his voice. "I could hurt you."

"I didn't know breath play would make me pass out," Leehman said later, thankful it had occurred only the one time. "I didn't expect injuries," she added. "In the past 'play' didn't have injuries."

For the remainder of the weekend Leehman made the best of a bad situation: "I was trying to make nice and live through it ... I was just trying to figure out what the heck I'd gotten into, and how to get out of it."

On the morning of January 15 Leehman drove Bashara back to the *Portland International Airport* in dead silence. Bashara caught the 6 a.m. flight for Detroit, and Leehman was left to her own devices.

In testimony Leehman later said she had "no plans for any future with him at this point." However, she remained in contact with Bashara via phone, text, eMail and Instant Message for at least another 10 days. Bashara left behind a leather collar and a pair of light blue briefs in her possession, leaving little doubt of his expectations.

§

This time Rachel Gillette was adamant. She would not move to Kensington until she had the Bashara's divorce papers in her hands, and the closing date of January 27 was rapidly approaching.

"He told me he lost his copy," said Gillette. "When he went to get another one several weeks later his attorney was on vacation."

"We were about to embark on a big deal," lamented Gillette, "and I was going to be moving, putting my name on financial documents with him. I wanted to know for sure that he was really divorced."

> **January 20** eMail:
> *"So if I am wrong for insisting on seeing the divorce papers before I can believe You, I will apologize once I see them. We started our relationship with lies and there's been lies all through it. Every few months I find something else out. So why should it be different now? If You have not lied to me about your divorce then You'll be able to say I was wrong for not trusting You. But until I see those papers You can not say that to me."*

In mid January of 2012 Bob Bashara found himself in a tough spot. He'd made arrangements to purchase a home for his new lifestyle; he'd laid plans to bring a second submissive into their relationship and his mistress had finally laid down the law: No divorce papers – No new life!

Bashara didn't have the finances to complete the transaction on the Kensington property without either the support of his wife's income or the full proceeds from the sale of their home. Or ... was there some other way? Unwittingly perhaps, Rachel Gillette's ultimatum may have forced tragic consequences ...

Chapter 4

Conspiracy Rising

Conspiracies coalesce in the wind, born of apparent necessity and often lacking clear conception. In the first half of 2011 Bob Bashara had a problem, and by all appearances he could think of nothing else. Merely an eery coincidence or well planned foreshadowing, correspondence with Rachel Gillette alluded to an evil tiding:

> **March**: *"My situation is secondary to what we have and yet ending soon."*
> **April**: *"We are close to our time coming."*
> **July**: *"My situation, now coming to a close."*
> **July**: *"The wait is over. The promise of our life, a life for us that you dream of, is at hand."*

A typical warm and humid August in Michigan enticed many to seek cooler weather up north, but Bob Bashara was longing for a different kind of vacation. As the landlord of multiple rental properties, he often frequented a seedy east side Detroit furniture supplier called *Steve's Furniture*, located in a rough and forgotten neighborhood on Warren Ave. at Chalmers, owned and operated by Steven Tibaudo.

Tibaudo was a man in his mid fifties who fancied himself as a quasi 'connected' type, a sort of low rent 'wiseguy.' To Bashara he was a man who could get things done. The two became acquainted in the late 1990s as Bashara patronized the outfit looking for cheap deals on a variety of appliances. It was late summer when Bashara strolled into *Steve's* looking for Tibaudo:

"Hey Steve, can we go talk in private?"

"He kept staring at the corners of the room," recalled Tibaudo. "I had these cameras. I have one camera on the back door so I can see who's coming in an out."

"Well, this is private here, Bob, what do you need?"

"No," Bashara insisted. "I really need to talk to you in private." All the while he continued looking back and fourth, eyeing the cameras.

"Want me to send everybody away?"

"No, I want to talk in private," repeated Bashara. "Can we go outside?"

"Yeah, if it'll make you feel better."

Tibaudo later said that in the 12 years he'd known and done business with Bashara, he'd never made such a request. "Bob put his hands on my shoulders and started pressing down on me and he says, 'can I trust you?'"

"Yeah Bob, what do you need?"

"Can I really trust you," he said again, his voice betraying his urgency. "I got this Grosse Pointe tenant that's making my life miserable. Do you know anybody that can take care of her?"

"What do you mean?" gasped Tibaudo.

"Do you know anybody that could run her over, or T-bone her," (with a car) Bashara persisted, never eluding as to who or how this person was a problem: "She's making my life hell."

"I've got two cop buddies who can handle this for you," replied Tibaudo.

"What, are you fucking crazy," Bashara half stated while forcefully pushing Tibaudo away, his voice cracking with anxiety.

"I just looked at him," said Tibaudo, "and then he got in his car and drove away."

The two never again spoke of this exchange.

§

By all accounts Joseph Gentz is a big man. Standing nearly six foot five and weighing over 225 he has a distinct resemblance to the actor Ron Pearlman, star of the television program *Sons of Anarchy,* a likeness he often points out to strangers.

Early in his adult life Gentz worked as a merchant marine but more recently he held down numerous odd jobs in and around metro Detroit. During this period Gentz lived in various suburbs including Warren and St. Clair Shores. Known to be 'a bit slow,' he actually had mild mental retardation due to a stroke suffered during child birth which also left him blind in his left eye. His I.Q. is believed to be 67, equivalent to that of a third grader.

Gentz suffered a long list of mental problems over the years. Court records indicate diagnosis from countless physicians of bipolar disorder, organic mood disorder, intermittent explosive personality disorder, seizure disorder and he often exhibited chronic antisocial traits. He was hospitalized three times between 1998 and 2001 for psychiatric problems and suicidal tendencies. His explosive tempter led to a 1999 hospitalization after he threatened to break every bone in his brother's body for stealing his leather jacket.

Gentz married Donna Lowery in 2000 and within a couple months they had a daughter. However, the union was doomed from the start and they filed for divorce only a few months later. Lowery lost parental rights in November 2001 due to neglect – as did Gentz – but the child was eventually returned to Gentz's care following a court ruling. Sadly, Gentz's daughter is also developmentally disabled.

Three weeks after an arrest for domestic violence involving Lowery, Gentz had another explosive outburst when he threatened to shoot both Lowery and her companion. A gun and hunting bow were reportedly confiscated by police following the incident. Soon after they each filed for personal protection orders. An April 2002 court document reads: "There was significant violence throughout the relationship on both sides … however, the majority of … incidents were situations where (Joseph Gentz) was on the offensive."

Court documents also shed light on a July 2009 visit from *Children's Protective Services* which revealed the family home to be 'filthy; the bathtub was black and moldy' and exposed wires were found in the bathroom. The child's bedroom was covered in trash and dirty clothing. In addition, the family dog had an untreated injury causing mouth bleeding, and blood splatter was found on the floors. That visit preceded an order placing the child into *Foster Care*.

Following a diagnosis of impulse disorder in May of 2011, Gentz was rejected for unsupervised visits with his now teenaged daughter. At that time it was determined that he did not have the cognitive capacity, behavioral controls nor judgment to function as a primary parent. As a result, the child was ordered to remain in *Foster Care*. From that point on, Gentz was consumed with the overwhelming desire to regain custody.

§

A chance meeting in mid 2010 at a St. Clair Shores *BP* gas station brought Gentz to the attention of Russell Achatz, who owned a burger joint on that city's *Nautical Mile* along Lake St. Clair.

"I was getting gas and I come in the gas station and he asked me if I was a police officer," remembered Achatz. It was strange because he was not wearing a uniform, nor did he have a badge or police car.

"I told him I owned a restaurant down the street," continued Achatz. He said why didn't I give him a job?"

So that's just what Achatz did, and Gentz began cleaning *Achatz Burgers* for a couple hours a night; and why not? The gas station clerk said Gentz was a good guy, and for a while at least there were no problems.

Achatz noticed quickly that Gentz had perpetually poor work habits, but he continued to employ him to mop the floors anyway. Although he was 'rarely on time' Gentz remained in Achatz's employ for nearly a year.

When given a task or if someone worked along side him Gentz was perfectly able to do the work. "But if he was left alone he couldn't stay on it … He *might* be able to continue a task from day to day, but not always."

"Joe, get back to what you're supposed to be doing, get off that phone," recounted Achatz, describing the day to day exchanges. "He was always on his phone. You couldn't take it from him. He'd put it back in his pocket. He lost concentration quick and he couldn't stay focused."

Achatz also noticed that Gentz always had a business deal going with his attorney, there was always a scheme to get his daughter back and he was always telling Achatz 'I gotta talk to my attorney.'

Another problem troubling Achatz was that Gentz had no actual mode of transportation, instead relying heavily on friends to get him to and from work. Sometimes he walked, but more often than not he got rides from a friend named Steve Virgona.

Virgona was well known for driving Gentz all over town in his white van. The two had been friends off and on for more than a decade but had lost touch. Early in 2009 they became reacquainted when their daughters turned up at the same high school.

Virgona spent increasingly more time with Gentz, along with mutual friends Daniel Fritch and Greg Barraco. Virgona also helped Gentz with a police matter in 2009 stemming from a domestic incident allegedly involving a shotgun.

In the late winter of 2011 Gentz got hurt. "He was helping people who were stuck in the bad snow," recalled Achatz. "He got injured and he brought a doctor's note. That pretty much ended his employment because he couldn't come back to work without a doctor's note stating that he could work again; and from my understanding he fell behind on stuff with his apartment and he just moved on."

Gentz spent the rest of 2011 unable to work and trying, vainly it seems, to regain custody of his daughter. "He was always talking about her," remembered Achatz, "and something to do with the courts."

§

Rebecca Forton, a woman in her late forties and a Grosse Pointe Park landlord, was having difficulty finding a suitable tenant for her duplex at 1226 Wayburn. After a short discussion she decided to act on her mother's advice and seek the services of an agent.

Looking up property management companies, the elder Forton came across Bob Bashara in "*the little blue book*", Grosse Pointe's local answer to the *Yellow Pages*. Based on her mother's advice and positive experience with Bashara, Forton decided to engage his services.

"I mentioned that I had a property that I needed a tenant for," explained Forton. "He said he would be interested in showing it and finding me someone."

A short time later Bashara called to say it was a very nice property. "He said he shouldn't have a problem finding an adequate tenant," remembered Forton. Soon after the two met.

Although the available unit was the upper, they actually met in the lower flat where Forton's father lived. "We talked about the rent and what type of tenant I was looking for," explained Forton. "I told him I didn't care about the details of tenants."

"I didn't want more than two people there because of wear and tear on the property," clarified Forton. "Plus I was concerned because my father was living below, that there not be a lot of noise to disturb him."

A month later Bashara indicated he had a tenant living in Detroit with children who wanted to move to Grosse Pointe. It was a family of four but Forton held fast to her limit of double occupancy. The next attempt came in the package of a middle aged single mother with a teenage daughter. This would have been ideal for Forton, but Bashara never followed through and the deal never materialized.

§

Steve Tibaudo is a dog lover, and particularly fond of terriers. Sometime in the late summer of 2011 he received a call from an old friend and fellow terrier owner Roy Lawson, an elderly gentleman with a soft southern drawl who walked with a cane. Tibaudo was particularly fond of his accent and the two often engaged in friendly conversation."

"I met him at the corner of my street at *Joseph's Party Store* in St. Clair Shores," said Tibaudo. "We started a conversation, he had a terrier and I had a terrier."

The two shared a long history of helping each other, usually concerning dog needs such as leashes, collars and kennels. "I tried to help him with whatever he needed done," remembered Tibaudo.

Lawson shared with Tibaudo that he had a friend who needed help and a job. "I told him I didn't have any openings ... business was slow," recalled Tibaudo.

"Maybe you can buy some of his furniture?" suggested Lawson.

As a favor Tibaudo went over and took a look. A few days later Roy showed up at Tibaudo's home with a familiar face in tow ... "It was Joe Gentz."

Gentz had worked for Tibaudo once, a decade ago. "He only worked for me for a short spell," said Tibaudo. "He worked for my wife's cousin's pizzeria."

"Roy said Joe was being evicted. He was living at the *Eagle Pointe Apartments*," in St. Clair Shores. Again Lawson asked Tibaudo for help.

Believing he knew the owner at *Eagle Pointe*, Tibaudo agreed to see what he could do.

"I called Bob," said Tibaudo. "I thought Bob owned the building." Thinking Bob could stand to save some money, he offered to help. "If you evict someone you gotta pay the bailiff, so I might be able to keep Bob from calling a bailiff and getting Joe a few extra days to help him move, as a favor to Roy," explained Tibaudo. But when he asked Bashara if he owned the *Eagle Pointe Apartments* and he said no.

"I got this guy," Tibaudo explained to Bashara. "He's being evicted from there and I thought if you owned it we'd move him out so you wouldn't have to get the bailiff."

"Maybe he could be a good handyman for you?" suggested Tibaudo. "He's being evicted. He might be able to help you. He does plumbing, he's a big guy, he can help you move stuff."

"Give the guy my number," Bashara said, clearly not expecting much.

So Tibaudo gave Gentz Bashara's number and vice versa. Bashara made first contact on September 27, the first of nearly 500 calls the two shared over the next five months.

§

On the last day of September Bashara contacted Rebecca Forton with news of a single male parent who was in the midst of a custody battle. "He would make the perfect tenant," Bashara told her. Then he explained that he'd already shown the apartment and was ready to close the deal so Forton agreed to meet on October 8.

"When I arrived Mr. Bashara was already there with the potential tenant," recalled Forton, "and he introduced me to Joe Gentz."

"He was a large man," continued Forton. "He was dressed in blue jeans and a casual shirt. He didn't look at me or make much eye contact. They were in the kitchen and Mr. Bashara was standing beside him."

Bashara had the rental agreement in hand, already partially filled out, but according to Forton much of it was illegible. "He handed it to me," said Forton, "and then began talking about Mr. Gentz."

> "This is Mr. Joe Gentz ... "I've known him a long, long time. He's a really great guy. He made an excellent tenant. He is currently in the process of trying to gain custody of his daughter, so you would not have to worry about the house being a mess. He would always make sure that everything was perfectly in order, in the event (that) the case workers would come by."

"He also told me Joe was extremely handy," remembered Forton. "He would be able to work on the apartment, he'd be able to work odd jobs. He'd make a great overall tenant."

Joe Gentz hadn't spoken a word as Bashara continued his sterling reference, adding that Gentz had lived in his former residence for nearly 10 years. Then Bashara asked Forton if she had any questions.

"Mr. Gentz, you've been at this residence for nine or 10 years? Why did you suddenly want to move?"

Keeping his eyes trained on the floor, Gentz remained mute. Then Bashara said: "Well, the property he's at, which is at 9 and Jefferson, has been bought out by a new management company. They are in the process of renovating all the apartments, they've increased the rent and they're in the process of trying to drive out all the current tenants. If you don't believe me you can drive by and look for yourself."

"I don't think I'm going to take him," Forton said flatly. There were far too many unresolved issues, she thought, particularly troubling was the fact that Gentz had lived at his previous residence for 10 years and was suddenly moving. In her experience this was not usually a good sign.

"At that point Mr. Bashara became a little agitated," said Forton. "He began posturing … the tone of his voice, the look on his face, his body language."

"Oh, come on, this is a great guy," pleaded Bashara, pressing his knuckles on the counter. "Why won't you take him? He's going to make a great tenant."

Another nagging issue troubling Forton was Gentz's lack of monthly income, which reportedly was a mere $1,000. With rent running at $750 plus utilities, Forton knew he'd have virtually nothing left for food or living expenses.

"He's recently had surgery," added Bashara. "He normally works more, but he's not able to at this time."

"Well, I also get (an additional) $1,000 a month," stammered Gentz, finally breaking his silence.

"He spoke very slow, very deliberately," described Forton. "He made no eye contact … I believed that he was either mentally handicapped or perhaps he'd had a closed head injury." He also indicated that he'd be coming into some extra money soon.

"Based on what Gentz told me," explained Forton, "I finally decided he would have the means to live at the apartment and that he would have additional income."

Later the same day Bashara, Gentz and Forton met at the apartment of Forton's mother. Bashara had already written up the rental agreement along with the appropriate receipts, which he partially filled out and printed while waiting in his car.

Oddly, Bashara signed the agreements but Gentz did not. In fact, Forton said that Gentz never paid any money either, but Bashara forked over $1,100 cash to cover the first month's rent and a security deposit.

Finally, Forton and Gentz discussed the transfer of utilities. Gentz moved in about a week later, everything went smoothly for the first month and in November rent was transferred as expected from Gentz's account to hers.

§

It's not difficult to entertain the possibility that a plot to kill Jane Bashara existed well before the characters were cast. But in Joe Gentz Bob Bashara may have found exactly what he was looking for: Gentz was large and physically threatening, easily manipulated and less than intelligent. Possibly the best characteristic of all, he was desperate for anything, such as cash and transportation, that could help him regain custody of his child.

It was an unusually warm fall afternoon when Bashara summoned Joe Gentz to his home for some random cleanup projects. But Gentz said there was far more to it than that, Bashara actually wanted his wife dead.

Out of nowhere Bashara said: "I'll give you five grand."

"First I thought he was joking," Gentz said later. "And I'm like, OK Bob, whatever ... I thought he was bullshitting. It don't make sense. Why would he want his wife dead?"

There are differing accounts of the incident: on *Dateline NBC* Bashara said Gentz "met Jane out in the back ... She brought iced tea one day when we were cleaning up shrubbery and preparing the backyard for the winter."

On another occasion Bashara said the two never met. Nevertheless, Gentz spoke, in an interview with retired Detroit police detective Tom Berry which aired on *Dateline NBC*, as if she was there.

"When I checked out the back yard after she left, I looked on top of the roof and there's tools up there," said Gentz. "I'm like, this guy's serious. He wants his wife taken out."

"He said 'I'll give you a grand if (you) knock out (my) wife,'" recalled Gentz. "He wanted it to look like an accident, like she fell off the roof of the house." But Gentz decided not to go through with it.

"He goes, 'I'm ticked off,'" remembered Gentz. "'You're supposed to take care of my wife' and I'm like, Bob! I says, I don't know. He says 'you're chicken.' I'm like Bob, you know what? Maybe I am. I got a lot to lose here."

Then Bashara said he was on a deadline. "Now I'm like, what do you mean you're on a deadline?" explained Gentz. "He says I gotta have this done immediately."

"I should'a went to the police department, I should'a went to the cops," Gentz said regretfully. "This man's for real, this man's crazy." But Gentz didn't go to the police, and the plot continued to fester.

§

"The first time I heard of 'Bob' was when Joe was getting evicted," recalled Steve Virgona. "Joe got injured ... he was pushing a car that got stuck in the snow and he had a hernia." Incapacitated, Gentz was forced to quit working at the burger joint and money problems quickly ensued.

"Joe said he knew a guy named Bob," explained Virgona, and that he was helping him get the new apartment in Grosse Pointe. "Joe showed up and was asking about the ... gas and electric utilities."

"I saw 'Bob' there," continued Virgona. "I was over at Joe's, I saw him the day he was evicted. Joe was trying to get some money," and a few days later Virgona helped Gentz move.

Virgona said Gentz came to him with a far fetched scheme to make some extra money. It was a mid October evening and the two were inside Virgona's white van, parked outside a Roseville *McDonald's*. Gentz said he was approached by a guy who wanted him to do harm to someone for money.

"He mentioned something about a hit and run," said Virgona. "What do you mean about a hit and run? You mean an insurance job?"

"Yes," whispered Gentz. "Steve, you need to make money."

"I don't want nothin' to do with it," Virgona said flatly.

"He mentioned there was an offer," said Virgona. "I believe it was $10,000 … Then he offered $4,000. We'd split it in half, so it would be $2,000" (each).

"I said I still don't want nothing [*sic*] part of it," said Virgona. "Then I asked him 'what about your family?' He didn't act like he really cared about it at the moment."

A few weeks later the subject came up again while the two were eating at the *National Coney Island* at 11 Mile Rd. on Gratiot. The two were again in the white van in the parking lot.

"Joe said basically the same thing as he said the first time," reported Virgona. "I remember … a conversation about a *Cadillac*. … and he showed me a quick flash of some receipts that supposedly 'Bob' gave him."

The specifics of the plot varied, but the idea surrounding a hit-and-run solidified around the use of a drug known as heparin, an anticoagulant that could either be injected at a lethal dosage or, if combined with an open wound, could cause the victim to bleed to death. (The idea may have come from the Dan Brown book and film *Angels and Demons,* in which heparin was used to kill the Pope).

Evidence suggests that Bashara dispatched Gentz to obtain a supply of heparin and insulin "any way he could get it." However, Gentz was unable to spell or pronounce 'heparin' so Virgona, unaware of why he was looking for it, wrote it down on a scrap of paper so it wouldn't be forgotten.

On October 16, Steve Virgona received a text message from Gentz asking for help; his reply read: *"Joe, I can not help you with your bills by putting my name on them, I won't do this."*

§

In late October Joe Gentz began corresponding with a woman he met on the *Metro PCS* singles website named Lorna Beth Riikonen, who was in her early forties and living in a small apartment in Romulus, near Detroit's *Metro Airport*.

Riikonen had a history of bad, dead end relationships and was weary of the whole rat race, and yet, she was tired of being alone. After a conversation with her nephew, who shared his recent success with online dating, she thought she'd give it a shot. "I was working and came home bored, that's why I did it."

"First we texted, because it was on that *singles.com* thing on my phone," explained Riikonen. Gentz shared a photo of himself in a leather jacket and sunglasses and Riikonen mistook him for a biker, which she found instantly intriguing. Soon Gentz said he wanted to speak via telephone and Riikonen was open to that as well.

The two found they had a few things in common, which fueled their conversations. "He had a daughter in *Foster Care* and my children had been in *Foster Care*," Riikonen pointed out.

Riikonen was the mother of three and had recently lost a daughter to an accidental drug overdose, which was often the topic of their discussions. One exchange in particular caused Gentz to became agitated, so much so that it appears he was intent on exacting revenge for the teen's untimely death:

Gentz:
"I have FD high pls." (I have friends in high places).
"I will not let this go."
"They heve ak47. I will let them know."
"It did happen in det ok but was it the e side or the w side?"
"I am getting a handgun."

In another exchange on November 17 Gentz revealed some oddly disjointed details:

Riikonen: *"What have u been doing did you get the cadillac from your buddy?"*
Gentz: *"No I did not get it but i am working on it."*
Riikonen: *"Is he really giving it to you?"*
Gentz: *"Yes. I am get the car."*
Gentz: *"No i move to this very nice place."*
Gentz: *"It is Grosse Pointe."*
Gentz: *"I am playing with the big dog big money."*
Gentz: *"i messing around with those rich people."*

§

Bashara again reached out to Forton in late November. He was looking for a referral fee, but according to Forton he had never sent a bill. She instructed him to do so and said she'd gladly take care of it.

In December, Bashara called again, still looking for a referral fee but according to Forton she still hadn't received a bill. By this time issues had arisen over rent payments from Gentz, or more accurately the lack of it. Bashara assured her he'd speak to Gentz and would personally take care of paying any past-due rent.

The extent of Gentz's financial desperation was increasingly evident on December 27: while Bashara was in South Carolina attending the wedding of Rachel Gillette's daughter, he sent the following text to Bashara:

> **Gentz**: *"Bob i do not have any money or food in this house i need to get some i need 50 dollers [sic] can you lone me that tell the 3td."*
> **Bashara**: *"I am out of town, will call."*
> **Gentz**: *"ok."*

The bill for the referral fee never materialized, but somehow Gentz's rent got paid and it would be nearly two months before Forton would again hear from Bob Bashara.

§

Fifty-one year old Frances Natale (na-TA-lee) became 'acquainted' with Joe Gentz via *singles.com* during the summer of 2011. "I met him on single line," explained Natale. "He gave me his phone number. I called him and I proceeded to meet him, acquaint him as a friend."

Natale is a few inches short of five feet and has a round face. Her thinning hairline displays an unforgettable image. Shortly after meeting Gentz she became an item with his friend Greg Barraco. Along with Steve Virgona the group was increasingly social, often meeting for coffee or a bite to eat. Their usual stomping ground included various *McDonald's* and local greasy spoons such as *Travis Coffee Shop* on Mack Ave. in St. Clair Shores.

Through numerous conversations Natale became aware of the many odd jobs Gentz ventured through, but in the late fall, around Thanksgiving, he began speaking of one in particular. When Natale pressed him about it Gentz simply replied: "To make good money ... around $6,000."

"Doing home repairs or what?" probed Natale, trying to learn something about the mysterious employer. But Gentz wouldn't budge, refusing to reveal his full name.

"It's a secret, and he's out of town a lot," Gentz said, escalating the intrigue.

In December Natale said she began to hear the name 'Bob' in connection with Gentz's new Grosse Pointe apartment.

"He explained to me that someone helped him get the apartment," said Natale. "I thought, OK, he had to apply for the apartment ... So I guess the gas or ... electric ... was not going to be in his name? But why not?"

"Well, I owe some money," revealed Gentz, "and I can have it put in my friend's name." At this point another pattern began to emerge, that of 'friend' versus 'boss' when referring to the mysterious 'Bob'.

"One time he talked about making $6,000 when the 'boss' was out of town," explained Natale. "I couldn't figure it out; how does his boss go out of town when he worked at the restaurant? I never knew what kind of work he was doing."

But Natale was eventually able to put some of the pieces together although she couldn't make heads or tails of the reasons behind it. 'Bob' was Gentz's 'friend' who was helping him with the apartment and utilities, but apparently a 'boss' when referring to the $6,000 and the car, which appeared to be compensation for the mysterious job. If she was right, and 'boss' and 'friend' were the same 'Bob', but Gentz still never revealed his last name, nor volunteered any details.

§

Joe Gentz and Greg Barraco were longtime friends before a falling out separated them for several years. They were reacquainted in 2010, and a year or so later, in the late fall of 2011 between Thanksgiving and Christmas, Gentz and Barraco were having a discussion over sliders at *Travis*. Gentz said he had a question he needed to ask.

Gentz said he needed help: "To hurt some lady in Grosse Pointe … Try to kill her or something." Gentz also said he would be paid.

"I think he said $5,000," recalled Barraco, "and he wanted to hit her with a big car."

As usual Gentz was short on the details, not giving any indication who the woman was or specifically who wanted him to do it.

"He mentioned it was 'Bob', I think," continued Barraco, emphasizing the lack of a surname.

"He said he wanted to hit her with a big car and he asked where he could buy one." But he never shared any other details.

"I don't want to hear it, I don't want to hear that crazy stuff," replied Barraco, brushing Gentz off. "I walked back inside and ate my hamburger."

Three times Gentz asked Barraco for help, each one receiving the same cold shoulder. "I told him the same answer, I'm not gonna do it."

§

On December 10, 33 minutes after a four and half minute phone exchange between Bob Bashara and Joe Gentz (and the very next phone transmission from Gentz), records reveal a mysterious text conversation between Gentz and an unknown person in the 302 (Delaware) area code:

> **Gentz**: 5:40 p.m.: *"When you get up i really need to talk to you about something, if i know something about someone about to do someone in."*
> **Gentz**: 5:40 p.m.: *"Were do i go to."*
> **Gentz**: 5:41 p.m.: *"I have to watch my ass."*

Gentz: 5:41 p.m.: *"Pls call me hun."*
Gentz: 5:42 p.m.: *"I do not went [sic] to die."*

§

It was mid December and Steve Virgona and Joe Gentz were again engaged in a familiar conversation in Virgona's van, this time near the service drive at I-94 and 12 Mile Rd.:

"He asked me again, and he turned around and he goes 'Hey Steve,'" recalled Virgona. "He's on the phone talking to some guy named 'Bob', and he goes 'you know Steve, you need some money,' and he's giving me more detail about the hit and run."

"What's going on here?" demanded Virgona.

"This guy 'Bob' wants to knock off ..."

"He used the words 'do a hit and run' on his wife, do an insurance job," remembered Virgona. "I kind of caught on what he was saying the third time."

"What do you mean insurance job, Joe? 'Cause this makes no sense. Is this leading to murder?"

"Yes," replied Gentz, the word slowly creeping from his mouth in a whisper. "She works downtown in Detroit."

"I want nothin' to do with it," Virgona said forcefully, putting his hand up near Gentz's face.

But Gentz persisted with more details while 'Bob' was still on the line. "He provided the route his wife usually took to get home and the approximate time," remembered Virgona. "She gets up around 6:30, she gets off at 5/5:30, sometimes later like 6/6:30 and she'll be home around 7; she drives down Jefferson."

"They were planning to do it in the next day or so," continued Virgona, adding that Gentz mentioned 'wife' and a guy named 'Bob', but still wouldn't reveal 'Bob's' last name. Then, according to Virgona, Gentz showed him a recent text from 'Bob' saying he would text the plan and deposit money into his bank account.

"After the conversation … he turned around and showed me that the money had been deposited in his bank account … he had a picture of the receipt," continued Virgona. "He was showing me that this was real, it was gonna happen."

"Steve, I'll call you in the morning," Gentz said excitedly. "I'll give you more information and I'll let you know what's going on."

"I don't want nothin' to do with it," Virgona pleaded again.

Armed only with information that 'Bob' wanted to kill his wife, Virgona says he contacted an unnamed Macomb County Detective as early as October, but he "wanted more information (and) I didn't have it".

(Neither the text or deposit slip was introduced into evidence).

§

Although they corresponded for nearly two months, Lorna Beth Riikonen laid eyes on Joe Gentz just once. It was an icy, cold and damp December night, a week or so before Christmas. She was working at *Einstein Bagels* inside Detroit's *Metro Airport*.

"While I was at work somebody blew out my phone," explained Riikonen. "Basically, they called my phone over and over again. I didn't answer it because, usually when it was something important I would call my daughters, to make sure they were OK."

Once quitting time arrived Riikonen checked the phone. "I was hoping it was the guy that I liked," she said with a frown. But the phone was dead and required some plug in time first. Once she reached the car she plugged in the phone and was instantly disappointed to find Joe Gentz on the caller I.D. "When … I seen it was him I was like … honestly? It was not the guy I hoped was calling."

Unfortunately, while plugging in the phone she accidentally answered it. She had no romantic interest in Gentz, but they did have a few things in common.

"He asked me previously, 'do you want me to come see you' and I said yes, that would be nice," explained Riikonen. "But I didn't think he'd come that same day, and he did."

Gentz said he was near by and wanted to see her. "The guy's got a kid in *Foster Care*," Riikonen thought to herself, so maybe some time together would be OK. But once Gentz arrived he said the bus stopped running for the night so Riikonen was forced to drive him home; and that's when Gentz started talking.

"He mentioned a car," recalled Riikonen. "He said somebody had offered him some money, I can't recall the exact words he used. He said somebody offered him some money to put a hit on somebody."

"What about that car your friend was giving you," asked Riikonen, remembering Gentz said he needed a car and a job to impress the court in the upcoming custody battle. "Is something wrong with it?"

"No, it's a nice car," insisted Gentz before repeating that somebody had offered him money and the car in return for knocking somebody off.

"Who is behind all this?"

"Basher ... Basher," Gentz mumbled.

"Who is that? A drug dealer?"

Gentz said nothing, absolutely nothing. Then Riikonen pressed the issue and asked if it was a friend or acquaintance who'd made the offer and Gentz said 'friend.'

"Maybe they're not serious," posed Riikonen. "People say stuff like that, like 'I'm going to kill you,' maybe he wasn't serious."

"Oh, they were serious all right."

"When he said that, he didn't sound serious," Riikonen remembered later. "He had a way of talking."

"I can take you to the police station tonight," proposed Riikonen. "'Somebody offered you money like that ... you should go to the police ... Those kinds of people aren't your friends. You could go to jail for life if they do something like that."

Then Gentz suggested they go back to Riikonen's apartment and she declined. "I have a daughter. I didn't know this man like that. I didn't want to bring anybody home."

"We could hang out at your place," Gentz said, pressing his luck. But Riikonen would have nothing of it.

The rest of the drive was in silence, and increasingly troubling for Riikonen. "I was very distressed," she said. "But I had the feeling I would never see him again." And that was just fine by her.

§

According to phone records, five calls were placed from Bob Bashara's cell phone to Joe Gentz originating in Eugene, Oregon and Salt Lake City, Utah between January 12 and 15. Janet Leehman later recalled overhearing a "three to four minute" conversation between Bashara and someone she assumed, based on the one-sided conversation, to be a handyman. Bashara was in the kitchen when she heard him bellow: "What the fuck is wrong with you? I want this done. I want it done before I get back."

Chapter 5

January 24

(The following depiction of the events of January 24, 2012, is culled from multiple sources including courtroom testimony and exhibits, media interviews, ATF/FBI telephone records and Bob Bashara's own words from law enforcement and media interviews.)

It began like any other mid-winter day in Michigan, overcast, chilly, 13 mph winds and temperatures struggling to reach the mid 30's. It was exactly the kind of day that drives snowbirds south seeking refuge.

Jane Bashara awoke at her usual time, around 6:20 a.m., and went about her morning routine. Passing Bob in the bathroom, they had a brief conversation concerning the evening's plans: prep work on Bob's tax documents from the rental business.

While Jane was getting ready for work, records show that Bashara made three phone calls to Joe Gentz starting at 6:24, the first of seven between them that day. His fourth call was to Rachel Gillette at 6:58.

After grabbing breakfast, Jane was out the door and off for work by 7:15.

Today was a special day for Jane, anticipation mounting for word from little sister Julie Rowe: "It was my first day of a big, major meeting at a new job," recalled Rowe. "Jane helped me create the agenda."

Growing up Julie and Jane had a special relationship, not uncommon for siblings born 13 years apart. "I was presenting," continued Rowe, "at lunchtime I sent her a text that said the morning went really well."

"I'll call you tonight," was Jane's simple reply.

At 8:54 Bob received a text from Janet Leehman: *"Good morning, Sir."*

At 9 a.m. the Bashara's house keeper, Maria, arrived and found a handwritten note:

> *"Dear Maria,*
> *I have lost my wedding ring. Please keep your eyes open for it.*
> *Thanks, Jane."*

Minutes later Jane made the first of two phone calls to longtime friend Eileen Stratelak (the second was just before noon). Stratelak hoped to talk Jane into attending the high school basketball game with her that evening, but Jane declined, she'd been gone lately and "just wanted to go home and relax."

At 9:03 Rachel Gillette received an eMail from *DTE Energy* confirming residential gas/electric service would begin at 1011 Kensington on January 30.

According to Maria (the housekeeper) Bob left between 10:15 and 10:30. He had a big day planned as well, particularly a meeting with *Johnstone & Johnstone* realtors, but first he headed south to a *Rotary* function at the *Wyandotte Arts Center* where he remained from noon until 2 p.m. before heading back to Grosse Pointe.

Bashara called Joe Gentz at 2:33. According to Gentz, Bashara offered him a job, instructing him to meet at his home on Middlesex at "seven o'clock sharp, and do not be late." *(Evidence suggests the actual time was 6 p.m.)*. Phone records indicate Bashara's phone connected to a *Verizon* cell tower located on East Jefferson Ave. near Connor St., about one mile from Grosse Pointe Park.

"I'll be there," Gentz replied.

At 3:30 Bashara arrived at *Johnstone & Johnstone*, located on Kercheval in the Grosse Pointe Farms Hill business district. He was meeting with Lorraine Muccioli and Kathy Young to pick up the closing packet for 1011 Kensington, where Bashara was intending to set up shop with his two 'slaves,' Rachel and Janet. The realtors easily recalled the meeting, noting: "It was very cold … he had no overcoat or gloves, just wearing a sport coat."

Bashara brought his conditional certification of occupancy (dated January 17, 2012) and once the short meeting was over Young realized she'd neglected to set up the final walk through so she phoned Bashara around 5 p.m. and made arrangements to do so on Friday, January 27 at 2 p.m., an hour before the scheduled closing.

§

The FBI is home to the *Violent Crime Task Force* (VCTF), which is a coordinated effort including the *Wayne County Sheriff*, Detroit Police, *Michigan State Police* and the ATF.

Among other things, the VCTF is empowered to recover forensic phone records containing the exact location of each cell tower a particular cell phone connects to, plus the time and duration of activity. Essentially, anytime a cell phone is connected, either on an active call or simply receiving or retrieving a voice message, the information is archived. In January of 2012 this task force was coordinated by FBI special agent Christopher Hess, who was also involved with the *Cellular Analysis Survey Team* (CAST) within the FBI.

According to these forensic phone records, on January 24 Bashara (or his cell phone at least) was at or near 552 Middlesex at 3:48 p.m. and connected to the nearest *Verizon* tower, #994, which is located a block west of Connor St. at East Jefferson Ave.

Upon leaving work at *Kema Services* in downtown Detroit, Jane called her daughter Jessica at 4:11. "She said she was on Jefferson," remembered Jessica.

Jane was heading east, making her way back to Grosse Pointe. The conversation primarily concerned a summer job she was arranging for Jessica with the help of Sandra Ennis at *DTE*.

Jane concluded the conversation saying she needed to get something to write on just as she pulled her black *Mercedes SUV* into the driveway at 552 Middlesex at 4:33. Records indicate her *Blackberry* was connected to *Verizon* tower #994, where it would continue to do so until 6:26.

"We were going to have another phone call," explained Jessica. "I had to speak to … her friend regarding the job that summer." Jessica said her mother would normally park in the garage on the right hand side, closest to the house.

Jane called "specifically at 4:40," Bashara told police, adding that he'd missed the call because he had his hands full cleaning up the alley behind the *Hard Luck Lounge* and *Dylan's Raw Bar*, both housed in the solid block of buildings along the east side of Mack Ave. in Grosse Pointe Park. (In actuality, he didn't answer the call because he was in the midst of an eight minute conversation with Rachel Gillette that began at 4:38).

According to those who knew him, cleaning up the alley was odd, uncharacteristic behavior for Bashara. "He told me he'd been having a drink," remembered Venita Porter. "He said he'd gone to the back alley to pick up some trash, which I thought was really funny. I've never seen him pick up a damn thing."

"When I had my hands free I dialed Jane back at 4:46," Bashara told police. "She called me and said she was on her way home, and that she'd be home at 5:15." However, records indicate Jane was already home at the time of the call.

Between 4:52 and 5:20, Bashara's cell phone accessed *Verizon* towers #144 and #156, both servicing the vicinity near the *Hard Luck Lounge*.

"Jane asked me what I was doing," Bashara told an interviewer, "I said 'well, I'm involved in this project and I'll probably be home around 7:30 - 8 o'clock.'"

It was blustery and the mercury was rapidly falling, so Bashara decided to go inside to warm up. Kristy Sample, *Hard Luck Lounge* bartender, noted that Bashara entered around 5:15. Bashara asked when Mike Mouyianis (owner of the *Hard Luck*) would arrive and Sample said she expected him around 9 p.m. Bashara then ordered a *Captain&Coke*, seemingly significant only because he always drank *Pabst Blue Ribbon*. In fact, Sample recalled having served him nothing else before.

Sample then watched as Bashara took a seat in the back lounge area of the bar, an obscured view from the front. Noting the emergency door (exit only) in the back and the main door in front, Sample said she always tried to position herself with a view of both. Bashara returned and initiated a brief conversation.

According to Sample it was unusual for Bashara to spend so much time at the *Hard Luck*, and shortly after "he left through the back door at approximately 5:45."

§

Joe Gentz talked to his friend Steve Virgona sometime in the late afternoon, and said he was going to 'Bob's' to clean the garage. "I offered to drive him and he said he could walk faster," recalled Virgona. Gentz declined, incorrectly saying he was just around the block.

At 5:33 Gentz received a text message that read *"I'm done eating hun,"* from an unknown sender. He typically would respond immediately but in this case he didn't get around to it until 8:04 p.m. when he replied: *"I am home babby."*

Walking briskly due to the winter chill, Gentz covered the one and a half miles from 1226 Wayburn to 552 Middlesex in just under 20 minutes, arriving at almost exactly 6 p.m. Bashara was waiting at the door between the garage and the main entrance, which led directly into a small mud room. Gentz then followed Bashara out to the attached garage.

"Bob, you want me to move these boxes out?"

Abruptly, according to Gentz, Bashara said, "I want you to take out my wife."

At that moment Gentz realized Bashara's intentions had little to do with moving boxes. "He goes, 'eight grand, car!' ... I was told to hurry up and do it," explained Gentz, adding, "there's a deadline."

Then the two men apparently created a ruckus sure to alienate Jane, who was in the kitchen.

"Bob turns around, she's (Jane) yelling and screaming at Bob," recounted Gentz. 'I want this fucking shit out of here, take your Goddamn fucking golf clubs to *Lochmoor* ... and Bob says 'Shut the woman up now.'"

A short hesitation, according to Gentz, was enough to push the issue with Bashara, who brandished a .32 caliber *Smith & Wesson* revolver and aimed it directly at Gentz. Bashara pulled back the hammer ..."All I heard was c-l-i-c-k!" remembered Gentz.

"I looked down the barrel and I'm like 'oh shit!' and he (Bashara) says, 'take her out, or I'm takin' you.'"

"He hit her with a right hand chop to the back of the head," Steve Virgona said, eager to share the account to a TV interviewer several days later.

"I hit her," Gentz confirmed, "back of the neck. I knocked her down. She goes 'Bob!' and Bob says 'choke her.'"

"We struggle ... she didn't get knocked out. She was more like "What cha doin' Bob? Help me Bob!' and Bob says 'take care of her.'"

According to media reports, Gentz got down on his knees and began choking her. She continued to struggle so Gentz stood up. "Finish her," ordered Bashara, "finish her!"

"I went like, bam," described Gentz, displaying a crushing kicking motion with his leg. "I took her neck out with my boot."

In testimony a medical examiner described the loud pop the two men must have heard as her larynx was crushed, adding that three to four minutes of constant pressure to the neck would normally be required to cause asphyxiation.

"Bob saw the whole damn thing," observed Gentz.

"Make sure she's dead," Bashara instructed, adding, "load her up in the car." Then he shoved the gun into his back pocket.

"So I went to pick her up," explained Gentz, and for a brief second, "her shirt opened up. I didn't see a bra, I seen tits. Bob goes over there and goes (in a childish voice), 'I'm sorry baby' and covers the tits up. Then we put her in her vehicle."

"I put her feet in," continued Gentz, "Bob put her head in." Then Bashara went back into the house, retrieved Jane's purse and threw the contents around the front of the car, her *Blackberry* falling on the passenger side floor with a single thud. Then he stuffed Jane's arms inside her black *North Face* jacket, backwards, leaving her hands barely peaking out through the sleeves.

As Gentz got into Jane's *Mercedes* Bashara barked, "Don't fuck up!"

"I'll pay you," Gentz remembered Bashara promising. "Don't worry about it. I'll catch up with you later."

"I'm like OK, fine," said Gentz.

As the garage door slowly opened, Bashara climbed into his mud colored *Lincoln Navigator* and the two drove off in opposite directions. At 6:26 p.m. Bashara called Jane's cell phone, both phones accessed *Verizon* tower #994 (which provides service exclusive to the vicinity of the Middlesex home) before Jane's phone transferred to *Verizon* tower #156, which services the entire area between 552 Middlesex northward into Detroit.

At 6:28 p.m. Bashara made a second call to Jane's cell phone, this time connecting though *Verizon* tower #156. That call then transferred to *Verizon* tower #94 (located at Lennox St. north of East Jefferson Ave. and also services exclusively the area north towards the *Hard Luck Lounge*).

(Forensic analysis indicates tower #94 is not accessible from 552 Middlesex, suggesting the call must have originated near 552 Middlesex but terminated near or in the vicinity of the Hard Luck Lounge).

Jane Bashara's *Blackberry*, nestled precariously on the passenger side floor of her *Mercedes*, received the 6:28 call utilizing the same *Verizon* tower #94, suggesting her *Blackberry* was also in transit.

Hairdresser Missy Keller, a tenant of Bashara's who lived in the second floor apartment above the *Hard Luck Lounge* (and at one time next door to Rachel Gillette) was entertaining friends, who began arriving shortly after 6:30. A few made comments about someone in the alley cleaning. Peering out her back door Keller could see Bashara, "sweeping up the back parking lot," something she had never seen in the three years she lived there.

Between 6:41 and 7:15 Bashara's phone interacted with *Verizon* towers #156 and #144 (both provide service near the *Hard Luck Lounge*) by placing calls to his mother Nancy, daughter Jessica and son Robert.

Jane Bashara's *Blackberry* received another call at 6:43, connecting to *Verizon* tower #323, located just south of 7 Mile Rd. at Gratiot Ave. in Detroit, indicating the *Blackberry* was still in transit, moving further and further northeast.

Kristy Sample observed Bashara reenter the *Hard Luck*, alone, at approximately 6:45. "He ordered another cocktail (*Captain & Coke*) and returned to the lounge area," then stayed out of sight for about 10 minutes.

"He returned to the bar and ordered a beer and a glass of water," said Sample. "He informed me that he was going to have a friend join him, then he moved back to a booth ... Soon after that he left out the front door. He said he was meeting a friend and that he would return."

Ten minutes later Bashara reappeared with a man looking to be in his late '50s. Upon later reflection, Sample said Bashara "never talked of his comings and goings before, it was unusual."

The mystery man was Michael Carmody, fellow Grosse Pointer and Rotarian. Having been friends for several years, he and Bashara often met for a beer and a chat.

"Bob called me at 6:40," recalled Carmody. "He said he was working in the alley behind his Mack Ave. investment property ... At 6:55 I called him and said 'I'm almost there' and I was, at that point, about five minutes away. I went down and parked in the front."

Arriving just a couple minutes after seven, Carmody greeted Bashara with a handshake. "He was coming around the parking lot on the end of the property ... We went into the *Hark Luck* cafe'. Bob had a table ready and we sat down."

"One of the first things Bob said to me was, 'I talked to Jane on the way home from work today and we'll be at the fellowship dinner on Thursday night," remembered Carmody. The Rotary Fellowship Dinner was an annual event the two had long planned to attend with their wives.

"Having a beer with Bob was not uncommon," Carmody explained. "We did it quite frequently." After a few drinks they parted ways around 7:50 p.m.

§

At 7:47 p.m. Joe Gentz was captured on security video entering the *McDonald's* at the corner of Gratiot Ave. and 7 Mile Rd. The video shows him at the front counter and in and around the bathroom area. He was still inside when video ended at 8 p.m.

After leaving *McDonald's* Gentz boarded a downtown bound Gratiot bus to the *Rosa Parks Terminal*, then took the East Jefferson Ave. bus to the Grosse Pointe Park border. He walked to *Art's Liquor* at the corner of Kercheval and Wayburn, just a stone's throw from his residence at 1226, to purchase a pack of cigarettes. Later he was seen with a friend known as "J.J." at *My Dad's Bar*, located a single block west at the corner of Kercheval and Alter Rd. from approximately 9 p.m. until just past midnight.

§

Bashara arrived home around 8 p.m. to find the television on, Jane's backpack in the mudroom and her work credentials upstairs, but no sign of her or the *Mercedes*. A three minute outgoing call was placed at 7:58 from the Bashara's home phone to Bashara's sister, Laura Mauer in Utah.

Then Bashara texted Jane's close friend, Deborah Breen, at 8:15. Jane and Breen's friendship went back more than 20 years. Their children attended kindergarten together and she was, along with Patti Matthews and Roxanne Flaska, a fellow Middlesex neighbor, one of Jane's closest friends.

Breen was attending a jewelry party that evening and Bashara wanted to know if she'd heard from Jane. He then left a similar message with Flaska a few minutes later.

At 8:30 Bashara's cell phone received a text from Janet Leehman: *"Home, Sir."*

Eleven minutes later Bashara made two consecutive calls to Jane's *Blackberry*, which connected through *Verizon* tower #42, located in northeast Detroit.

Breen said she responded to Bashara's text with a call around 9:15. "I asked him what's going on and he said that Jane hadn't returned home."

"She usually leaves a note if she's not going to be home," added Bashara. "She was supposed to be home at eight to do the taxes."

"He wondered if she was with us," remembered Breen. "He was worried she might be missing."

"So I called Roxanne," added Breen. "I picked her up and we went over to his house."

Breen said that in more than 20 years Bashara had never called her regarding Jane's whereabouts.

Bashara made two more calls to Jane at 9:21 and 9:24, then he called Jessica.

"I believe there were two or three calls," remembered Jessica. "He asked if I had any idea where she was ... He said she wasn't home, and didn't leave a note. She's usually very organized ... That was unusual for her, and he wanted to know if I had any information."

Jessica characterized the call as odd. "She was a woman in her 50s, I thought she could take care of herself, so I didn't find it concerning that she wasn't home. I thought she would be at *CVS* (pharmacy) and I didn't understand the concern."

"She would do yoga," continued Jessica, "and she went out to dinner with friends on different nights." But still, her father never called her with this kind of concern before.

"The first call, he gave me no instruction," said Jessica. "But when I hung up I called her repeatedly and called different hotels in the Detroit area to see if she had checked into one. I thought maybe she'd gotten in a fight with him and wanted somewhere to stay away from the house ... I thought it was a little strange that I couldn't get a hold of her because she knew I was speaking with someone about ... the (summer) job. But I figured I'd talk to her the next day."

At 9:25 Bashara called his son Robert, who was still settling in at his new home in Burlington, Iowa.

"He asked if I'd talked to my mom," remembered Robert. "I said no. I'd tried to call her earlier and she didn't answer." But despite failing to reach her, he saw little cause for alarm. "I assumed she was coming home from work ... that she would call me back later; and he just said it was weird that she wasn't home when he got home."

"I did mention she was probably at *CVS*, potentially picking up groceries or doing errands," added Robert, who made no attempt to call anyone else nor was he concerned.

§

At 9:29 Bashara called Gillette: "That's when he first told me that he came home and found Jane's work bag, and that she wasn't there, and he was starting to worry."

Gillette asked him why he was so concerned. "I thought it was unusual," continued Gillette. "He said she had been the one that was adamant that they get together that evening to work on taxes. They were trying to separate financial documents with the impending moving apart, and she had been the one that insisted they work on it. Then she wasn't there, so he was kind of frustrated."

Breen and Flaska arrived around 9:45, entering through the mud room between the front door and the garage. Bashara led them inside. "I was expecting Lance (the family poodle) to come up and greet us because he was always all over anyone who came in the house," remembered Breen, "and that didn't happen."

"We started in the kitchen," explained Flaska, noting Jane's backpack was still leaning against the wall in the mud room.

"I remember asking him what's happening," said Breen. "He said she didn't come home. I walked over to the dog bed with Roxanne and Lance was laying there and it was extremely unusual, he wasn't moving."

"Bob asked Roxanne and I to go downstairs," continued Breen.

"Jane must have been home," Bashara said, half explaining as they descended the basement stairs, "because she'd been taping something, a program or something."

The basement was a large space with several adjacent rooms. The three of them stayed there for about 15 minutes, searching for any trace of Jane.

"He took us into each room, which I thought was unusual," explained Breen. "He would turn the lights on and say, 'well, she's not in here.'"

Bashara never explained why he wanted them to look around the house. "Eventually, we went back upstairs to the kitchen," remembered Flaska, "and then we started asking Bob questions … Initially, I felt it odd that he said he was so worried, but he wasn't visibly upset."

Thus far Flaska had remained unconcerned. But after several failed attempts to reach Jane on her cell phone she began to worry. Bashara seemingly led them all over the house, but it was much later when she realized that he never took them out to the attached garage, located on the far side of the mud room.

At 10:08 Bashara called his mother, who was now in her early 80's but still a capable and feisty woman. "He was very upset," Nancy recalled. "He said Jane's not home. I don't know where she is, and I said 'Bob, she's always on time and she always leaves notes.'"

"Could you come down," begged Bashara.

"He sounded very upset," Nancy said later. "So I said yes, I'll come down and he asked me on the way if I would stop at *St. John Hospital*, there was a 'Jane Doe' there ... But I could tell by the description this person wasn't Jane, so I left and went down to Bob's house."

(Phone records indicate a single call was made from the Bashara residence to St. John Hospital at 11:01 p.m.).

Without a word to any of his guests, Bashara made his first call to Grosse Pointe Park Police at 10:36, asking to speak directly to the on-duty sergeant.

"My name is Bob Bashara, I live on Middlesex and (sigh) I don't wanna overreact, and maybe it's just too soon to call, but my wife is not around and she's not answering her cell phone and it's been three hours since I – since I've been home, and she's not here. Her car, her purse and her are gone – and – just a little concerned."

Dispatch: "So she wasn't supposed to go anywhere?"

"No, nothing on the calendar, nothing I know of."

Dispatch: "OK, so what do you need the Sgt. for?"

"I just wanted to ask what the procedure is, as far as like a missing person or ..."

Dispatch: "No, I'd be happy to explain that to you sir."

"OK, I'm sorry, go 'head. I didn't mean to minimize you or belittle ..."

Dispatch: "No, that's OK. So you don't know where she is or where she was supposed to go?"

"So here's the deal: we talked about working in my – the office Tuesday, to work on the taxes, and she called me at 4:30 and said she's on her way home and I said great, I'd probably not be home until 7:30, quarter of eight, because I own some rentals and I had some work to do over at my Mack building, and I got home at ten to eight and she's not here. Now, she's been home because her backpack that she uses for work with her computer and her I.D. that gets her into the building is up on her jewelry box. But she, her car and her purse are gone."

Dispatch: "OK."

"That was at ten to eight. In another … 10 minutes it's been three hours … I've been calling her cell phone and I called all of her good friends to find out if maybe she went to dinner with someone. I called her brother, I called both my kids just to say hey, have you heard from mom and they haven't … I called her … multiple times."

Dispatch noted information on Jane's automobile make, model and plate, then offered to put out a LEIN, an information network which connects virtually all law enforcement agencies in Southeast Michigan, designed specifically to aid in finding missing persons.

"I don't want to panic anyone," hesitated Bashara, "but at this point it's been three hours … At 4:30 she called, we talked, and she said she was on her way home," repeated Bashara. "She normally gets home at 5:30, but she was coming home early. I said I got a couple things I have to do over at Mack and I've been working over at my Mack building for, at that point it was probably from quarter to five to – it was probably about 4:30, I left here to go over there. Came home, let the dog out, went over there and worked for probably two and half hours."

Dispatch: "What time was she supposed to be home?"

"She called me at 4:30 and said she was on her way home and she works downtown, so … five o'clock?"

Ending the conversation, the dispatcher told Bashara to call back if he heard from his wife and the two agreed to reconnect in an hour.

A few minutes later, at 11:02, Grosse Pointe Park Public Safety dispatch officer Jodi East called and left the following voice message on Jane Bashara's cell phone. *"We're trying to find out where you are ma'am, your husband's very worried."* Then she initiated the LEIN notification detailing information about Jane Bashara's car.

At 11:13 Bashara made a second call to police for an update: "Yeah, hi, this is Bob Bashara calling back ... I've still not heard from her and she's not shown up. Did you tell me to call back in 25 minutes?"

Dispatch: "That's fine, I can send someone over to take a report."

"I called *St. John* and *Bon Secours* (a second local hospital) to see if she was there ... I've been working my stupid rental ... If you could send an officer by I guess I have to fill out a report."

Dispatch: "Unfortunately, we can't enter her as missing but we can take a report that you haven't talked to her ..."

"Well, then why not just wait? Why have the officer come over if ... what is a missing person, after 24 hours?"

Dispatch explained to Bashara that at this point they could only do a missing person's report for a juvenile or if foul play was suspected.

"Why don't we just hold off, that's not going to help us in any way. She's got to be at work at eight o'clock in the morning and she goes to bed around 10, 10:30. This is way out of the norm for her, so I'm very concerned. I don't want to say anything about foul play as there's no evidence of it. I'm looking in my house, I went out in the garage to look and I didn't see anything scattered about."

Dispatch: "I'd be happy to send somebody over if you want to talk to them and they can take some more information from you."

"Well, given everything I know, why don't we just hold off for a little bit."
Dispatch: "OK, call me back whenever you want, when you decide."

Around 11:30 Deborah Breen asked Bashara if he had called the police. "It was getting later and it was more emergent. He was concerned," she recalled. "He said he had already called earlier and they put out a notation regarding the type of car that she had. I said I think you need to get an officer over here."

At 11:33 Bashara made a third call to police in less than an hour, this time saying his neighbors encouraged him to call. "Any word on your end," he asked.

At 11:38 Officer Terry Hays was dispatched to 552 Middlesex to take a report from Bashara. He first checked the exterior of the home for signs of forced entry but found none. Flaska described Bashara's demeanor while the officer was there as "concerned but not excited."

Meeting him at the mudroom door near the laundry, Bashara invited the officer inside. According to Hays nothing was out of the ordinary. He entered the kitchen where he found Breen and Flaska talking quietly.

Bashara told Hays that he last spoke to his wife "at 4:46. We were supposed to meet at eight to do some tax work."

The officer searched the garage area but found no sign of 'struggle'. He did note the presence of boxes, styrofoam and plastic wrap on the floor. In the bedrooms upstairs were several items of value left in plain sight, all but ruling out any suspicion of theft.

"He said her brown purse wasn't there," noted Hays. "He couldn't describe clothing or jewelry she was wearing or anything else to help identify her."

Bashara indicated there was no marital problems and even volunteered that his relationship with her was like they were "ships passing in the night," which of course begged the question, thought Hays, why was he acting so concerned?

"I asked him to look to see if there were any suitcases missing," said Hays, "but there were none." Oddly, Bashara offered up that his wife was going through menopause and was taking medication.

"I asked him if anyone would want to hurt him or his family," recalled Hays, standard questions under the circumstances.

"I knew of two previous reports involving Bashara," explained Hays. "The first one was filed in February 2011, and the second in November of 2011 ... He was worried about threats and possible violence ... Actually, to the point where he had us come to his house the following morning. He wanted a police officer parked in front of his house in case that individual returned."

Hays said Bashara seemed to be at a complete loss as to who might want to do harm to either Jane or the family.

"Roxanne and I stayed upstairs," recalled Breen, wishing to keep out of the way. Around midnight, after Officer Hays left, Flaska decided it was time for her to head home.

After walking down the street to speak to a neighbor who Breen knew to be a *Comerica Bank* executive, Breen and Nancy Bashara drove around Grosse Pointe, stopping at various *Comerica* ATMs, "thinking that maybe we'd see her car," suggested Breen. "We drove down Jefferson and Fisher, Kercheval, trying to locate her car." Discouraged, they returned empty handed shortly after 1 a.m.

At 1:16 Bashara again phoned Gillette, but this time from Nancy's cell phone, and left a short message. Gillette returned the call two minutes later.

"He started using his mother's phone," recalled Gillette. "He sounded very upset, very worried." He said, "Jane's still missing. Something must have happened, like a car accident." He went on to tell her it made him feel better just to hear her voice.

At 1:37 Bashara again called police, this time to enquire whether Jane's phone had been used. At 3:01 Bashara called a fifth time and was given the phone number for *Michigan State Police*, which he called a few minutes later. Disappointed and exhausted, Breen went home around 3:30.

At 4:47 Bashara made a sixth call to police and provided them with Jane's Social Security number. With still no sign of her, Officer Hays returned around 5 a.m. to make a more formal missing person's report. Nancy Bashara let Hays in through the front door.

Officer Hays saw Bashara rubbing his eyes as he exited the master bedroom before descending the stairs. In their second encounter Hays said Bashara told him that he and his wife had been to marital counseling six months ago.

Hays filled out the missing person's report while Bashara provided a picture of Jane and then he filed a consent form to formally add Jane to LEIN.

(In an interview with WDIV's (NBC) Marc Santia, Bashara later said: "I called her throughout (the night) from 8:30, when I couldn't find her car ... to 4 in the morning, a dozen or plus – many times." Forensic records indicate that Bashara

made nine calls to Jane's Blackberry during the overnight hours of January 24-25).

§

At 6 a.m. Bashara's cell phone received a two minute call from Debbie Breen. The phone connected through *Verizon* tower #94 (which does not service the area near the Middlesex residence) before being transferred to *Verizon* tower #156, which services the area north of and including 552 Middlesex.

Breen said Bashara never revealed his location during the call and at 6:26 she texted him the following message: *"Can the police do a GPS locator on Jane's phone?"* There was no reply.

At 6:18 Gillette sent the following Instant Message (IM) to Janet Leehman in Oregon:

> *"Not sure if He told you ... but the ex wife went missing yesterday sometime after work I will let you know if I find out anything and if you hear from Him please let me know .... it's gonna be a hairy day!!"*

At 6:28 Bashara made a seventh call to police, this time mentioning the GPS function of Jane's *Blackberry*. He called police again at 6:48 asking if they could put a GPS trace on it. A few minutes later, at 6:51, *Verizon Wireless* customer notes indicate Bashara asked about the possibility of tracking Jane's phone.

At 7:03 Gillette received another call from Nancy Bashara's cell phone and a few minutes later Gillette again IM'd Leehman:

> *"MB has asked that you not text or call Him until you hear from Him He is trying to keep his phone records clean ... I will keep you updated as I can but He is not going to be contacting a whole lot either... she has been missing since 6pm yesterday."*

At 7:26 Bashara called *Kema Services* and asked about the possibilities of activating the GPS on Jane's phone. Six minutes later he made his ninth and final call to police to inform them of his call to *Verizon Wireless*.

§

Beginning at 8:42 p.m. and lasting throughout the night, Jane Bashara's *Blackberry* connected exclusively to *Verizon* tower #42, located due north of where 7 Mile Rd. and Gratiot Ave. intersect on Detroit's northeast side. Nearly 50 calls were met with the same eery response: *"Hello, this is Jane Bashara. I am not available to take your call at the moment. Please leave your name and number and I'll be happy to return it as soon as possible, thank you."*

Chapter 6

Annott Street

In the early morning hours of January 25, Frank Leone, a tow truck driver with *H&B Land Towing* in Detroit, was out doing his usual early morning routine.

"I go out and look for cars," Leone said innocently. As an extra source of income this practice is not unusual and many urban tow truck drivers cruise the city in search of abandoned vehicles. Once police process them the drivers pick up some extra cash hauling them away.

Leone saw his first vehicle of the day "in an alley amongst a bunch of abandoned houses" near Pinewood and Annott Streets on Detroit's burned out, and nearly uninhabited northeast side near Gratiot and 7 Mile Rd. It was a black *Mercedes*. Leone thought to himself: "It's gotta be stolen."

Leone scraped the frost from the windshield before noting the last six digits of the VIN in his notebook. Climbing back out of his truck he scribbled '*HB Land*' on the rear windshield with a grease pencil, signaling his rivals that he'd been there first.

"Then I called the Detroit Police," recalled Leone, before returning to the search for more.

Within a few minutes Detroit Police officers, initially responding to the report of an abandoned vehicle, began to arrive. Their expectations were turned upside down when the lifeless crumpled body of a woman in her mid 50's was discovered on the floor of the back seat, and the front passenger side strewn with what appeared to be her personal belongings.

Capt. David Loch, a 26 year veteran of the Grosse Pointe Park police, who had been promoted to Capt. only three weeks before, arrived for work at 7:30. He was already aware of the missing person report filed overnight, but was now getting a more detailed report. About an hour later he received a call from Detroit Police; there was good reason to believe they'd located Loch's missing person.

Meanwhile, at Annott St. the victim's driver's license, found in her purse, was used to positively identity her as Jane Bashara of Grosse Pointe Park, reported missing by her husband Robert eight hours earlier.

Loch and fellow Grosse Pointe Park detective Michael Narduzzi arrived around 9:15 a.m. to find a black *Mercedes* SUV, surrounded by Detroit police officers, tucked into an alley just off Pinewood St. behind 19416 Annott St. They walked around the vehicle before peering inside to view the deceased woman. "It was Detroit's scene so we didn't have jurisdiction," remembered Loch.

Responding to reports indicting a victim was found at the scene, DPD (Detroit Police Department) homicide Detective Donald Olsen, along with Sgt. Kevin Hanus, arrived around 9:45. Olsen, who had been involved in thousands of homicide cases, noted the weather conditions to be around 32 degrees and cloudy.

Minutes later DPD homicide Sgt. Moises Jimenez arrived and assumed command due to the nature of the crime. Jimenez, a 21 year veteran of the department, had worked over 800 homicide cases.

"The SUV was 17 feet from the street in the alley east of Annott," noted Jimenez. After canvassing the surrounding area for possible witnesses he noted that the neighborhood was mostly abandoned; there were few to ask and none who could offer any helpful information.

Photos documented the crime scene including the inside of the vehicle, verification that nothing was changed since the initial discovery. "From the information gathered," observed Jimenez, "the vehicle wasn't tampered with, from the point of when the responding officer got there; everything's just like the first officer found it."

The outside of the 2004 *Mercedes Benz ML 350* SUV was splattered with dust and road grime. Not so dirty as to have caked mud "but enough ... to tell that it was dusty, except for the driver's door, outside, and the rear driver's side door, like if somebody smushed themselves up against the doorway," Jimenez noted.

DPD Crime Scene Evidence Tech Lori Briggs, who arrived shortly after 10 a.m., also noted the state of the outside of the *Mercedes*: "You could tell where the dirt had been, like, smeared away."

There was no sign of footprints or a struggle surrounding the outside of the vehicle. "It seemed like there was some kind of action or physical altercation," remembered Sgt. Jimenez, but "obviously it didn't happen here."

Detective Olsen agreed, adding "it did not appear to be the original crime scene."

Noted items of street value left intact on and within the vehicle included the catalytic converter, electronics, GPS, engine, seats, air bags and even the keys, which were found on the driver's side floor. Carjacking was initially ruled out due to the fact that the wheels and tires were still present (had it been carjacking the vehicle would likely have been striped and placed on blocks).

"The ignition was intact and the radio, it didn't look like it was tampered with," noted Briggs.

"This is like a one in a million chance for you to have the keys of a *Mercedes Benz* inside the vehicle itself," said Jimenez. All but closing the door on a possible robbery gone wrong theory was the fact that the vehicle was left unlocked.

"If this had been robbery the purse, phone and other valuable items would be gone," said Olsen. "It looked like the scene was staged to look like something it wasn't."

The inside of the *Mercedes* offered still more intrigue. "Somebody placed this person in the vehicle, and the contents of the purse, in a show to make you believe that it was something it wasn't," observed Olsen. "Like a street robbery or a carjacking."

"There was a pill bottle assigned to the victim on the passenger seat," Jimenez pointed out. "It's a one chance in 3,000 that your gonna actually have her pills, her phone, her keys, her purse, her checkbook laid out on display."

The victim was in the backseat on the floor, facing backward in a very awkward position. "She was laying face down on the seat, with her feet and knees on the floor board," reported Jimenez.

"She was placed there, then the driver's seat was moved back, and it crunched her in," speculated Olsen. This began one possible lead, that the person who had most recently driven the SUV must have been relatively tall.

"She had an injury to one of her ankles," continued Jimenez, "where they scooted the seat back, jamming her foot between the driver's side door and the seat."

Olsen noted a "black nylon coat," and that the hood was detached and lying on the floor next to her lifeless body, the rest of it forced onto her in a haphazard and backwards fashion, her hands barely peaking through the sleeve ends.

The coat itself appeared to have been an afterthought, placed on the victim post mortem. "It was like the coat was still on her arms, and her arms were twisted almost under her, still stuck in the jacket," observed Briggs.

"Her slippers were under her, not on her feet, and they were clean, there was no debris on them," noted Briggs, guessing they'd not been worn outside.

Several pieces of evidence supported the possibility of a struggle: Briggs observed a discoloring to the victim's face "that appears to be bruising, from either being struck, or pressure. One of her fingernails was torn off but still attached, it was just hanging there."

Olsen noted the victim had a "necklace, a watch and one earring." A futile search for the matching erring was conducted but it was never recovered.

"I came to the conclusion," said Jimenez, "that the homicide did not take place at Annott whatsoever. Because of the way she was placed, how her slippers were thrown in the vehicle, the vegetation on her foot, the way the pill bottle was on the seat, the purse, the *Blackberry*, the keys on the ground, the smudges on the car, there was no vegetation on that side by the driver's door, the totality of all the circumstances shows and indicates that Mrs. Bashara was not killed on Annott Street."

After the area was secured and the preliminary investigation concluded, Jimenez and Narduzzi made arrangements to transport the vehicle with the victim still inside in order to preserve evidence. Loaded onto a flatbed truck, the vehicle was transported directly to the Wayne Country Morgue for positive ID and evidence processing.

§

Between 7:50 and 8:07 a.m. Bob Bashara made three calls to Grosse Pointe Park Police (totaling 12 since 10:36 the previous night). This time he asked to speak directly to Capt. Loch. Later, just before 9, he called Debbie Breen and asked her to come over.

§

In a series of Instant Messages, Rachel Gillette kept Janet Leehman, all the way out in Oregon, appraised of the day's events:

> **8:48 a.m.**:*"she called Him at 5:30 on her way home from work they were supposed to work on taxes and get it done... He was working on a rental and got home around 7:45 and she had been there left work stuff but was not home."*

> **8:51**:*"talked to Him this morning and still nothing He is worried about her of course but also worried about how it will look for Him with 2 girlfriends etc.... this may blow the house deal and everything else... He wants all of us to lay low for a while just to not make it any worse."*

> **9:14**: *"she doesn't even know He is planning on moving out on sat.... He didn't tell her yet He was going to tell her Friday."*

> **9:46**: *"He told me He had not told her He was moving yet and that she didn't know about the house."*

§

"Have you heard from Jane," Bashara questioned Julie Rowe in a 9:30 phone conversation. "She's been missing since last night." (Rowe is Jane's youngest sister, who lives in Chattanooga, Tennessee).

"No. What do you mean she's missing," returned Rowe, who's guard instantly escalated every time she heard Bashara's voice. "Did you have a fight?"

"No, we didn't have a fight," Bashara said defensively. For the next hour several calls flew back and fourth between them as Julie tried to secure news of Jane.

§

At 9:50 a.m. Bashara called police asking for a detective (his 13th call) and nine minutes later he called Gillette at work, again using his mother's cell phone.

Just after 10 a.m. Bashara, still using Nancy's phone, called Loraine Muccioli of *Johnstone & Johnstone* to say he needed to delay the closing on Kensington because his wife was missing and he was getting nervous.

"Why does that matter?" Muccioli protested, believing him divorced.

"That's where I'm getting the rest of the money," Bashara said matter-of-factly.

(Believing him to be engaged, it was the first time either woman from Johnstone & Johnstone heard Bashara use the word 'wife').

§

A flurry of communication between *Master Bob* and his two submissives began at 10:03 a.m. First Bashara called Gillette at work from Nancy's cell phone followed a minute later by several IM's between Leehman and Gillette:

Leehman: *"I woke to a cryptic message from Him from some other cell number."*

Gillette: *"His mother's maybe."*

Leehman later said the message read: *"MB here; family emergency, cease all communication."*

Two minutes later Bashara again phoned Gillette and after ten more minutes Gillette Instant Messaged to Leehman:

"He is incapable of harming anyone ... I think He feels so guilty for what He has done that He's worried about getting blamed for this ... I keep telling Him an affair doesn't make you a murderer."

§

"Bob, have you found out anything, do you know anything?" came the discordant voice of Julie Rowe just minutes before 10:30 a.m.

"Hold on a minute," Bashara said distractedly before the call was abruptly terminated.

§

Although jurisdiction was under the control of the Detroit Police Department, Capt. Loch, because of his familiarity with both the area and Bashara, was asked to accompany Olsen and Hanus to the Bashara home for official notification.

The trio arrived at 10:30 a.m. Following a brief huddle at the curb to coordinate strategy (what they would and would not reveal to Bashara) they approached the front door. The meeting would be brief and confined to the most basic of facts.

Bashara was already standing on the porch. "Mr. Bashara directed us inside," Olsen recalled. Keeping to the plan the trio volunteered no details of the location or cause of death, nor did they reveal they were 'homicide' detectives.

The four men entered the kitchen and Bashara invited them to sit down. "We found your wife's vehicle," Olsen began. "She was inside and she was deceased when we found her."

There are conflicting reports of Bashara's initial reaction:

"Bob cried out, 'they've killed my Jane!'" reported Nancy, who said she was in the next room. "I could hear everything ... Bob's voice was in anguish."

But that's not what Olsen heard. "It took about 10 minutes before he even asked what happened."

Loch described Bashara's reaction as "kind of subdued, not much emotion, a flat response. I don't recall him asking a lot of questions. He was pretty quiet."

In a television interview broadcast several months later Bashara stated: "I think I fell to my knees. It was absolutely the worst news I could have gotten. I was just grieving."

"The whole conversation at that point ... was to my thinking, a scripted event," recalled Olsen.

Establishing a victim timeline was essential, so Olsen began a series of questions: "There's a generic statement that I give," Olsen explained. "I need more information from the family about the victim's events of the day and he proceeded to tell me: at 6:15 in the morning she got up and went to work. He laid out the entire day from that point all the way up to 7 p.m. when he met with Michael Carmody. From there it went to what time he got back to his house at 8 o'clock or so, throughout the day when he received certain phone calls. He was exact on the time."

After a short break Bashara asked what happened but was given precious few details. That prompted a question about a recent high profile investigation, known as the *Backpage Murders*, which received a great deal of media coverage. Four young women had recently been found dead in the trunks of cars on the far east side. Bashara asked if Jane could have met the same fate. But despite the fact that detectives said there was no evidence pointing in that direction, Bashara repeated the theory for local media cameras on several occasions.

Then "Bashara asked about Jane being found in the back," Detective Olsen said, clarifying that he was only told she was found in the vehicle, not in the back.

Bashara volunteered that he and Jane had planned to meet the previous evening at 8 p.m. to go over taxes. He said they were married 26 years, had two children and lived at the Middlesex home for 22 years. He also admitted there was financial strain; the couple was losing money and had a bad credit score.

Considering Bashara was just notified of his wife's passing, Olsen believed this type of information was odd coming so soon. The conference lasted less than a half hour when Olsen suggested a full interview would be necessary the following day.

Suddenly, Debbie Breen, in hysterics, burst through the front door, just in time to witness the final minutes of Bashara's meeting with police. "Bob was sitting at the kitchen table facing me," she said. "Capt. Loch was sitting across from him at the table and Bob was holding his head, crying."

"She was very emotional and that signaled it was time for me to leave," recalled Detective Olsen.

"Bob said Jane was dead," remembered Breen, "they found the car." Looking for comfort, Breen called Roxanne Flaska who immediately left work to join them at the Bashara's home.

10:52 a.m. Instant Message: Gillette to Leehman:
"They just found her in Detroit dead omg I am going home now will get in touch with you soon."

Then Bashara phoned Julie Rowe, arranging for a three way connection including her brother John: "They killed our Jane," Julie remembered hearing Bashara say.

"I was speechless," said Rowe. "I heard my brother say 'Oh no,' and then Bob was yelling at me over the phone to respond."

Lorraine Englebrecht, mother of Jane, Janet, Julie and John, happened to be visiting Rowe, who was instantly shocked to her core. Julie handed the phone to Lorraine, who remembered that Bashara said something happened to Jane and that she was dead, but he gave no details.

"He was crying," Englebrecht recalled, not surprised at that display of emotion.

"I don't know what happened to your daughter," Bashara said.

§

Almost immediately after Roxanne Flaska arrived Bashara asked her to accompany Nancy on the hour long drive to Ann Arbor to fetch Jessica, who was still in the dark over the fate of her mother.

"I stayed back," Debbie Breen recalled. "Bob was going to make phone calls and he wanted me to stay and clean up the kitchen."

Once Flaska and Nancy departed for Ann Arbor Bashara reached out to his son in Iowa. "The human resource manager called and got Robert to the phone, and Bob talked to him," explained Breen. "I was standing right behind him with my arm on his shoulder. I knew this was going to be tough."

"I got a call to go up to the office, which I thought was weird," remembered Robert. "It was my dad. I guess he couldn't reach me on my cell phone so he called my work number instead."

"Robert, they found your mother, she was murdered," Breen remembered hearing Bashara say. "She's dead. They found her car … I'm so sorry. I'm not really sure what happened."

"He was really distraught," continued Robert. "Obviously, I was pretty out of it at the time, I was pretty distraught about it too."

"I don't have more details," Bashara added. "But, please come back home as quick as you can."

Minutes later Jessica received a call from her father. "He told me I was coming home," explained Jessica. "I was to pack a bag … Roxanne Flaska and my grandmother would be at my apartment to pick me up. When he heard they were in the driveway he told me my mother was dead."

"I was to call upon arrival," Flaska said, remembering Bashara's instructions. "He would call to say her mother had died, and I would be there to have my arms open for her."

114

When she arrived Flaska watched Jessica descend from the apartment building flanked by her roommates. She remembered Jessica was visibly upset and the two hugged before climbing into the backseat.

"When we got in the car Jessica said, 'Mrs. Flaska, someone murdered my mother.'"

"No honey, we don't know what happened. She could have had a heart attack. Who told you that?'"

(Roxanne Flaska and Debbie Breen gave similar testimony, indicating they each heard the word 'murder' used to describe Jane's demise, Breen when she overheard Bashara's conversation with Robert, Flaska when Jessica described her initial discussion with her father. However, neither Robert nor Jessica used the word in their own testimony).

§

Once Flaska returned with Jessica, the sticky note left for Maria (the Bashara's housekeeper) was found in the kitchen garbage. "Jessie was next to me," recalled Flaska. "I said 'can I have this, because it's probably … her handwriting. I wanted it as a memento."

"She told me her wedding ring was missing …" Jessica said, addressing no one in particular. Knowing Jane and Roxanne were close Jessica willingly handed over the note. Flaska knew the ring Jessica spoke of and later described it as a single, large solitary diamond.

During the lunchtime hours on January 25 local media began breaking the story of the grisly discovery at Annott Street. At about the same time Janet Leehman, all the way out in Portland, Oregon, received a cryptic text from an unknown phone number:

"Family emergency here, Stop all communication."

§

115

Between October 2011 and March 2012 Joe Gentz lived but a stone's throw from the *St. Vincent de Paul Thrift Shop* on Kercheval Ave. in Grosse Pointe Park. He began volunteering there shortly after moving to the neighborhood and quickly became aquatinted with Mary Moray, part owner of *Eastern Market Antiques*, who often hired him to do manual labor.

"I would pick him up at *St. Vincent* and transport him downtown, two to three days a week," remembered Moray. She noted that Gentz was chronically short on cash, except for one noted exception.

"On January 25 when I picked him up ... he showed me quite a bit of money ... from what I could count it was between $800 to $900 ... He said he was expecting a large sum of money and he wanted to purchase a vehicle with it."

"When I was bringing him back to *St. Vincent* he asked to stop at a cell phone store," continued Moray. They stopped at a now defunct *Metro PCS* shop at the corner of Mack Ave. at Alter Rd. "Joe came out with a brand new cell phone," (*LG MS910*) said Moray, "and he had $200 to $300 left over ... he was flashing it: $100s, $50s, $20s ... he had it fanned out."

§

Late that afternoon, around 4 p.m., a mystery man in a white SUV began casing the neighborhood surrounding Pinewood and Annott Streets, knocking on doors and offering anyone who answered a $10,000 reward for information leading to the arrest and conviction in the death of Jane Bashara.

Media reports suggested residents were uneasy about the stranger, pointing out there hadn't been reports of a reward. Days later the man presented himself to Grosse Pointe Park police and explained he was merely a family friend who wanted to help. Later it was revealed the man was former Bashara business partner Jim McCuish.

§

"Dad, you won't believe what happened!" Jim Wilson recognized the excited voice was his son. "Jane Bashara's been murdered!" News was spreading fast, especially around Grosse Pointe.

Acting solely on impulse Wilson placed a call to Bashara: "What happened Bob?"

"Jimmy, she's gone," Bashara said, shock stifling nearly all emotion from his voice. Wilson could tell there was a house full of people from the noise in the background. "I can't talk now," Bashara said.

"We hung up and I waited a while, and I called back when he could talk a little bit," remembered Wilson.

"They think there's trauma to her neck," Bashara explained, "but they're going to do an autopsy."

"He was very upset and he acted like he really didn't want to be on the phone," reflected Wilson. "He acted like there was still a lot of people in the home."

"Did you do it?" Wilson said abruptly.

"No, I didn't, Jimmy. But I'm probably gonna have to defend myself."

§

Courtney Johns was a tenant in the small frame house on Cadieux Rd., technically owned by Rachel Gillette, but Bashara was her contact. Whenever she had problems it was always Bashara that would arrive with a handyman in tow to make repairs.

In the late afternoon on January 25 police made a house call and found John's boyfriend, whom they questioned. The boyfriend relayed the information back to Johns, who in turn called Bashara. She was clearly not aware of the events of the past 24 hours.

"I … received a phone call," hesitated Johns. "The police were at the house on Cadieux."
"Where were they from?" asked Bashara.

"I don't know."

"Well, they're trying to do their job and get information," explained Bashara. "If they ask you anything, just say that Rachel and I are friends, nothing more, nothing less." According to Johns he never said a word about Jane.

Later that evening, after learning about Jane's murder on the news, Johns called Bashara a second time: "He didn't answer, and then I text messaged him and told him that I was sorry about his loss." Bashara never told her anything more.

§

On the evening of January 25 nearly 200 people gathered on the front lawn of *Grosse Pointe South High School* to mourn the death of Jane Bashara. Both Jessica and Robert were graduates and Jane had volunteered on various school committees such as the *Band and Orchestra Boosters* as well as serving as president of the influential *Mother's Club*.

Organized by Jane's longtime friend Amy Graham, word quickly spread throughout the community via social media for people who wanted to remember Jane to come to the school at 6 p.m. The vigil was led by the Rev. Marianna Gronek, rector of *St. Michael's Church*. Attendees sang songs and exchanged hugs in the dark, January chill, exchanging stories of Jane as they struggled to understand how a person so loved and respected could succumb to such a horrible end.

Bashara begged Gillette to attend and after some persuasion she agreed. They shared a private moment near the end when they hugged. After the gathering Bashara followed her home to her St. Clair Ave. apartment in Grosse Pointe where they discussed recent events.

"We were still under the supposition that maybe this was a carjacking," recalled Gillette. "Did they take her credit cards, her jewelry, that kind of thing?" Bashara said he didn't know. "He told me they didn't find her jewelry or her diamond ring either."

According to Gillette Bashara speculated that possibly "Jane went out somewhere that evening and was carjacked ... He said he thought some niggers did it."

In any event, before he left Bashara instructed that Rachel and Janet should continue to lay low during the investigation.

§

Back at the Bashara's home on Middlesex around 10:30 that evening Eileen Stratelak and Bashara had a short private discussion, not an easy task considering how many people were still there. "I did tell him I'd talked to her that day," remembered Stratelak. "He was very calm, and all he said to me was I was the last person, the last friend probably, who had talked to her."

To her surprise Bashara asked no questions and simply "babbled on about something on Jefferson, you know, a car jacking or something like that."

§

Lounging in front of his television that night, Steve Virgona switched on the 10 o'clock news and, seeing coverage of the candlelight vigil at *Grosse Pointe South High School*, suddenly had a revelation: 'Bob' and 'Bob Bashara' were one and the same! He remembered meeting him at Gentz's old apartment, and another time at the Wayburn flat when he helped Gentz move in, but he still hadn't made the connection. Now the mysterious 'Bob', whom Gentz had said wanted his wife killed in a hit and run scheme, finally had a last name.

"I knew Joe Gentz was involved," said Virgona, and "I guess to a point I knew what happened."

§

The next day (Thursday, January 26) Mary Moray observed Joe Gentz again hanging out at the resale shop. "He was anxious, he was pacing ... He asked if anyone had dropped off a package."

At 10:33 in the morning a single 82 second call occurred between the cell phones of Nancy Bashara and Joe Gentz, the sole instance these two phones connected.

A short while later Laura Callaway, an employee at the *St. Vincent de Paul Resale Shop* saw Bob Bashara step inside the door. "He asked me if Joe worked here … He told me Joe had done some work for him, and then he handed me an envelope to give to him." Then Bashara left without another word.

Around lunchtime Joe Gentz exited the font door of *St. Vincent de Paul*, crossed the street and entered *Art's Party Store*. He handed proprietor Paul Samona a check to cash for $452. Written out to 'Joe' and signed by Robert Bashara, the check (#89 from Bashara's *B&B Investments*, LLC account) was postdated January 29, 2012.

"How did you get this check?" Samona asked Gentz.

"I did some work."

Samona watched closely as Gentz endorsed the back and, although he'd been a regular in the neighborhood for a few months, on the back Samona wrote 'Big Joe' and 'JJ', referring to an elusive neighborhood friend of Gentz's named John 'J.J.' McKee. The two were frequently seen together, most recently late on the night of January 24 at the nearby *My Dad's Bar*. The check never cleared.

§

Continuing to utilize his mother's cell phone, Bashara made another call that day to realtor Loraine Muccioli. He told her that because his wife was just found dead he would need to again postpone the closing on Kensington. "I have to wait until after the funeral," Muccioli remembered him saying. "Let's wait until February 10."

§

At 1 p.m. that afternoon, Bob Bashara arrived at the Grosse Pointe Park police department for his first forensic interview. In many cases this type of interview is directed toward family or friends who might possess vital information to the case, whether or not they are aware.

Although detectives already held suspicions that Bashara had not been truthful, they had no actionable evidence and at this time no one was considered a suspect. However, often in this type of investigation the perpetrator turns out to be the husband, and in Bob Bashara they knew they had someone who was already acting suspiciously.

The interview was voluntary and Bashara was free to leave at any time. As the case was currently under the jurisdiction of Detroit police, Detective Olsen took the lead while Capt. Loch assisted him.

In addition to the draw of information, this type of interview is designed to eliminate suspects. In many cases detectives ask questions to which they already have answers in order to judge the level of truthfulness of the subject. More often than not, what the interviewee doesn't say is equally valuable than what they do. Because of this, detectives often say pretty much whatever they need to keep the interviewee talking, often embellishing or even conjuring from thin air, scenarios to create a comfortable camaraderie. For instance, Olsen talked about his family and wife while he admittedly has none. He was particularly looking for non verbal responses such as a show of emotion or body language.

Bashara was not made aware of any specific items recovered in the *Mercedes*, but he was told that nothing had been removed in an effort to preserve the crime scene.

"Captain Loch mentioned the car," Bashara said as he took a seat … "The garage door opener? Was that in the car?" Olsen noted that Bashara was uncommonly light hearted and talkative.

"The other thing was the keys … you know what, I'm just gonna have the locks changed," said Bashara, "and I'll recode on my garage door opener." Olsen noted it was strange that more than 24 hours had passed and Bashara still hadn't changed the locks nor accounted for the missing garage door remote.

Bashara told detectives he had two children, ages 20 and 23. Despite the fact that most people's cell phones hold a wealth of contact information, he left his in the car. He explained that he owned several properties in Grosse Pointe Park, Detroit, St. Clair Shores and Eastpointe.

"My tenants called me, someone from your office has already contacted them, a couple detectives showed up I think. One to the Guilford property and the Cadieux property, I don't own (that one) any more. I sold that. It actually went to foreclosure (and I) recommended someone to buy it, and that person bought it."

It was Rachel Gillette who bought the house and Bashara did not reveal his continuing involvement. He also didn't mention the whole transaction was ultimately funded by a $20,000 loan from his mother. In fact, Rachel Gillette, nor their three year relationship, was ever discussed in the interview.

Bashara also said he owned several more properties and described two of them: the 26339 Jefferson duplex at 10 1/2 Mile Rd. and *Lakeside Apartments*, the 40-unit complex in St. Clair Shores.

Bashara said he was a manufacturer's rep for *United Laboratories* and gave Olsen his business card. "I sell a product called *Sun Solv* that will clean the yellow fire suits from soot and charcoal," explained Bashara. "I try to convert people from using bleach and hazardous stuff to using nontoxic products."

"Yeah, I wish they'd use that on our station floors," observed Olsen.

"Well, I'll leave you a sample of it and, certainly if you like it you can buy it from me. See how I made this a sales call?"

Refocusing the interview to Bashara's January 24 timeline, Olsen's objective was to expand the scope from the initial conversation the day before, and Bashara responded with an abundance of detail:

> "She gets up around 6:20, 6:15 (a.m.) … showers, dresses and leaves for work between 7 and 7:15 … Sometimes I hear her and we talk briefly. Sometimes I have to use the facilities while she's in there, then I actually go back to bed and I get up about 8, 8:15 … That morning we talked about doing work on taxes and then reconfirmed that I had nothing Tuesday evening and neither did she. So I let her go about her business, and we talked one time during the day. I may have called her during the day or she called me … At 4:40 she called … I was over at my Mack building.
>
> I arrived around 4:30 … I was doing three or four different tasks. For whatever reason my commercial tenants aren't

cleaning the back of the building, so leaves, cigarette butts, paper ... So I was out there sweeping. I was cleaning the stairwells that had leaves in them and I have a storage unit in the back of the photographic studio.

I have some stuff there that I'm going through and cleaning and processing. These are remnants of tenants, they've left things in the apartments ... I don't know if they have any value. I have bags of stuff, clothing to furniture, and I'm just going through them ... So between 4:30 and ... she calls me at 4:40, and ... I have – something was in my hands. I was doing something, so I just ignored her and, (I) saw it was her. When I had my hands free I dialed her back at 4:46. She called me and said that she was on her way home, and that she'd be home at 5:15. She asked me what I was doing, and I said, well, I'm involved in this project and I'll probably be home around 7:30 - 8 o'clock; and that's the last time we talked."

(Although there is confusion as to who placed the call at 4:46 p.m., phone records indicate Bashara was actually on a call with Rachel Gillette at that time).

Despite remarkably clear details on several matters of fact, Bashara said he had no memory of the clothing Jane wore on January 24 nor did he reveal anything concerning the BDSM dungeon underneath the *Hard Luck Lounge.*

"So you're behind the Mack building," Olsen said, blurring the distinction between question and statement.

"Because it was cold, I was working mostly outside," Bashara said defensively. "I had to go in the *Hard Luck Lounge.* I think I went in there about 5:15, had a drink. I drank *Captain Morgan and Diet Coke.* ... Then I came back out, went back to work and, three or four times I was in and out of the bar between 4:30 and my friend Mike Carmody, I talked to him around quarter to seven."

"I can give you a cell number or two ... I know I gotta verify my time and where I've been. I understand that," offered Bashara. "Believe me, I had a number of my attorney friends tell me what ... you were gonna say and what you were gonna ask and what I should look forward to. That's why I want to cooperate fully."

"I've had people like Mike (Carmody), who's an attorney, and others, tell me that 70 percent of the time it's someone close to the victim," added Bashara. "I know him through *Rotary*. He and I are very, very close friends. He was at bowling Monday night, watching me destroy myself as a bowler. I can't even believe, I bowled a 111, a 160 and a 109 ... how do I do that? I had a 140, 150 average, I only hit it but once."

"Anyway, I called Mike, I said 'Mike, I'm up here workin', why don't you come up here for a beer,'" continued Bashara. "That was at about ten to seven."

"You called him?"

"Correct. I said, 'I'm up at the *Hard Luck* working.' He said, 'I can be there in ten, fifteen minutes.'"

"I said 'great'. I went back to working. When he came by, I came back into the bar, he was just pulling up. (He) parked out front, walked in and we had a couple drinks ... that was about 7:10 ... He lives on Kensington ... I don't know his address."

"We stayed until eight o'clock, when we parted company and I came home," continued Bashara. "I saw her backpack there in the mud room ... I have a garage that's connected to the house ... So when she pulls in, she drives right into the garage. For years – not years – months, she said, 'When am I gonna be able to park in the garage?' ... I had shit everywhere, and I said 'I'll clean the garage up for ya.' Finally I got her, in the fall, I got her into the garage."

"It was then I decided to search the garage," remembered Olsen. "It seemed odd to me at the time that the ability to park in the garage was something recent." Olsen already had doubts about the location of the crime scene, and this interview heightened this suspicion.

"I called her around 8:30, quarter to 9," continued Bashara, referring to Jane. At "8:10 I was home. I'm sorry I didn't bring my phone, but in my phone are all my records, of phone calls I made. I like to be as precise as possible."

"Around 9:30-10 o'clock I called my mother," Bashara went on. "I told her to come over. I said I need you over here, I don't know where Jane is, will you come on over?"

"I don't know why, I started calling the hospitals," continued Bashara. "I don't know why I did that, I just thought to myself, you know? And I called *St. John* 'cause I figured if something happened on the east side she'd have to go to *St. John* or *Beaumont* ..."

Bashara told Olsen and Loch that he and Jane lived at 552 Middlesex for 22 years and that Jane's "closest friend is Patti Matthews."

Bashara was chatty throughout the interview, and the topics cut a broad path, as if he didn't have a care in the world. Commenting on people who have affairs Bashara said: "I can't believe there are people out there like that, it's pathetic."

"I don't want to narc on my wife," said Bashara, going out on a limb, "but she did smoke marijuana. She took a couple puffs before she went to bed, helped her sleep. I saw no trouble in it, I used to smoke when I was in High School. I haven't touched it in a while. Maybe she went to buy something ..."

Olsen asked about social media Bashara might be involved in such as *Facebook, Twitter* or *Skype*. Bashara said he did "none of that stuff". However, records show that after he arrived home that evening he deleted his *alt.com* profile at 10:57.

Bashara continued to add information about Jane, that she was *Mother's Club* President in 2007 or 2008 at *Grosse Pointe South High School* and a member of the *Vestry* at *St. Michael's Church*. Then, in an abrupt change of subject Bashara asked: "Do you have cameras along Jefferson and that type of thing?"

"There are some," Olsen offered up. "Some are good, some are not."

"I did ... these two interviews with 4 and 7," (local television news) stammered Bashara, "and one of the gals just took me by total shock. She said we understand how your wife was strangled to death ... Tell me, was that the cause of death, strangulation?"

"There was some trauma to her obviously, that caused her death," replied Olsen, mindful not to reveal specifics.

"People are asking me, and my kids want to know, how did mom die, and I have no – I have nothing to say to them," said Bashara. Then he asked about the possibility of sexual assault.

"There's no indication," replied Olsen.

"It's just that you lie awake at night … and what she must have gone through," Bashara speculated, tapering off.

At the end of the interview Capt. Loch asked Bashara for permission to take a DNA sample to eliminate his from recovered evidence. Bashara complied and Loch swabbed the inside of his cheek. Loch made arrangements for a second interview for the next day and the interview ended before 2:30 p.m..

Upon reflection, there were two things that particularly caught Olsen's attention: Bashara "never said anything about returning to the Middlesex home between 4 and 8" … and he said "he didn't know (Michael) Carmody's address on Kensington," despite their close friendship. (Olsen was also unaware of Bashara's plan to purchase the home next door).

Immediately following the interview, detectives initiated a request for a warrant to search the Bashara residence.

As Bashara exited the police station he was forced to wade through a mass of media, which was camped outside. In a statement he said he was doing everything in his power to cooperate with authorities. However, he clearly had not disclosed many pertinent details. Two hours later tips began arriving concerning Rachel Gillett and her links to 5935 Cadieux … and the suspicion continued to escalate.

When he arrived home Bashara made yet another statement to waiting media, beginning what became a six week 24/7 vigil:

"Please come forward, the police need your help," Bashara begged on camera. "In addition to those four women that had been put in the trunks. Terrible things. Anyone that knows anything, please come forward."

That evening an acquaintance of Bashara's through *The Lifestyle*, Richard Falcinelli, reached out. Falcinelli had been in and around the same *Lifestyle* haunts as Bashara and Gillette, and was well aware of their relationship. The next day, on Bashara's invitation, Falcinelli came to the Middlesex home where he expressed his condolences.

§

Early on Friday, January 27, Robert Bashara, Jr. finally made it home. His father was eager to bring him up to date, and particularly to recount his experience.

"He said he was at his rental, one of his rental properties on Mack," said Robert. "He was doing handyman work, then he was with one of his friends, Mr. Carmody."

Over the course of the day Detective Olsen observed several interview clips of Bashara on the local news:

> "I have no clue. I have no idea what happened. I've lost my girlfriend and my partner and it's absolutely ... unthinkable."

> "Someone did this to my wife, and now I'm doing what I need to do to cooperate with the authorities, to find who did this to my wife."

Late in the afternoon at the Wayne County Morgue Bashara positively identified Jane's remains. As is common practice in homicide cases, her entire body was obscured by a white sheet to conceal her injuries, leaving only her face visible. The procedure was conducted via closed circuit TV.

At 5:40 p.m. a second forensic interview, actually a polygraph test, was conducted at the Grosse Pointe Park police station. It was administered by *U.S. Secret Service* agent Mark O'Reardon with assistance from Detective Olsen and Capt. Loch.

Prior to the 'interview' agent O'Reardon read Bashara his *Miranda rights* which he waived.

Previous to the interview O'Reardon received a briefing by local police and was made aware of several matters of fact, such as marital issues concerning the Basharas and the impending purchase of the home on Kensington. "I concluded there were no health issues that would preclude me from speaking with him," observed O'Reardon.

Bashara told O'Reardon that although his marriage was going well, they did have some marital issues eight years prior which resulted in counseling. Going further, he admitted having had extra marital affairs, although there were none going on currently.

Bashara also said he "borrowed approximately $250,000 from his mother to purchase another house in Grosse Pointe."

"He told me he was purchasing that house to live in with his wife," said O'Reardon, "and that they were downsizing, as his children were getting older."

"I thought his affect was a bit out of character," observed O'Reardon, "given the fact that earlier that evening he had identified the body of his deceased wife."

"Midway through the interview he made a comment regarding his *Rotary* pin," explained O'Reardon. "He referred to the pin and said 'how can I have killed my wife if I was president of the *Rotary* club?'"

"The *Rotary* comment sounded odd," said O'Reardon. "It seemed like something he would say to try to convince me that he had nothing to do with the homicide."

After the session O'Reardon was reasonably certain that Bashara had not been "forthcoming about his extramarital affair," and other details. However, he believed further review was necessary before confronting Bashara about any conflicting statements.

§

Minutes after Bashara began the polygraph, law enforcement officers descended on 552 Middlesex. Led by Officer Eugene Fitzhugh of the *Detroit Police Department's* CSI (Crime Scene Investigation) unit, he was assisted by officers that included Sgt. Jimenez (DPD), David Babcock (DPD), Detective Narduzzi (GPP) and members of the *Michigan State Police*. The expedition lasted four hours.

"The information I had was (the homicide) occurred either in the garage or the mud room," recalled Fitzhugh, so those two areas were searched most thoroughly, assisted by cadaver dogs.

Officer Fitzhugh took photos of the front of the house, driveway, the attached garage as well as the mud and laundry rooms. The garage "has a garage door opener," observed Fitzhugh. "However, it wasn't plugged in, so I had to operate it manually." He also produced a sketch of the garage area, taking note that it was a two car garage with boxes and debris on the left side and open space for a vehicle on the right.

Sgt. Jimenez was particularly hopeful of finding the matching earring to the one Jane Bashara was wearing, but there was no sign of it. Several items were taken into custody, including multiple computer components as well as Jane Bashara's *Will and Trust* and the Bashara's *Certificate of Residency*.

Curiously, leaves, similar to those found on Jane Bashara's slippers, were discovered just inside the garage door on the left hand side ...

§

Bashara returned home after a grueling three hours of police questioning around 9 p.m. Media began reporting that he had actually taken and failed a polygraph test and would be officially named a *Person of Interest* in the case. This action was seen as premature by some and met with great controversy as the Detroit Police, still technically in charge, were not consulted on the decision.

At home that evening Bashara began to solidify his 'timeline' of the events of January 24. He told family members he was working at his rentals between the hours of 4 and 8, that he had spoken to Jane around 4:40 and had previously arranged to meet with her to go over taxes at 8 that evening. He said he'd been in and out of the *Hard Luck Lounge* to get warm between 4 and 7 and met Michael Carmody for a drink between 7 and 8 before arriving home to an empty house just before 8 p.m.

Chapter 7

Deception

As the days slowly wore on since Jane Bashara's murder, reality was quickly closing in on Rachel Gillette:

> "Wednesday, Thursday I believed we were still on track. He was still a divorced man, we were still going to be together, we just had this horrible tragedy.
>
> But Thursday night when I saw him interviewed on TV, and he's talking about his wife ... he's just lost his wife and his girlfriend ... When the news people are referring to somebody as your wife, that could be a mistake. But when you're being interviewed in person and you keep calling her your wife, that's not a mistake. So at that point I knew he was (still) married and we weren't getting a house, and everything, our whole life, had been a lie."

§

During the final week of January 2012, Bob Bashara publicly maintained his belief that carjacking was the most likely scenario surrounding his wife's murder. He mentioned it to police, he mentioned it to waiting media outside police headquarters and again in front of his home, he even mentioned it to family members and friends.

It is also important to note that at this time Bashara's account of his whereabouts the evening of January 24 was that he was solely at his Mack Ave. rental properties between the hours of 4 and 8 p.m., including a quick drink with friend Michael Carmody at the *Hard Luck Lounge* between 7 and 8 p.m.

But on the Friday afternoon of January 27, while preparing for his second interview with police, those close to him were made aware of a new twist:

"That was the first I heard his name ... Joe Gentz," said Stephanie Samuel, Bob Bashara's first cousin. The two had been close their entire lives. Stephanie, 13 years his junior, often referred to him as her 'big brother' and she characterized the family as 'extremely close.'

"I overheard Bob tell my mother, Gwen, that he had received a phone call, or a voice mail message from Joe Gentz," remembered Samuel. "He told Gwen that on the message Joe had said, 'I need my money, I want my money ... and soon.'"

"You make sure you tell the police that when you go in for your appointment, that's huge," counseled Gwen, who is Bashara's Aunt and Godmother.

"Gentz is a guy down on his luck," is how Bashara explained it to Stephanie. "An OK handyman and he seemed like a nice guy." So naturally Bashara thought it all right to help him find an apartment.

Bashara also said Gentz was harassing him for money, but never said he was violent, or even threatened physical violence. He certainly hadn't made threats against the family or Jane. Ultimately, he elected not to alert police of his presence, nor the recent voice message when he met with them only 90 minutes later.

§

Rachel Gillette was becoming increasingly antsy about *Master Bob* and their current predicament. Something just wasn't right. "In an Instant Message I told him to leave me alone," explained Gillette. "I had my locks changed." But *Master Bob*, however, was not eager to let go.

§

"Bob said I hadn't been over to give him a hug," remembered Lorraine Englebrecht, who had just arrived in Michigan with her daughter Julie Rowe.

Bashara insisted they come inside.

"Don't worry," Bashara assured them, "they're gonna get this guy, 'cause she'll have DNA under her fingernails."

The remark so upset Rowe that she simply rose to her feet and walked out.

§

That evening around 10 p.m. after Bashara returned from his second 'forensic interview' (actually a polygraph) Grosse Pointe Park Police Chief David Hiller, along with Capt. Loch at his side, publicly named Robert Bashara a *Person of Interest* in the homicide of his wife.

There is reason to speculate that Hiller's decision to name Bashara a *Person of Interest* was due to pressure brought on by local media and residents demanding progress in the case. Widespread fear within the community of a killer on the loose was mounting and Hiller believed his duty as police chief was to reassure residents that the murder was not a random act.

Meanwhile, mourning family and friends, seeking solace and comfort, continued to flood the Bashara's Middlesex residence. Carrying home-baked goods to share, they were forced to navigate through an ever expanding sea of television news trucks, sometimes numbering into double digits.

§

Despite personal relationships with several local attorneys, on the evening of January 27 Bashara retained the legal services of a complete stranger, criminal defense attorney John Brusstar. The arrangement occurred at the Grosse Pointe

Park police station before either was made aware of the *Person of Interest* designation.

Following a brief introduction, Bashara and Brusstar drove to the Bashara's home where they met alone for a short while before agreeing to a more substantial meeting the following day.

"He was in legal trouble," recalled Brusstar, "and we had some issues on what course to take ... We started by going through anyone that he had disagreements with or would have any vendettas with ... I wrote a letter to the chief of police ... It was (Bashara's) idea."

(The information initially gleaned from Bashara was intended solely for this letter and not subject to attorney client privilege).

Brusstar took notes during the discussion, which quickly focused on a single person Bashara wanted brought to the attention of police. To begin the letter Brusstar indicated that he was representing Bashara, that the two had met the previous day and that he wanted to reveal someone who should be considered a suspect.

"There was a call yesterday at 9:46 in the morning ... a disturbing call demanding money," Brusstar quoted Bashara, "because (he had) helped (him) out." Bashara showed Brusstar his phone with the exact time of the call from Gentz.

Brusstar explained that Bashara owned a business of rental properties, that he sometimes hired handymen, and that one in particular, "a part-time worker named Joseph *Goetz*," was someone they should look into. The letter described him as having a "disgruntled and aggravated relationship with" Bashara.

The incorrect spelling of 'Goetz' "came directly from Mr. Bashara," reported Brusstar ... "It's not Gentz but, Goetz. I think that's what he told me." Despite the fact that Bashara was given the chance to review the letter, he made no attempt to change the name or spelling.

"Mr. Goetz went into a rant about the death of Jane Bashara in the same phone call," Brusstar wrote, again quoting Bashara.

"He might have used the word rant," Brusstar said later, "but it was ... nonsensical gibberish as far as Bashara was concerned. But it seemed like Gentz had seen something on the news."

The letter continued into detail about Gentz, a roofing project he was supposedly hired to do and another disagreement concerning electricity being cut off by *DTE Energy* (for non payment).

"I don't know whether Bashara was responsible for that house (on Wayburn) or not," Brusstar said later. "Ownership wasn't clear to me, but I assumed he did." Brusstar made no enquiry of the nature of the problem with *DTE Energy*, he "just wrote it down."

"Veiled threats were made by Mr. Goetz," Brusstar continued. There was "a sense that Bashara was being constantly badgered ... Mr. Bashara thought nothing of it until yesterday (Friday, January 27) ... It was just some sort of agitation on the part of Mr. Gentz and I think I was paraphrasing some anger there."

(Although Bashara first made family members aware of Joe Gentz prior to the 'forensic interview' on January 27, he elected not to mention him to police that day. Therefore, it is reasonable to speculate that his motive for doing so just two days later was in direct response to his designation as Person of Interest, which occurred between the two events).

Near the end of the letter Brusstar and Bashara provided Gentz's name, address and phone number, concluding with: "It is our intention to assist your homicide investigation in any way possible. We will provide any and all relevant information as quickly as we can."

The following day Brusstar returned with the typewritten letter for Bashara's final approval before delivering it to Chief Hiller. Having served his purpose, a few days later Brusstar was replaced by high profile defense attorney David Griem, well known for defending convicted wife killer Stephen Grant (who murdered and dismembered his wife Tara in 2007).

In a statement Brusstar made more than a month later, he claimed Bashara never said he was threatened nor made any indication there had been physical threats, harm or extortion involving Joe Gentz.

§

The following day Bashara began spinning stories about Joe Gentz to Rachel Gillette. Her reaction was to pay a visit to the Grosse Pointe Park police where she spilled the beans on their relationship. She made no secret of her intentions: "We didn't discuss it," remembered Gillette. "I just told him I would."

In several messages Bashara told Gillette to "lay low," but she couldn't recall whether or not he told her to actually avoid the police. She is certain, however, that he did not ask her to lie. Initially, she neglected to share the whole story, particularly anything concerning Janet Leehman. But eventually even she couldn't keep it a secret any longer.

After speaking with police Gillette decided it was time to finally end her relationship with Bashara. "I realized that ... after lying to me for eight months that they were divorced ... we were not buying a house, that he had strung me along and ... I was done, as far as he and I were concerned ... I changed my locks and told him to stop communicating with me." However, the two were still regularly communicating via Instant Message for at least another week.

§

Designation as a *Person of Interest* brought Bashara a great deal of attention from the public and media alike. Local ABC affiliate WXYZ (Ch. 7) kept up the pressure, reporting that police were looking to talk to a possible witness who may have seen a white male driving Jane's black *Mercedes* on or near Middlesex on January 24. Bashara's reaction and body language began to betray him, pushing sideways his carefully constructed alibi, which slowly began to evolve.

"After he was taken in for questioning with the Grosse Pointe Park police he changed the story," explained Jessica. He said "after (Jane) had come home he ran home to grab keys from the house ... He said he was at home for less than five minutes."

Both Robert and Jessica described their father's keys, usually there was a single ring with all or most of them on it. It was "one very large key chain," described Jessica, and "he carried it with him all the time."

Jane Bashara.

Robert Bashara, Jr., Junior Class President, *Grosse Pointe North High School*, 1975.

Above: The Basharas celebrate the wedding of Jane and Bob at *St. Micheal's Episcopal Church*, Grosse Pointe Woods, MI, April 26, 1985. (l to r); Bob, Jane, Suzanne and the Hon. Robert, Sr.

Below: Jane and Bob Bashara's home at 552 Middlesex, Grosse Pointe Park, MI.

Right: Steps lead down to Bob Bashara's dungeon beneath the *Hard Luck Lounge*.

Below: The alley behind 19416 Annott Street, northeast Detroit, where Jane Bashara's remains were discovered on January 25, 2012.

Above: Bob Bashara embraces a friend at the candlelight vigil held at *Grosse Pointe South High School*, January 25, 2012. Rachel Gillette can be seen to the right.

Photo courtesy of the Grosse Pointe News.

Below: (l to r); Robert, Jr., Bob and his mother Nancy Bashara address reporters in front of the Bashara home at 552 Middlesex, February 1, 2012. *Photo courtesy of Kathy Ryan.*

Above: Joe Gentz pleads guilty to Second Degree Murder, December 21, 2012.

Right: Law enforcement reads charges against Bob Bashara, April 17, 2013. (l to r); GPP police Chief David Hiller, Wayne Country investigator Corey Williams, Wayne County Prosecutor Kym Worthy, Wayne Country investigator Tim Matouk and Assistant Wayne Country Prosecutor Robert Moran.

Photos courtesy of Kathy Ryan.

Rachel Gillette, testifying on October 16, 2014.

Photo courtesy of Kathy Ryan.

The Hon. Vonda R. Evans.

Photo courtesy of Kathy Ryan.

Janet Leehman, testifying on October 22, 2014.

Photo courtesy of Kathy Ryan.

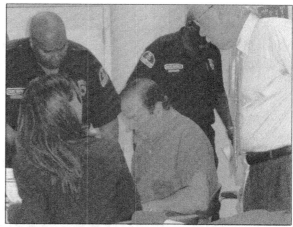

Bob Bashara is flanked by sheriff's deputies and his first legal team of David Griem and co-council Christine Utley; summer 2012.

Photo courtesy of Kathy Ryan

Above: (l to r); Assistant Prosecuting Attorney Lisa Lindsey challenges Bashara public defenders Mark Procida and Nancy Shell in a pretrial hearing in early 2014.

Left: Bob Bashara at trial with attorneys Lillian Diallo and Michael McCarthy; fall 2014.

Photos courtesy of Kathy Ryan

Left: Bob Bashara addresses the court on the day of his sentencing, January 15, 2015.

Below: Lorraine Englebrecht delivers a scathing rebuke of Bob Bashara in her Victim Impact Statement during his sentencing hearing, January 15, 2015. She is flanked by Wayne County prosecutors Robert Moran on the left and Patrick Muscat on the right.

Photos courtesy of Kathy Ryan.

Right: Back in green scrubs, Bob Bashara with appellate public defender Ronald Ambrose during post-conviction hearings for a new trial, September 2015.

Below: With Judge Vonda Evans looking on Joe Gentz reads his stunning affidavit to the court, May 24, 2016.

Photos courtesy of Kathy Ryan.

Dedicated in the spring of 2015, *Jane's Walk* is a replica of a 13th Century French labyrinth that stands as a tribute to the life and memory of Jane Englebrecht Bashara on the grounds of *St. Michael's Episcopal Church* in Grosse Pointe Woods.

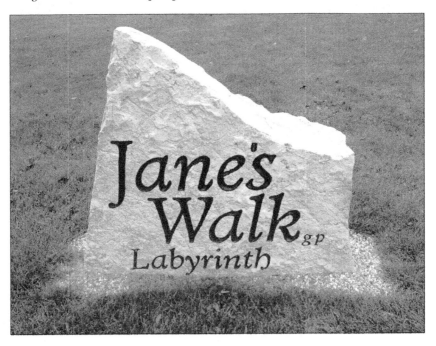

"Usually, what he carried around with him was a wad of multiple – dozens of keys – on one key chain," explained Robert. "A house key, car key and ... a number of master keys.

"There was always a big ring or mess of keys in Bob's cup holder in the *Big Bob Mobile*," remembered Michael Carmody, referring to Bashara's *Navigator*. "They were always present in the vehicle he was in."

All indications suggest that Bob Bashara never left home without his keys.

§

Jane's wedding ring was missing for weeks. Valued around $7,500, it featured a large, five carat diamond.

"Originally, she received an engagement ring that served as both the engagement ring and the wedding band from my father," explained Jessica. "Then at their 18-year anniversary she got a band that fit into the ring, as well as a larger center diamond."

Several family members recall the Sunday afternoon at Middlesex (January 29) when they speculated on the whereabouts of the ring. Julie Rowe began the discussion when she said she heard from investigators that it was not present among Jane's personal effects.

According to Julie and Lorraine, Bashara immediately left the room. After about 15 to 20 minutes he returned with something in his hand. "Look what I found," a beaming Bashara said as he held up the missing ring. "I found it in the bedroom, behind the flowerpot."

"He has Jane's ring!" Lorraine said in astonishment.

"After the police searched our house, my father found the ring," explained Jessica matter-of-factly. "He said he found it under a table in their bedroom and his explanation for it was that after ... the police came in and searched, it probably moved things and the ring became dislodged from whatever it was under."

The discovery was odd because Jane's nightstand (where you would normally expect such an item) was on the opposite side of the bedroom from the flowerpot.

Later that evening, just five days after Jane was found, *WDIV Defenders* (local NBC) reported Jane's sister (Janet) and mother were stunned to learn that Jane had been strangled. Janet said she didn't believe the crime was a random act, and her husband, Mark Gottsleben, struck a chord when he made public comments about Bashara: "I think the guy's not telling everything he knows. If he isn't, then somehow it just looks like he's hiding something."

In reaction mode Bashara phoned his mother-in-law and demanded she "put a muzzle on Mark."

"I said 'how do you expect me to do that?'" queried Englebrecht. "Because Mark never liked you anyway."

§

Around 10 a.m. Monday morning, January 30, Detective Michael Narduzzi and Officer Taylor of the Grosse Pointe Park police department knocked on the front door of 1226 Wayburn in Grosse Pointe Park. The officers felt the chill in the air as they waited for Joe Gentz to answer the door. When Gentz finally appeared Narduzzi asked if he knew Bob Bashara.

"No, why?" the big man asked with a shrug, then added, "well, I haven't talked to him in a long time."

Narduzzi said Gentz became visibly nervous and evasive. Gentz asked why the officers were there. "I think you know why," said Narduzzi, but Gentz insisted he didn't.

"It's on all the news channels," continued Narduzzi. "Did you have anything to do with it?"

"I don't watch TV," said Gentz.

"Is that so," Narduzzi said as he peered beyond Gentz and noticed three televisions within sight.

"We need to talk, Joe. You need to come with us to the station."

The two officers escorted Gentz to the car and drove him the half mile down Wayburn to the station. Narduzzi guided Gentz past the security door into the interview room where he was given a waiver, which he signed, stating he was there of his own free will. The two sat face to face, ironically, in the same spot Bashara had occupied just three days before.

Again Narduzzi asked Gentz about his last conversation with Bashara. "It was about a month ago," volunteered Gentz, becoming more agitated.

"Let me see your phone," demanded Narduzzi. Complying without argument Gentz handed over his new *LG MS910*. "Then why is his number right here," asked Narduzzi, pointing to the phone's 'recent calls' list. "You just talked to him three days ago."

"I don't know."

After a short 30 to 40 minute 'chat' covering topics as far ranging as Gentz's days playing high school football to Narduzzi's multiple assertions that he had *something to do with it*, all of which were met with the same denial, Gentz said he had to go. There was a custody hearing he needed to attend and he wanted to call a friend to pick him up. But before Gentz left Narduzzi obtained a DNA sample, using a swab on the inside of both of Gentz's cheeks.

Just before noon Frances Natale arrived. Slipping inside the reception area, which is partitioned by half inch bullet proof glass, she told the duty officer she was looking for Joe Gentz. "I didn't know why he was there," she said. "He asked me to come meet him at (the) Grosse Pointe police station."

Natale explained that Gentz needed to be at the Macomb County court for a custody hearing and that he had arranged with Narduzzi for her to pick him up.

"I told him he has to be to court on time, he can't be late," insisted Natale, as she whisked Gentz away to the hearing in Mt. Clemens.

After Gentz left, Narduzzi noted visible scratches on the side of his face, and he had no doubt there was far more to the story than Gentz let on.

In the car Natale immediately noticed the marks on Gentz's face and neck. It "looked like he was scratched or smacked across his face, even down to his neck ... It was red, and it was a dark color on his face, consistent with a bruise."

Noticing Natale looking at the scratches Gentz volunteered: "Someone got hurt."

When they arrived Gentz went inside the courthouse for the hearing while Natale waited in the car. When it was over they drove south on Gratiot Ave. to the *National Coney Island* at 11 Mile Rd. for a bite.

"He was very emotional," observed Natale. "He was losing custody of his child, who was already with a Foster parent." Over the course of their meal the two began a rather cryptic conversation:

"What's going on with your court case, and why would they come to the police station if you're coming voluntarily to your lawyer," asked Natale. "You had an appointment."

"My lawyer is still going to see me tomorrow," replied Gentz. "But I don't know what's going to happen to my case."

"Why is that?"

"They think I did something," Gentz said flatly.

"Did what, do you know?"

"It's about going to court tomorrow ... but someone got hurt," Gentz muttered a second time.

"Who got hurt?"

"People might know because it was on the TV and on the news," replied Gentz.

"What was on the TV and the news?" insisted Natale, slowly beginning to suspect that while she was talking about the custody hearing, Gentz was talking about something else entirely.

§

Richard Falcinelli was a heavy set man in his late 50's with a fully receded hairline and mostly full gray beard. He had been acquainted with Bashara through *The Lifestyle* for more than a decade and answered to two nicknames, *Sir Rick* and *Midnight Rider*. The two were never close but Falcinelli recognized a brother in need and he decided to step up.

Falcinelli arrived at *A. H. Peters Funeral Home* late Monday afternoon, January 30, for Jane's public reception before accompanying Bashara back to Middlesex, which was still bustling with grieving friends and relatives. Bashara wanted a favor and Falcinelli was all too willing to provide.

"I want you to contact Rachel and relay a message," Bashara said. The message was that he still cared for her, loved her and wanted to maintain the status quo, and that once through with the burial he would be there for her. Gillette's simple response was for him to shove off.

§

After about an hour at the coney island Natale left for the home of Greg Barraco (her boyfriend) and left Gentz to fend for himself. Barraco, a mutual friend, had recently been asked by Gentz for help with 'an insurance job.'

A short while later Gentz also left the coney island. Heading south on Gratiot, he walked across the I-696 overpass to the *McDonald's* just beyond the service drive. It was at about this time that Barraco recalled receiving a call from him round 10 p.m. "He called me five or six times ... and asked me to pick him up. He was in a hurry to get out of *McDonald's* ... but he wanted to talk to Frances."

"He sounded kind of nervous," added Barraco. "The voice sounded a little lower than before."

So Barraco and Natale headed over to *McDonald's* in search of Gentz. When they arrived Natale recognized a familiar scene: "Several people were talking in a white van."

As Gentz climbed out of Virgona's van, Barraco said he was acting strange: "He was walking back and forth smoking a cigarette ... he was talking on the phone ... saying he was going away for twenty years." He also noticed Gentz had a few "fresh scratches on his face."

Gentz was expected back in court the following day and, as usual, he was relying on Steve Virgona for transportation. So Natale drove him back to Wayburn to grab a clean suit and some personal items before dropping him at Virgona's. When they got there Natale waited while Gentz went through the back door in the alley. A few minutes later he returned carrying a black duffel bag. As Gentz climbed back into Natale's car a police car slowly drove past.

"Gentz was nervous," remembered Natale. "I didn't know why because his case was in Mt. Clemens and we were in Grosse Pointe."

"Why are they following me?" begged Gentz, sounding paranoid.

Without a word Natale drove the van north and entered Eastbound I-94. A minute or two later Gentz ask her to pull over. She exited at 10 Mile Rd. and, after crossing the overpass pulled into a *Shell* gas station. Clutching the black duffle, Gentz "got out for four or five minutes," remembered Natale. "I thought he was smoking a cigarette. He walked away – I didn't see exactly where – then he came back without the bag."

Later Natale said she thought Gentz threw the bag into a blue goodwill collection box. Around 11 p.m. they arrived at the home of a close friend of Virgona's, Shirleen Vancleeve.

"Where's Steve?" demanded Gentz as he stepped through the front door. Vancleeve simply motioned with a slight nod of the head toward the basement stairs.

"Joe was hysterical, very emotional," remembered Virgona. "He was acting like he was crazy, pacing up and down saying, "I'm fucked, I'm fucked ... I need to talk, need to talk."

Then, with little emotion, Gentz said, "I messed up."

"He must have said 100 times he screwed up," remembered Virgona. "He was praying to God ... please forgive me for what I did ... He had his head down and was shaking – his face was white as a ghost."

"I asked him some questions," continued Virgona. "He was scared to death. He thought Bob Bashara double crossed him ... He was very excited. He was sweating, swearing ... I've been around him a lot, and when he's panicking and he's scared, that's the way he acts."

"They got me on DNA," whimpered Gentz.

"He said Bob probably put a hit on him," Virgona said matter-of-factly. "He was scared of that, and he was also scared of someone else."

"Was it just you or did Bob do it," demanded Virgona. "He shook his head up and down, yes."

Then Gentz caught a breath and began to explain: he was at Bob's house. Bob said to kill her. Gentz balked and Bashara pulled a gun. Leveling it towards Gentz, Bashara said, "kill her or I'll kill you." Gentz described the blow to her neck, then said it was probably broken.

"He used the words neck and strangle," said Virgona, "and he kept on crying."

Virgona asked if money was discussed and Joe said: "Yes, $5,000." Virgona said Gentz also mentioned a used *Cadillac*.

"Joe said he wanted to leave town," continued Virgona, "and I said 'Joe, we gotta go to the police.'"

But before Gentz was willing to leave he wanted to speak with another man who was in the house, a pastor named Dan Fritch. Following a short discussion, Gentz went upstairs, took a shower and a shave, put on his clean suit and ate a full meal. Then all three climbed into Virgona's white van and drove directly to the Grosse Pointe Park police station around 2 a.m. When they arrived Gentz asked to speak with "Detective Dizzio" (Narduzzi).

§

Acting nighttime Patrol Supervisor Lt. James Hoshaw of the Grosse Pointe Park police received a radio transmission around 2:30 a.m. January 31 with instructions to immediately return to the station. When he arrived he found three men waiting to speak to him.

"I attempted to glean information from Fritch and Virgona," remembered Hoshaw. "Why they were there and what Mr. Gentz told them that prompted them to bring him in ... They were vague in describing what happened ... It was as though they felt they couldn't repeat Mr. Gentz's story word for word."

Hoshaw said he needed to speak directly with Gentz, who was outside smoking a cigarette and "appeared to be nervous," remembered Hoshaw. He also noted a minor injury on the side of his face.

Gentz abruptly said he was there because of Jane Bashara.

"Mr. Gentz," Hoshaw began, "is it your desire to turn yourself in?"

"Yes."

"I placed him in protective custody," continued Hoshaw, "because he'd come into the station and said he was in fear for his life … If he changed his mind then he was free to go."

Then Hoshaw contacted Capt. Loch, who arrived around 3:30 a.m. Detroit Police were notified and later in the day Gentz was questioned by Capt. Loch, Detective Narduzzi and two officers from Detroit.

Gentz told the officers about the disposal of his clothes on the way to Virgona's, specifically mentioning his boots, which he said he dropped inside a light blue clothing collection box on 10 Mile Rd.

Detective Narduzzi was immediately dispatched to retrieve the items but found the bin, owned by *Community Patriots* (a for-profit charity located in Melvindale, MI) empty. Thinking fast Narduzzi contacted the organization who was able to stop the collection truck, undisturbed, until he could get there. A short time later the boots and other items were recovered, still tucked neatly inside the black duffel.

§

Later the same day Steve Virgona turned up at DPD's homicide headquarters on Woodbridge and made a statement recounting Gentz's story. He acknowledged he'd been with Gentz on January 24 and that Gentz "mentioned going to Bob Bashara's house twice … he was going to clean the garage."

"I told him to go to the Grosse Pointe Park police station," Virgona told homicide detectives. "Me and Pastor Dan go [*sic*] with him." He said the two encouraged Gentz to strike a plea bargain and that the main reason for turning himself in was for his own protection.

§

In the days immediately following the two police interviews Bob Bashara began to exhibit odd and uncharacteristic behaviors. In an attempt to separate himself from Gillette and Leehman, at least to the prying eyes of law enforcement and the media, he stopped using his cell phone and instead borrowed phones from anywhere they were available.

Nancy Bashara had virtually moved in at the Middlesex home and her cell phone was readily available. "My phone was there for the taking," Nancy said with a shrug. "I never questioned when anyone picked it up or put it down."

Often Bashara asked to use her phone even while his landline and cell were fully operational. He never said who he called and always erased the call log. Nancy found out later he'd been contacting both Gillette and Leehman. Between January 25 and 29, more than 20 early-morning calls were placed from Nancy's phone to one of Rachel's three phones (home, cell and work).

On the last day of January, the day of Jane's funeral, Robert "Ponytail Bob" Fick, a longtime handyman and tenant of Bashara's, was at the Middlesex home fixing the screen door between the mud room and the garage, a shower door upstairs, screens in the back Florida room and a light fixture in the basement.

Leading the way down the basement stairs, Bashara turned and asked to use Fick's cell phone, a simple request but one he'd never made before. "He walked away," said Fick, "and left the area for 15 mins to make the call. When he came back he'd erased all records of the call." After Jane's death, Fick said Bashara continued to contact him from Nancy's phone.

§

Tuesday, January 31 was an uncommonly warm day in southeast Michigan and mourners attending Jane Bashara's funeral, which began promptly at 10:30 a.m. at *Grosse Pointe Memorial Church*, were clad mostly in lightweight attire. The limestone gothic structure, a stand-in for *St. Michael's,* was chosen due to the overwhelming throng of mourners. Pallbearers carried Jane's remains into the sanctuary, housed inside a glass enclosed liter. The hundreds in attendance forced an overflow room connected via closed circuit television.

Before the service began Bashara called Sandra Ennis, Jane's friend at *DTE.* "He wanted to know if I could help him out because the kids were in need of money, and he was trying to expedite getting the insurance money." So she passed on his request to the HR department.

At the funeral Roxanne Flaska said she overheard a conversation between Nancy and Bob Bashara: "Oh Bob, they're saying you have a girlfriend!"

"It's not true," Flaska heard Bashara protest.

"We walked through the procession line," remembered mortgage agent David Calcaterra. "I expressed my condolences and Bob said that he felt the investigation was not thorough enough and that he was going to hire his own investigators."

Ennis was one of several who gave a heartfelt eulogy to Jane. At the afternoon reception she finally got a chance to speak to Bashara: "Still invite us to that luncheon," she said, remembering that Jane and Bob had extended an invitation to an upcoming *Rotary* function: "We'll still be glad to attend, even though Jane won't be there."

"If I can," responded Bashara hastily, "because I'll probably be in jail. I've been told I'm going to be arrested right after this ... They think I killed my wife."

"After the funeral Bob sent a thank you card for speaking," said Ennis. "You know how much Jane means to me, and how much I loved her," he wrote. "You're going to hear some stuff in the media and you should just ignore all of it, because they're just out to get me, and you know how much I loved Jane."

§

During the funeral breaking news reported Joe Gentz's bizarre late night surrender to Grosse Pointe Park police. He had spun a wild tale and confessed to the murder of Jane Bashara, but more importantly, he said he had not acted alone.

Reports also speculated that Bashara was involved with another woman and that they were in negotiations to purchase a home on Kensington in Grosse Pointe Park. It was also reported that police did not believe Jane was killed in Detroit nor in her SUV and that the crime scene had been staged.

§

Lorraine Englebrecht was painfully aware of Bob Bashara's snub, he'd made no attempt to speak to her during or immediately following Jane's funeral. In fact, she said she didn't hear from him for nearly a week. Interviewed by local media after the funeral, the Englebrecht family admitted to having a 'tense relationship' with Bashara, all but alluding to the 20 year rift stemming from the child molestation incident involving Jane's then five year-old niece.

§

As negative media reports were piling on by the hour, the day after Jane's funeral Bob Bashara decided it was time to meet the press, who had been camped on his front walk for nearly a week. Moments before he passed through the front door, Michael Carmody, his long time friend from *Grosse Pointe Rotary Club*, noted he was acting unusual:

"He reached in his pocket, pulled out a hanky, looked at me and said something to the effect of, 'I'd better have one of these.'"

Carmody said the mood inside was 'somber' and added that Bashara's remark may have been designed to lighten the mood. "It was a little bit of a smart aleck comment," he remembered later. "Bob was a jovial kind of guy … I didn't take it as being something that was being viewed as serious, it was more … flippant … He didn't look energized or excited about doing it."

It was another unusually warm afternoon for February. Bashara, clad in a powder blue button down shirt and tan sweater vest, slowly descended the front walk with his left arm around his mother, his son pacing him on his right. Although his statement sounds scripted, it appears to have been delivered without notes.

Speaking in a slow and deliberate tone Bashara began with a head nod to his left: *"This is my mother, Nancy Bashara,"* then a slight motion to his right, *"this is my son Robert ..."*

> *"My daughter Jessica had to go back to school to resume her studies. We wish to thank the hundreds and hundreds of supporters and people who have shown their love and respect for my Jane."*

Then emotion began to creep into Bashara's voice:

> *"This is an unconceivable tragedy, and everyone needs to know how absolutely wonderful and how much this has meant, they'll never know, how wonderful this has been for us."*

As if on cue Bashara grabbed a tissue from his right pocket and dabbed his right eye, then the left before jabbing it back into his right pocket. The act was considered consequential to investigators and spectators alike as there is seemingly no evidence of moisture in Bashara's eyes.

> *"We have cooperated with law enforcement agencies, and will continue to do so. Both our families grieve, and in light of this horrific event ask for your continued prayers, ask for your support and respect of our privacy as we deal with this heartbreak, and try to cope. Thank you very much."*

> **Reporter**: *"Bob, what do you have to say about this new Joe guy who says that he was an accomplice in your wife's murder?"*

> **Bashara**: *"I have nothing to say."*

> **Robert Bashara** (son): *"My sister and I really support our dad throughout all this, and we just miss our mom so much and – we're just trying to get through this."*

> **Bashara**: *"Thank you ladies and gentlemen, I have nothing to say."*

> **Reporter**: *"Bob, do you have anything to say about this Joe guy?"*

The three pivoted in unison, breaking to the left before heading back toward the front door.

Bashara: *"No, thank you."*

Reporter: *"He says he was paid to kill your wife. What do you have to say about that?"*

Bashara: *"Have a good afternoon. Thank you, that's our statement."*

The three continued towards the font door without another word, son Robert falling in line behind Bob and Nancy Bashara. As they entered the door a final question was lobbed from the press corps: *"How did you know Joe, Bob?"* ...

When members of the media asked later why his client made the statement, David Griem said: "Bob wanted very badly, the day after the funeral, to say something because you all (the press) were camped outside his home. He thought it was the right thing to do. So I told him to just do it."

In a February 4 interview *WDIV's* (local NBC) Marc Santia asked Bashara about his apparent lack of tears: "People have talked about it. We watched it, and you were out there and you dabbed your eyes, but we didn't see tears?"

"You know, I have cried so much this past week and a half, that I have emotions that well up in me, and the emotions are so strong and so distraught that I don't know if I can cry anymore," explained Bashara. "I mean, I've cried so much. I've let myself go. I didn't want there to be tears ... I just dabbed my eyes because I thought there was a tear. I don't know. I didn't even think about that. Just a natural knee-jerk reaction."

During testimony Robert was asked if he ever saw his father cry. With little hesitation he answered with a swift "no." After further recollection of the incident he added, "he asked me to say ... that I support him and my family and everything else that's going through these times."

§

After the makeshift press conference in the front yard, Bashara pressured Jessica to sit for a similar interview with him on *Good Morning America*. His plan was to quash all question of his complicity in Jane's death as well as any lingering issues of infidelity.

"I was essentially told I was going to do something very similar to my brother," said Jessica. "My dad was getting a lot of negative media attention, so he wanted us to show support." The taping was set for February 8 and scheduled to air the following morning.

That night local media began a steady stream of reports alleging that Bashara was involved in the BDSM *Lifestyle*, owned and operated a private sex dungeon and that he had several 'sex slaves.'

David Griem began publicly speculating that Bashara would soon be arrested, although he still believed him innocent. Griem also said that Bashara had passed a second privately administered polygraph. Media also reported that Bashara and 'Joe' had 'known each other for quite some time,' were seen together on January 24 at the *Hard Luck Lounge*, and finally, that multiple sources had confirmed his affair with Rachel Gillette.

"The night after Jane's funeral Nancy, Laura and I were sitting in the TV room," recalled Stephanie Samuel. "The news came on and that was the night all of the *Lifestyle* broke open ... I don't know how Bob was, but I know for a fact that I saw on Nancy's and Laura's faces exactly what I was feeling, which was dumbfounded."

"After the news was over I stood up and I turned off the TV," continued Samuel, "and Bob was standing, and I looked him right in the eye, and I pointed a finger, did you have an affair?"

"No," protested Bashara, "it was just an outside lifestyle."

Both Jessica and Robert became aware of Bashara's affair that first night in February. "When the relationship with Rachel was first on the news he denied it," remembered Jessica.

"I have not had relations with these women," Bashara insisted to Robert. "There's a lot of things going on right now and I'll be able to explain it later." Although Bashara himself was the one who initially brought Joe Gentz to the attention of both family and police, he'd kept his son and daughter completely in the dark.

"He didn't give an explanation of Joseph Gentz until the media brought out the name," said Jessica. "Initially, he said he just worked exclusively at rental properties, and that he had never been to the house."

Later, after countless media stories, Bashara changed his story, saying, "Joseph Gentz came to the house on Middlesex during the fall to help rake leaves." He never told Jessica that Gentz and Jane had met and his details of the night of January 24 continued to evolve as new information came to light in the days leading up to the *Good Morning America* interview.

§

Beginning the first day of February, Janet Leehman received 14 calls originating from phone numbers of people associated with Bashara. In a voice riddled with agitation Bashara asked her to hide Rachel Gillette on her father's ranch in southeast Oregon, adding that he was concerned she would "turn state's evidence against me." He also asked her not to speak to the police.

"Absolutely not!" protested Leehman. She was so startled by the request that she slammed down the phone and immediately contacted the Grosse Pointe Park police and then Detroit homicide who immediately put her in touch with Wayne County Prosecutors.

"After the murder I tried to help Rachel get her life together," explained Leehman. "She was not a friend, but I tried to get to know her."

§

Michael Carmody did all he could to support his friend, including providing Bashara regular transportation. On one such occasion Bashara was conducting some phone business while Carmody drove. Finishing the call, Bashara said: "My phone's dead, can I use yours?" Carmody gestured positively and didn't pay much attention to the ensuing call, but he vaguely heard Bashara ask someone to make contact with someone for him.

"I believe it was at that time that he was trying to contact Rachel," Carmody said in hindsight, and "through that person he was trying to control her."

"Have Rachel call through this phone," Carmody heard Bashara say.

At this point Carmody began to feel as though he was being taken advantage of. "I don't know what all is going on," Carmody said to Bashara. "But I'm going to say it very clearly right now. Whatever you tell me, make certain it's the truth; and if there's something you don't feel you can tell me, your council has told you not to tell me, or that you choose not to tell me, don't tell me. But whatever you do tell me, I'm going to tell the truth if I'm ever put on the stand … the one thing you don't ever want to do is lie to me."

"Well, I would never do that," Bashara said reassuringly. "If I get a call back on your phone from Rachel I want you to let me know."

"I'm not going to do that Bob," Carmody protested as Bashara dialed another call, this time to his sister Laura. "He asked for Jessica and he had a conversation with her."

"Please try and relax," Carmody heard Bashara attempt to calm his daughter, "this is not as bad as it seems. Don't worry about what's being said on TV."

Later that evening Carmody had dinner with Bob and Nancy at the Middlesex home. "On a couple of occasions that evening I impressed upon Bob that it was best that he did not lie to me. Say nothing, but don't lie to me."

The following day Carmody received the first of a number of disturbing phone calls: "Four or five blocks away from the house my phone rings, I answer it, it's a woman on the phone, yelling for Bob," remembered Carmody. "The first call … bothered me by the mere language that was used." Carmody had no idea who Janet Leehman was, but he'd just gotten an earful from her.

The second call came from Gillette, who was "apparently beside herself … She sounded very excited, very high pitched in her voice and rapid in her speech," described Carmody. "She was probably somewhat tearful, (there was) an emotionality about the tone of her voice." It was at that point that Carmody realized that everything he'd been told about Gillette was pure fiction.

"I contacted Bob's attorney at the time (David Griem) and said that I had received some information that was highly disturbing," explained Carmody. "I wanted to discuss it with him because I wanted to have a face to face with Bob."

Carmody next placed a call to Bashara: "Bob, I'm gonna pick you up ... and we're going to go over to Windmill Pointe Park where we can have a private conversation." (At that time the front yard and street was a media parking lot and Windmill, just five blocks away, was a private resident-only park that would provide relative privacy).

"Bob, I've been informed that Rachel is your girlfriend and has been for a long period of time," began Carmody. "You've told me repeatedly she was only a friend ... and this is really disturbing in light of what's going on. What in the hell is happening?"

After a tense moment, Bashara, abruptly, confessed to Carmody that Rachel Gillette was in fact his girlfriend. "This is damaging to our friendship," warned Carmody. "I've asked you numerous times, please don't lie to me. You obviously have now lied to me. This is going to have a major impact on our relationship."

§

After four days Joe Gentz was released from police custody in the early afternoon of Friday, February 3. Similar to his release on January 30, Gentz was again on his way to a custody hearing in Macomb County. In an odd twist, police detectives actually delivered him to a waiting friend to avoid certain and unwanted media attention.

"I picked up Joe Gentz at Kelly Rd. and 10 Mile," explained Steve Virgona. "I'm not sure what day it was, I picked him up from the detectives."

After mulling it over a for several days Frances Natale, Gentz's friend who had picked him up and provided transportation on January 30, reached out to Grosse Pointe Park police and pretty much shared everything she knew about Joe Gentz, even handing over a scrap of paper Gentz left in her car with the word 'Heparin' scrawled on one side.

§

On Saturday, February 4, Bob Bashara, his sister Laura Mauer and their mother Nancy sat down at David Griem's office for an exclusive 35 minute interview with WDIV's *Defender* Marc Santia. It was taped for airing that evening and over the next two days.

In promotional spots Santia teased that Bashara had answered every question, and that the most interesting exchanges were directly about what the public wanted to know:

> **Santia**: *"Bob, did you kill your wife Jane?"*

> **Bashara**: *"Absolutely not. I had nothing to do with it."*

> **Santia**: *"Did you hire someone to kill your wife Jane?"*

> **Bashara**: *"No. No, I did not."*

> **Santia**: *"Talk to me about your marriage. How was your marriage with Jane?"*

> **Bashara**: *"Like any marriage you have your ups and downs. You have your rough patches that you come across. About a year ago we did go to a marriage counselor to sort through some things."*

> **Santia**: *"Was there talk of a divorce? Were you separated?"*

> **Bashara**: *"No. Not at all."*

> **Santia**: *"Were you having an affair?"*

> **Bashara**: *"No, I was not."*

> **Santia**: *"So the reports, and the other woman by the name of Rachel, you would characterize that as ...?"*

> **Bashara**: *"She was a good friend, that's it."*

> **Santia**: *"Were you involved in S&M?"*

Bashara: *"No … and I don't want to get into that because I have my children to worry about. There are so many peripheral issues that have been brought up. So many of them that I can't comment on that or say anything because of my children."*

Santia: *"Because of these other reports, what have you said to your children? I mean, because of talks of extra marital affairs and S&M?"*

Bashara: *"Don't believe what you hear. This has been sensationalized. Things have been brought up that aren't true … and the focus needs to be on finding Jane's killer."*

§

February 4 Instant Message: Therese Griffon (former Chicago police officer and the first prospective third member of the intended threesome) to Rachel Gillette:
"Impression I get from him is he's hiding … he is hiding something. He is a pathological lier. They believe their lies are reality, very sad … My concern is that the thought of the three of you moving into that house pushed him over the edge and her confronting him about his mistress."

§

"I have not spoken to the media because I feel the issue has been terribly exploited and I wish no part in what has become a distraction to a serious murder investigation. I would like to request that the media desist in contacting me, my friends, family and especially my children. I think the general public should be ashamed of their feverish appetite for gossip."
-Rachel Gillette statement,
February 6

§

165

Followers of the Bashara case, a group expanding by the day, became fascinated by an Internet blog known as *The Hinky Meter*, created and moderated by a woman in Oklahoma using the name Valhall. On February 6 several postings from Gillette's *Bella's Blog* began to surface there, giving the site a surge of attention.

"*Hinky* is an old law enforcement term," Valhall explained on a live interview broadcast on Detroit's *WWJ* radio. It was "first introduced to the public by Ann Rule in her book about the Diane Downes case," (Downes was convicted in the 1984 shooting of her three children). "It's just your inherent ability to pick up on bologna," Hall said.

Valhall began *The Hinky Meter* in 2009 in response to the Casey Anthony case. "I first started (it) with the intention of addressing bad information on forensics, on the science," she explained. Her sources, which had an uncanny level of accuracy, included media reports, public documents and firsthand knowledge from people who contacted her, primarily friends and family.

"My opinion is that Bob Bashara most likely had his wife killed," Valhall said. But "I don't know if his hands were on her … We've heard that (Gentz) said he was paid a little bit of money … He may have been offered a car, and then he may also have said that a gun was held to his head."

Valhall was certain of at least one thing, the motive was money. "Bob was not doing well financially and basically Jane was … keeping them afloat. They were very upside down in their house … and in 2009 they took out over $500,000."

As for BDSM, or *The Lifestyle*? "My sources are saying (Bashara's involvement went) all the way back to 2005," Valhall explained. "I have spoken with close friends of … Jane and Bob and relatives of Jane and also a couple of different sources in the BDSM community that know Bob and Rachel. They all say, from all sides, that Jane didn't know about this and wouldn't have approved."

Bashara's January trip to Oregon to meet Janet Leehman was already a hot topic on *The Hinky Meter*. "Just two weeks before Jane was murdered," continued Valhall, "he went out to test drive her … she was going to be his second … slave in the triad."

The three "were buying this big house," she said. They were "supposed to close on the 27th of January, the big house on Kensington … Over the course of months they got to know her long distance and then Bob flew out to Oregon somewhere around the 10th or 11th of January."

Once Gillette noticed *The Hinky Meter* was reposting items from her *Bella's Blog*, where she had documented much of her relationship with *Master Bob*, she discussed it with Bashara and in turn they discussed it with Therese Giffon, who was once again in Bashara's good graces. Upset by what he was reading, Bashara wanted revenge.

"Bob believed (correctly) the police and prosecution were monitoring *The Hinky Meter*," said Giffon. So he asked her to log on, which she did using the screen name *Across the Lake*, to post negative information, "making Jane not look so good," explained Giffon, "that she could have possibly had a boyfriend and he done [*sic*] it."

Giffon and Gillette exchanged several eMail and Instant Messages concerning *The Hinky Meter* on February 12:

"Hey, I could say Jane had a boyfriend," wrote Giffon, "and when she wouldn't leave Bob for him he'd kill her. Another scenario right? It would have a very bad effect because it would make them (the police) look in another direction, away from him."

In an attempt to explain herself, Giffon testified that her actions were due to the fact that, "I truly believed, at that point, that he was innocent, and I thought I was helping him."

Chapter 8

Broken Alibi

Shortly after noon on Wednesday, February 8, law enforcement officers from Grosse Pointe Park, *Michigan State Police* and the *Wayne County Prosecutor's Office* descended on 552 Middlesex to conduct a second search. Media reports noted that Nancy Bashara was seen cleaning in and around the garage prior to their arrival.

Apparently caught by surprise, Bashara promptly called attorney David Griem who advised him to leave the premises. He climbed into his mud colored *Navigator* and promptly left for Griem's downtown office. The whole ordeal, eerily similar to O.J. Simpson's odyssey through L.A. in 1994, was caught by media helicopter and broadcast live to television and live-streamed on the Internet while, at the same time, Griem was interviewed on local *WXYZ* News (ABC). He questioned the legality of the search, incorrectly claiming there was no warrant.

According to testimony, upon entering Griem's office at the 1 Woodward Building, Bashara called Gentz's Wayburn landlord, Rebecca Forton, who happened to be following the events on television. Although Forton was aware of Jane's death, she had not had any contact with Bashara for nearly two months.

Not recognizing the number on the incoming call, Forton made a note of it once Bashara identified himself. "I asked him why he was calling me," recalled Forton. "He said ... 'I'm trying to get the utilities on Wayburn out of my name.'"

"Why are they in *your* name?" Forton half demanded. "How long have they been in *your* name?"

"Since October ... and I really want you to get the gas out of *your* name," added Bashara in a feeble attempt at obscuring the significance of the situation. "I've already had the electricity removed," continued Bashara, "I don't want your pipes to freeze."

"I didn't know the arrangement he had with Mr. Gentz," Forton testified. "But as a landlord its illegal for me to tamper with or change utilities."

(A trial stipulation from December 1, 2014 indicates DTE service to 1226 Wayburn was in the name of Robert Bashara from October 25, 2011 to January 18, 2012. During this period the account was billed to an address connected to Bashara in St. Clair Shores. The record indicated that Rebecca Forton's name appears both before and after these dates).

§

Melinda Jackson arrived at 552 Middlesex along with two other forensic scientists from the *Michigan State Police.* A 29-year veteran, she is a forensic scientist and expert in collection of DNA evidence. Although they were aware the home had been previously searched, they were not informed of the date or nature of the crime.

Of particular importance in this second search was evidence of blood, so law enforcement arrived with a test kit containing luminol, a chemical that reacts with the iron found in hemoglobin that creates a "luminescence, a bright bluish green, like a glow stick," explained Jackson.

"I was there to process, or *trace* evidence," continued Jackson. "Originally, the search warrant requested that we collect a known hair sample from the victim," so the team obtained a DNA sample from Jane's hair brush.

When Jackson first entered the attached garage from the house she noted the left side was dominated by an overhang, and the right side, which was closest to the house, was filled with what appeared to be empty boxes.

"As I was going through the garage," explained Jackson, "I noticed there were a few stains on the inside of the garage door ... I went ahead and tested them ... It's a preemptive test and there are false positives that occur. However, when the samples are forwarded on (to the crime lab) ... if it was not blood we would not get a DNA result."

"There were three areas on the garage floor that fluoresced, so I circled them," continued Jackson. "Most of the stains were less than the size of a dime, or a pencil head, and weren't visible to the naked eye."

"I used a sterile cotton swab, moistened with distilled water, and collected the suspected blood stain," continued Jackson. "I allowed it to dry, then a cutting of that stain was taken off and put in a DNA extraction tube which was forwarded to the laboratory for further testing."

Once in the lab the samples were tested against known samples from Joe Gentz and Jane and Bob Bashara. Ultimately, both samples tested positive for human blood.

According to Andrea Young, Crime Lab Specialist and DNA expert with the *Michigan State Police*, among the three samples collected, the first two, recovered from the inside of the garage door, were a match for Jane Bashara. The third, collected from the center of the garage floor, was comprised of three donors, the major of which was Jane Bashara. Bob Bashara could not be excluded from the sample while Joe Gentz was.

In addition to evidence recovered from 552 Middlesex, Jane's nail clippings, forwarded from the Wayne County Morgue, contained no evidence of blood on her right hand, but the left had a blood stain containing DNA from which both Jane and Joe Gentz could not be excluded.

The boots recovered by Detective Narduzzi, allegedly owned by Joe Gentz, were also processed by the *MSP Crime Lab*.

"I believe the boots were recovered from a dumpster," reported Jackson, implying the identity of the wearer could be in question. So she swabbed the inside and laces. "Its important to place who was wearing the boots," in order to positively connect them to the crime.

"I also received information that it was possible the victim had been stepped on," explained Jackson. "So I processed the bottom of the boots by swabbing them for the possible presence of skin cells that could contain DNA."

The lab results were largely inconclusive. However, the bottom of the right boot contained at least three donors including Gentz. Jane's DNA couldn't be excluded while Bob's was. Samples collected from inside the boots tested positive for Joe Gentz.

Other known items, such as car keys and various objects inside Jane's *Mercedes* were sampled for DNA but none yielded significant results.

(The matter of whether or not a person's DNA can be excluded simply means the sample contains elements from more than one person, not necessarily a perfect match. Human DNA is 99 percent identical which leaves only one percent for individual uniqueness.)

§

Mid afternoon on February 8, Bob and Jessica Bashara were preparing for their first network interview at David Greim's office, which was set to air the following day on ABC's *Good Morning America*. While being pressed on the nature of his marriage Bashara denied having any motive for killing his wife and said: "We had a very good, open relationship," coded language apparently devised by David Griem to deal with pesky reports of infidelity.

Jessica was asked if there was any chance Bashara was capable of killing her mother. "No, not at all," she said without emotion. "Without a doubt in my mind I know that he didn't do it. There's no way … I just know how my mom felt about him. There was never any, even hint towards violence."

"Joe (Gentz) is reportedly telling us that you forced him to kill Jane," interviewer Andrea Canning pushed Bashara.

"I don't own a firearm," Bashara said flatly, "and I absolutely had nothing to do with this. That is a sick assessment on his part. It just shows how deranged he is." As for Bashara's alleged double life and affair with Rachel Gillette? Bashara had no comment (a pre interview agreement ruled the subject off limits).

But Griem doubled down, again using the coded language concerning the nature of the Bashara's marriage: "The term open marriage comes to mind."

"Jane was OK with that?" pressed Canning.

"My belief is that it was an open marriage," reiterated Griem without further explanation.

Jane's mother, Lorraine Englebrecht, was so shocked by what she heard on *Good Morning America* she immediately phoned Bashara: "Please don't bring Jane down to your level," she pleaded. "You didn't have an open marriage ... *You* had an open marriage."

"You didn't know your daughter," taunted Bashara.

"No! You didn't know her!"

"Do you know what Jane told me? I can go out and do anything I want as long as it makes me happy," Bashara said smugly. "You don't know your daughter ... she smoked pot!"

§

Although the release of Joe Gentz from police custody on February 3 was controversial, it was due to several factors, the most important being the perceived unreliability of his statements. Grosse Pointe Park police Chief David Hiller said they were lacking evidence, particularly DNA, to substantiate Gentz's story and therefore they were unable to arrest him.

Gentz was obviously mentally challenged and the tale he weaved was fantastic. However, details and evidence began to line up, backing his story. First was a simple observation Gentz made about Jane when he and Bashara allegedly loaded her lifeless body into the backseat of her *Mercedes*, that he had seen her breasts. In fact, at the time of her death Jane Bashara was not wearing a bra, rendering this statement quite believable and unlikely to have been fabricated.

The February 8 search at 552 Middlesex yielded blood samples consistent with Gentz's rendition of the attack. Not only was one sample found in the middle of the garage floor, where he said he knocked Jane down, but it was also positively confirmed to be hers.

§

On February 18 *The Detroit News,* quoting information obtained in a *Freedom of Information Act* request, reported Bashara had been the subject of a 1995 child molestation investigation involving his then five-year-old niece. The article noted there were no charges filed and that Bashara passed a polygraph test.

On the same day, Macomb County judge Kathryn Viviano ruled for the continuation of a suspension of visitation, effectively blocking Joe Gentz from his daughter.

Rumors surfaced that a car was involved in the plot to kill Jane Bashara, but it was on February 10 that local media actually put the price tag at $8,000, and identified the make as a used *Cadillac.* After seeing the news report, William Schatz, tenant and sometimes handyman at *Lakeside Apartments,* said he remembered Bashara's offer to sell him one two years before.

"When I first moved in he asked me if I wanted to buy it for $4,000," said Schatz. "It's been sitting there since then … but I never seen [*sic*] him drive it."

When Schatz declined Bashara cut the price in half. "It didn't run," pleaded Schatz. "He pushed it around with a riding mower," in order to avoid city ordinance violations.

Ralph (Raif) Lee, another handyman employed by Bashara and a resident at *Lakeside,* made his first statement to police on February 23. The questioning was particularly focused on the beige 1981 *Sedan DeVille* and Bashara's alleged sex dungeon in Grosse Pointe Park. After the interrogation Lee tipped off Bashara about the police presence and fingered Schatz as the instigator.

The next day Schatz had a run in with Bashara and was told to keep his mouth shut. "I'll throw your mother fucking ass out if you keep talking shit about me," threatened Bashara.

"Then he said he didn't kill his wife," added Schatz.

Despite obvious warnings, Schatz continued warning other residents: "Watch out for his temper … He's crazy and likes to yell at people … He might hurt you, he may choke you." This, of course, only served to bring more attention his way.

Schatz said that over the years he saw Bashara drive several vehicles including a pickup truck and "a big huge van with a big huge top on it," in which he said he saw Bashara together with Gentz in 2010. "Bob would collect rent money … Joe

Gentz stayed in the van." Schatz stressed that he never saw Joe Gentz before or after that day in 2010.

According to Schatz Joe Gentz was virtually unknown prior to Jane Bashara's death; and, despite the single glimpse he claims to have stolen of him two years previous, the fact is, he had no idea who he was until the day he saw his name in the media.

§

Practically overnight Bashara began linking Joe Gentz and the *Cadillac* as if it was always part of his narrative, and the shift caught Michael Carmody off guard:

> "Bob mentioned giving a check to Joe Gentz ... payment for some handyman work. It was an odd number, a four hundred and some dollar check ... but he'd never mentioned a car ... Now there's substantiation on the car story."

Others, too, began to notice the new pattern, that Bashara altered his story whenever new evidence came to light. Although the original rendition shared with family never mentioned Gentz, it was now a major component: "My dad said they met on one of his properties," explained Jessica, "and that Joseph Gentz commented on a car that he kept there."

On February 23 Grosse Pointe Park police impounded the *Cadillac*.

"I saw a (news) clip ... of a *Cadillac* on a flat bed truck being towed away," remembered Stephanie Samuel, Bashara's cousin. "I instantly recognized the apartment in the background ... I called him and that's when he told me about Joe and the *Cadillac*."

Bashara pressed further, explaining to Stephanie he was merely trying to find odd jobs for Joe. Gentz needed money so he hired him to do a couple roofing jobs, "to make enough to buy the *Cadillac*," Bashara added innocently.

The ensuing weeks at *Lakeside* saw William Schatz increasingly harassed and manipulated. Thomas Ramsey, another of Bashara's handymen and occasional plumber (and with whom Bashara had a close working relationship) became Bashara's de facto mouthpiece there.

"Tommy said to quit talking to detectives, quit talking to police," recalled Schatz, "because I'm making the apartment building look bad, having all the police come over and talking all the time."

It was on an early, unseasonably warm spring afternoon when Ramsey and Bashara cornered Schatz in *Lakeside's* cramped, ground floor laundry room.

"Tommy came in and shut the door," explained Schatz. "He started talking about how I don't know Bob's life. I better quit spreading rumors."

"You should leave Bob Bashara alone," Ramsey threatened. "He had nothing to do with his wife's death."

"He said for me to back off," continued Schatz, referring to Ramsey. "That him and Bob were best friends, they were buddies, and that I should quit spreading rumors."

"I was scared … I still am," said Schatz, "because of the way Bob would react around people … When tenants were late with rent Bob got mad. He would come around at three in the morning with sunglasses on and he'd be wiping his nose like he was high on something."

§

On the evening of February 21 Bashara once again contacted Rebecca Forton.

"Why in the hell are you calling me," demanded a clearly irritated Forton. "I didn't understand why this man was calling me, and I was becoming afraid."

"He got very angry," Forton continued, "and said 'I'm trying to get the utilities out of my name.'"

"We discussed this already," protested Forton. "It's illegal for me to put them in my name and take them out of Mr. Gentz's." According to Forton, Bashara again said he'd had the electricity removed, and that he tried to get the gas removed but was still unsuccessful.

"I yelled at Mr. Bashara to never call me again," explained Forton. "But I decided to call back. I called the number, a different number than the other numbers he'd called me from … and I got voicemail."

When Bashara returned the call Forton said: "I just wanted to make this very clear. I'm not going to remove the utilities from your name or put them into mine, and I don't want you to have any further contact with me."

According to Forton, Bashara responded in a threatening tone, that "he was going to do whatever he needed to do to get them (the utilities) out of his name."

This last exchange so unnerved Forton that she contacted police and requested special attention placed on the Wayburn flat. The following day she learned from *DTE* that the utilities were in fact not in Gentz's name. Digging deeper, after looking over the rental application Forton found that it said Gentz worked at *Steve's Furniture* (owned by Steve Tibaudo) and the application had different sets of handwriting on it, one in black ink in cursive, the other in blue ink in block letters.

§

On the final day of February, local *WDIV* (NBC) reporter Hank Winchester reported a police source as saying there was a neighbor on Middlesex who called police and said, referring to the night of January 24: 'I noticed that night Bob Bashara pulling his *Navigator* out of the driveway, and a short time later I saw Jane Bashara's black *Mercedes* leave the driveway. But Jane Bashara wasn't driving the car.' This person says Joe Gentz was driving the car.'"

§

As the days slowly crept into March, many of Jane's friends had become increasingly suspicious. Debbie Breen couldn't shake the nagging feeling that something just wasn't right. "I called Bob and I said with all this stuff coming out in the media, I want to … ask you some questions … I want you to be honest and truthful with me. I asked him first, if he was with Jim Wilson between Christmas and New Years … He said yes."

"Then I asked him about the sex dungeon and he said 'there is no sex dungeon, the media is just trying to make me look guilty. The room is no bigger than my dinning room at home, and I store equipment in there. It's a storage room, there's no such thing as a sex dungeon."

Patti Matthews was thinking much the same way, and she too called Jim Wilson in Florida, asking if he'd been golfing with Bashara after Christmas, but Wilson told her no.

Matthews didn't bother to confront Bashara, she took the revelation directly to Jessica. "I told her that Jim Wilson said Bob wasn't with him," Matthews said. "He hasn't seen him in three years, and Bob called and asked him to cover for him in case Jane called."

A short while later Bashara called and left Matthews a disturbing message: "Don't ever talk to my daughter again. That was terrible what you told her."

Roxanne Flaska, the neighbor who'd been dispatched to Ann Arbor to fetch Jessica on January 25, also received troubling information concerning Wilson. She passed it on to Jessica as well and almost immediately Bashara's demeanor toward her changed for the worst.

It was well known among Jane's friends that Bashara harbored no love for the family dog, a dark grey Labradoodle named Lance, and they knew something sinister must be afoot when soon after Jane's death Lance mysteriously died.

"I said to him, all of these are lies that you're telling me," insisted Debbie Breen. "Lance dies and now all the stuff that's coming out in the media, everything is lies!"

"Debbie, I was advised by my attorney (David Griem) to lie," insisted Bashara. "Because all of this is going to be investigated, so I had to lie."

Eileen Stratelak and Bashara spoke often about the night of January 24, and she said he always repeated the same story, "he was at a rental property up on Mack." But when she asked about the eyewitness who saw him at the house that evening Bashara told her "not to believe it."

When she pressed him further he said simply: "Bad timing ... wrong place at the wrong time."

But several weeks later Bashara's account changed, and he began to admit he'd run home about 6 o'clock to get keys. He said he stopped briefly in the bathroom and noticed Jane's bag leaning against the wall outside the door, but he was in a hurry, so he left without confirming whether Jane was there or not.

"When I confronted him about the car being moved he said maybe Joe was in the garage," said Stratelak. "He knew Jane's car wasn't in the driveway, so he figured it was in the garage."

(Bashara did not tell Stratelak (or anyone else) there were signs of forced entry or a struggle, nor was anything out of place. He apparently made no attempt to find Jane, but he did tell Stratelak that after he left, "nobody left after me". It's difficult to determine how he could be aware of this fact).

§

Dissatisfaction with the investigation, said Bashara, was the reason he and David Griem hired a private investigator, a retired FBI man named J.D. Gifford. Now they had "more eyes looking into the whole murder," Bashara explained to his son Robert.

"They were looking for a person who could have done this," explained Jessica. "They hired (him) because they weren't happy with the progress of the Grosse Pointe Park police." Ironically, not once did Robert or Jessica ever speak to Gifford, nor was any other form of contact made between them.

§

On February 22 an investigative subpoena was issued in the name of Rachel Gillette. This powerful legal tool, signed into Michigan law in 1995, allows prosecutors to summon a witness to a hearing in which they are questioned under oath. Refusal to cooperate could invoke heavy fines or even jail time and is subject to perjury as well.

In response Gillette retained Dearborn based attorney Doraid Elder, "mainly to help me deal with the media," she said. A week later she instructed him to send a letter to Bashara asking him to cease all contact. In eMails she began to tell family and friends that she believed she was the motive in Jane's murder.

§

On Friday, March 2, Joe Gentz was arrested immediately upon arrival at a custody hearing at Macomb County Court. He was held on probable cause without a warrant. Bashara's reaction was to correspond via Instant Message with one of his few remaining friends, former Chicago police officer and prospective *Lifestyle* submissive Therese Giffon:

> **Bashara**: *"They have made an arrest of the man who did this."*

> **Giffon**: *"I am glad. How are you doing?"*

> **Bashara**: *"I'm just ok, but still very depressed about all this."*

Three days later Gentz was charged with first-degree murder and conspiracy. He was denied bond at his arraignment and a competency evaluation was ordered. Detroit-based attorney Susan Reed was appointed by the court to represent him which sparked another exchange:

> **Bashara**: *"Not good. They charged Gentz with conspiracy."*

> **Giffon**: *"I worry for you."*

> **Bashara**: *"Really? Well then I guess I am next. What does that mean, not manslaughter."*

> **Giffon**: *"With charging him with first degree murder and conspiracy means that whoever the co conspirator is will also be charged with first degree murder."*

> **Bashara**: *"He should be first degree."*

> **Giffon**: *"It's first degree but also conspiracy. The conspiracy is to implement [sic] another, possibly you."*

§

Days after Jane's death Venita Porter received a message from *St. Michael's Church*. "I was on the prayer list," explained Porter, "and they sent out an eMail informing of her death. I didn't know how or why, and my heart went out to Bob and the children." Shortly after, she sent a condolence eMail and Bashara responded with his appreciation.

"We had a couple contacts in the first months (after the breakup) ending some business," recalled Porter. "He owed me some money. We had some conversations ... I think there was an IM every couple months. I didn't trust him, and I wanted to know what he was up to."

In March, out of the blue, Bashara gave Porter a surprise visit. "I was home ... I looked up and in through my front door, because the door was unlocked, he walked in with my mail and a big smile."

Greeting him with a simple 'hi', Porter gave Bashara a condolence hug. "He said things had been rough since Jane's death." Porter testified that she simply tried to get the encounter over with, and get him out the door as quickly as she could.

"I know it sounds crazy," Porter said in a preliminary hearing in September 2013, "but I've been to the Bob, and I didn't want to make him mad, I didn't want to set him off, so I acted normal."

"He asked me to go to a *Rotary* wine tasting," continued Porter. "I couldn't understand what he was doing here after all this time." Bashara suggested they could go together as Rotarians – and his date – and they could meet there so people wouldn't know.

"I told him no," Porter said emphatically.

Then the conversation veered toward Rachel. Bashara, apparently not mindful of their single encounter, said she wasn't standing by him or cooperating with his private investigation. He was concerned she'd turned on him. Then he wanted to talk about the night of January 24.

"Bob seemed to want me to understand and know what happened, he seemed desperate," said Porter. "He told me that he'd been at the *Hard Luck* above the dungeon, that he'd been having drinks at the time it happened."

"He told me ... he'd gone back to the back alley to pick up some trash," Porter continued. "At some point it changed to the fact that he needed to go back to the house, he'd left for five or 10 minutes to get some keys at the house and had come back."

Promptly after Bashara left Porter made contact with Wayne County Prosecutors.

§

Minutes before 9 a.m. on Tuesday, March 6, five unmarked police cars from Grosse Pointe Park and the Wayne County Sheriff arrived at Rachel Gillette's yellow brick California bungalow on St. Clair Ave. in Grosse Pointe. The search was intended to unearth evidence of a romantic or sexual relationship between her and Bashara.

Conducted by the same evidence technicians as the February 8 search at Middlesex, investigators repeatedly emerged from Gillette's home carrying bags of evidence including a computer, seven cardboard boxes, a paper bag and an evidence box. Broadcast on live television and streamed on the Internet, the search was concluded in time for lunch.

Days before Gillette offered to return jewelry Bashara had given her but he declined. "The ring I believe he gave me in early 2010, the necklace ... was Christmas 2011," said Gillette. "We were breaking up, they were both tied to his family. I didn't want them anymore. I wanted him to give them to his children or whatever he was gonna do with them."

However, before Gillette could convince Bashara to accept they were seized by police, along with several other items. "They were taken from my home with everything else," she said, "I lost a lot of stuff that day."

Three days later Bashara and his mother Nancy left town on a driving trip to Iowa for a long weekend visiting Robert.

As his relationship with Gillette disintegrated, Bashara increasingly relied on Therese Giffon and Richard Falcinelli (*Lifestyle* friend) to act as intermediaries, keeping tabs on Gillette and at times urging her to communicate with him. He continued to reach out through Gillette's children as well.

In a March 15 eMail to Giffon, Bashara expressed his feelings for Gillette:

> *"Why is it that I can not get her out of my head? Like you said, she is not a beauty queen, but to me something special."*

Giffon was continually asked to intercede, but nothing it seems would change Gillette's mind. On March 29 Bashara asked Giffon to send her the Tammy Wynette song *Stand By Your Man*, because "she relates songs to life."

Bashara just couldn't get Gillette out of his mind. "He didn't want to approach the house, he didn't want to approach her," explained cousin Stephanie Samuel, but he did continue his daily drive-by surveillance of her home. Keeping the pressure on to the point of obsession, Bashara left a cross made of palm leaves for Gillette on Palm Sunday (April 1).

Following a second kiss-off letter, which was also ignored, and countless overtures by Giffon and Falcinelli, on April 26 Gillette finally requested a Personal Protection Order (PPO) against Bashara, which apparently caught him off guard.

§

When Bashara first shared the news with his cousin Stephanie that he'd hired a private investigator, he told her the move was designed to find the truth of who was Jane's killer. He then began talking about two people she was unaware of: Paul Monroe and April Montgomery.

Paul Monroe was an ex-con, convicted of various crimes including bank robbery, assault and felony firearms. He was also a drug dealer who occasionally provided Bashara with cocaine. Monroe was a tenant at *Lakeside* since 2006 and the two had become fairly well acquainted.

Days after hearing of Jane's death Monroe went out of his way to contact Bashara to express his condolences and phone records indicate the two maintained regular phone contact for the next six months.

In April, Bashara approached Monroe for a favor. First, he wanted him to make contact with J.D. Gifford (Bashara's private investigator). Second, he wanted him to call in a false tip concerning Jane's murder. In return he offered "money and getting (traffic) tickets (totaling $11,000) to go away," Monroe said in testimony.

(There is no evidence suggesting Bashara had the necessary connections to fulfill his end of the bargain).

The plan surrounded April Montgomery, Monroe's former fiancé, and Charles Wilson, her current boyfriend. Both were tenants of Bashara's and there was bad blood between Wilson and Monroe: Wilson "tried to do an armed robbery on me in 1995," explained Monroe. "So I really didn't like him."

Monroe enlisted long time friend and fellow coke dealer Daryl Bradford. "He wanted me to call in to give a report that his girlfriend and her boyfriend had something to do with the murder of Jane Bashara," recalled Bradford.

Monroe gave Bradford a cell phone and instructed him to make the call. Having no idea where he was calling, Bradford told the person on the other end: "I have information that April Montgomery and Charles Wilson had something to do with the murder." For his trouble Monroe paid Bradford $20.

After the call Bashara pressured Monroe to go a step further and submit an affidavit … "But I didn't feel comfortable doing it," recalled Monroe. However, intending to get even with Charles Wilson, Monroe made "twenty calls saying April and Charles were involved with Jane's murder." For his trouble Bashara paid him $89.

§

On April 11, Wayne County Prosecutors obtained a warrant ordering Bashara to submit handwriting samples to the court. Bashara and Griem appeared before Judge Timothy Kenny to fight for the right to have Griem present. Following a twenty minute in-chambers discussion, and a fiery exchange in court, the request was denied.

Reacting to continuous legal pressure, Bashara and Griem requested character letters from both Richard Falcinelli and Therese Giffon.

Giffon had recently been interviewed by law enforcement officers in Chicago where she was questioned about her relationship with Bashara. Insisting they were merely friends, she described a past visit to Bashara's sex dungeon: neither wore clothing and Bashara utilized a vibrator and nipple clips. Giffon insisted the session was properly considered 'play' rather than 'sex', because "based on his body parts ... he's not getting off on it ... It's his control over the female."

Griem carefully instructed Giffon on what he'd like to see in the letter, "all good things" she said later, and nothing about their past. "I've taken it upon myself to show support," Giffon began, continuing by writing that Bashara had been treated unfairly by media and law enforcement. "One cannot meet a gentler or caring person with an enormous generous heart."

Falcinelli, who self-identified as 'all in' with respect to *The Lifestyle*, was first contacted by investigators in early April. Before he could get to Bashara's character letter he wrote an eMail to Bashara and Griem seeking instructions and to inform them that Tim Matouk, a Wayne County Prosecutor's Office detective, had contacted him directly.

"I don't know where this detective got my name and cell phone number," wrote Falcinelli. "But I can tell you that no matter what direction he's coming from, he's not going to get anything but positive things about Bob."

In the same eMail Falcinelli suggested the three of them might get together to prep for his inevitable encounter with law enforcement. "Bob well knows how much I hate what all these other people, media, law enforcement, prosecutors, etc. are all trying to do to him, and how much I want to help him successfully get through this all, shut it down as it appropriately should be."

A week later Wayne County prosecutors took statements from Falcinelli and Giffon, neither of whom were cooperative, and the latter was forced to later admit to making false or incomplete statements.

§

On May 11, NBC aired *Dateline NBC: Secrets in the Suburbs,* an hour long exposé into the Jane Bashara slaying. It was taped in late April and shows a confident, if not completely naive Bob Bashara in interviews in and around the

Middlesex home. In one segment he is seen with his "You're the man BOB" oversized coffee mug at his side.

It is suspected that Bashara's distrust for local media caused him to make the assumption that their national older siblings might give him a better shake. Heavily utilizing footage taken from the February Marc Santia interview and typical Monday quarterbacking by local *WDIV* reporter Hank Winchester, the program dove in head first, beginning with a dig on the high standard of living found in 'the Pointes' and progressing to the heart of the matter, including interviews with Steve Virgona and former Detroit detective Tom Berry.

Joe Gentz's account was aired but voiced by Berry (a subsequent airing nearly a year later broadcast Gentz's voice in place of Berry's). A mysterious BDSM submissive known as 'Lynn' recounted a single encounter in the dungeon with Bashara and Gillette.

According to *WDIV* (local NBC), the following day an angry Lorraine Englebrecht lashed out in response to Bashara's comments from *Dateline* in another phone exchange with Bashara: "Stop dragging my daughter's name through the mud," she demanded.

In a very familiar exchange, Bashara twice returned her call to plead his innocence and told Englebrecht that Jane said he could go out and do anything he wanted.

"Oh, so she allowed slaves and dungeons?" Englebrecht spat sarcastically.

"Well, she didn't know anything about that."

On May 15 Englebrecht contacted police and accused Bashara of having changed mentally and was possibly "unstable enough to harm her."

As this conflict played out in public, a new one was brewing on the horizon … the fate of Jane's ashes, which since January were languishing in a file cabinet drawer in Bashara's home office.

§

It was a warm, sunny early June afternoon when Bashara again approached Will Schatz, this time with a smile and a request to write a character letter on his behalf. Introducing him to his cousin Stephanie, Bashara said she could help.

"Bob asked if I would take a dictated letter from one of his tenants who has very poor handwriting," said Samuel.

So Bashara, Schatz and Stephanie, armed with her laptop, sat down at a picnic table in the courtyard at *Lakeside* to write the letter.

"He didn't know how to start and I suggested dear sir or madam," explained Samuel. "I was helping him be grammatically correct with the opening."

Schatz said he instructed Samuel on what to write but also that Bashara threatened him as before: "If I didn't say what he wanted he was going to throw my ass out."

The letter alleged 'rude and persistent' behavior by detectives from Wayne County and Grosse Pointe Park over the course of multiple visits to the complex.

"They asked me about a *Cadillac* parked on the property," wrote Schatz. "They were asking me how long I've lived at the apartment building, if Bob Bashara carried guns and if I knew anyone that he would pay to kill his wife."

"I was so shocked at how rude and mean they were," complained Schatz. "They intruded into my home, they wanted to know if I knew there was a sex dungeon in Grosse Pointe and if I ever partied there."

Once the letter was finished Samuel and Bashara abruptly left to have copies made, leaving Schatz alone in the courtyard.

§

After three months in custody, on June 5 Joe Gentz was ruled mentally competent to stand trial. The exam was performed by a psychologist with the Michigan Department of Health. In a June 10 hearing, Gentz's attorney, Susan Reed, was granted a second, independent evaluation and a hearing was scheduled for July 23. It was widely believed the competency exams were a precursor to a possible Gentz plea bargain.

§

Bob Bashara had grown increasingly desperate by the middle of June. His odyssey since January had taken it's toll. The news concerning Joe Gentz and his competency exam was troubling and he was physically wiped out. On June 20 he got in touch with Paul Monroe (the now former tenant who phoned in the false tip concerning Jane's murder) who had recently moved to Highland Park.

"He picked me up on the corner of 6 Mile and Woodward," explained Monroe, "near the gas station. I met him at the *Valero*. He wanted to talk."

According to Monroe, Bashara was looking to score some coke, and he wasn't in the best of shape. "He looked bad, he looked like he'd lost weight. His eyes were red ... he had bug eyes."

The two sat in Bashara's parked *Navigator* for a time before aimlessly driving around Highland Park for a while. According to Monroe, Bashara paid him $2,300 cash for two ounces of coke. Bashara ingested some and the two began to talk.

Without warning Bashara abruptly pulled the *Navigator* to the curb. "He looked crazy, strange," remembered Monroe. "He asked me if I was wearing a wire and he patted me down ... I said, 'What you patting me down for? I don't have no wire."

Then Bashara abruptly started talking about Jane and the murder, which triggered a breakdown. "He started crying," Monroe said in testimony. "Then he said he had his wife killed."

"Why would you do that?" Monroe was astonished by the admission.

"Because divorce is like losing money," muttered Bashara.

"Was Joe Gentz there?"

"Yes."

"You know they're going to hunt you down ... get you convicted."

This encounter was their last conversation.

Chapter 9

End Game

The most illusive element of Joe Gentz's account of Jane Bashara's murder was his assertion that Bob Bashara held a gun to his head. Bashara was asked about it on *Good Morning America* February 8 when he replied: "I don't own a firearm, and I absolutely had nothing to do with this." However, despite the lack of supporting evidence, the claim continued to dog Bashara.

"He said he only owned a BB gun to keep the squirrels out of his garden," said Bashara's cousin Stephanie, and that was good enough for her. The two discussed the issue on several occasions and Bashara was adamant that he didn't own a 'real' gun. Despite the multitude of media stories to the contrary, she believed him.

Bashara and his mother Nancy had long shared a safe-deposit box at *Comerica Bank*, using it over the years for various family valuables and each had their own key.

"Near the end of February I'm putting laundry away," remembered Stephanie. "I'm hearing the conversation … between Bob and Nancy, and I see over my shoulder, Bob putting a couple of his father's watches into this squishy bag and knotting it up."

"Hey mom, I've got a couple of dad's watches, a couple jewelry pieces and some collector coins I've been saving for Robert," said Bashara. "Will you do me a favor? I can't find my key and I've got a lot to do today. Could you take this to the safe-deposit box?"

"He handed it to me … in a plastic bag," recalled Nancy. "I had to go to my apartment to get my key, went to *Comerica* and signed in, and without opening the bag I just put it right in my box. I wasn't there more than two seconds … the box was closed and I left."

§

Beginning in late February Bashara was making increasingly more calls to *Steve's Furniture*, always insisting on speaking directly with Steve Tibaudo. It was not uncommon as business interests caused their paths to cross many times over the years. But following the death of Jane, Tibaudo began to feel that things just weren't quite right.

Tibaudo called Detective Narduzzi and made a statement to Grosse Pointe Park police on February 29. He described his first meeting with Joe Gentz some years before: "He was working at my wife's cousin's pizza parlor in Roseville. They told me it wasn't working out so they asked me if I could straighten him out."

"Joe worked for me for one week," continued Tibaudo, "but he was such a hot head. He would kick things, he was so out of hand when he worked for me. I fired him after a week … for saying 'nigger' and kicking stuff around."

Tibaudo admitted he never mentioned these negative traits of Gentz's to Bashara. His intention at the time was simply for Gentz to become a tenant handyman.

A few weeks later Tibaudo contacted investigators from the homicide division at the Detroit Police Department, the Wayne County Sheriff and directly with Tim Matouk and Cory Williams, investigators with the Wayne County Prosecutor's Office. "We were asked every time (Bashara) showed up to let them know," explained Tibaudo.

"I feared for my life, that's why I called them," continued Tibaudo, despite admitting in court he regularly carried knives and owned three Beretta 380 handguns. When asked by defense council if he was scared he replied: "Not when I had back up around me."

"He's crazy, a hot head," Tibaudo said of Bashara. "An asshole who screws people out of their money. He screws everyone."

Tibaudo began regular dialogue with detectives in April that intensified in May as the frequency of conversations with Bashara steadily increased. After several meetings late in the spring, detectives and Tibaudo discussed the possibility of using a recording device on Tibaudo's telephone.

FBI Special Agent Christopher Hess delivered the recording equipment early on the afternoon of June 18 and later Tibaudo made his first call to Bashara from the bugged phone. The two exchanged pleasantries and Tibaudo recounted his recent health issues, standard practice for him.

"I got a fridge that's bad," began Bashara, getting down to business. "It never worked."

"If you've got a fridge that's bad I got a form to take care of it," explained Tibaudo. "But here's the deal, you got a bill here for two refrigerators."

"No, I paid for one of them, Steve."

"I know Bob, but you have a $900 bill with me."

"And I paid five," pleaded Bashara. "OK, I'm happy to pay you that, but that's for the one fridge that was bad ... Lookit, I will give you a check today my friend."

"I got all these people coming down here fuckin' up my business man," Tibaudo lobbed enticingly.

"Who?"

"Fuckin' Wayne County Prosecutors and everybody else have been coming down here."

"You think I got 'em comin' there?" choked Bashara. "Shit, I don't want nothin' to do with these guys. Your friend Joe Gentz has got me fucked up big time."

"You know Bob, listen, he ain't my friend. He's an acquaintance, like you are. I don't need this shit," said Tibaudo, mindful of who would be listening to the recording.

"Absolutely, and you know what? I appreciate you referring the guy to me, to get an apartment. But I didn't realize he was as loose of a cannon as he was, holy mackerel!"

"I got all these fuckin' people coming down here," Tibaudo pressed.

"There's only one person I want you to talk to," insisted Bashara.

"Who's that?"

"A guy named J.D ... J.D. is my guy, and he can help me."

"Is he an investigator?"

"Well, he's an investigator who used to be with the FBI," explained Bashara. "He's not though, he's a private eye that's workin' for me. If you would talk to him I would be most appreciative, OK?"

"This prosecution is terrible," added Bashara, "terrible what they're doin'. OK? They asked ... tenants of mine, were they fuckin' my wife? I mean, this is the type of shit they pull."

"But you come down here and you're bangin' at my door, sayin' I'm throwin' you under the fuckin' bus," said an agitated Tibaudo.

"Who said that?"

"My guys are tellin' me shit like this."

"Not from me. No, that's bullshit," protested Bashara. "What I said – I never said anything about you throwing me under the bus. I don't believe you would do that, OK? So first of all, there's nothing for you to throw, I've done nothing wrong."

"Secondly," pushed Bashara, "I buy refrigerators and stoves from you. I see you occasionally at the bar ... That's the extent of our relationship, OK? Are you there?"

"Yeah, I'm here," Tibaudo said distantly.

"First of all … every time I come in I ask Eddie how you doin', OK? So I don't think you threw me under the bus at all … I don't know what you said to these guys other than we had a business relationship."

"And we want to take care of ya's as long as we got paid," finished Tibaudo.

"Steve, it's the chicken or the egg … I wanna pay you for an appliance that works, but you delivered one that never worked … get me a (working) fridge, and I'd be happy to pay you."

"What about Joe Gentz's people coming down here and questioning me?" probed Tibaudo.

"Well, I have no idea – what do you mean Joe Gentz's people?"

"It's the attorney," replied Tibaudo. "They want to ask some questions and shit."

(This reference is to the fact that Gentz's lawyer, Susan Reed, had been seen walking around both Bashara's properties and Steve's Furniture looking for people to talk to).

"Well, you do what you gotta do," Bashara said flippantly. "I have nothing to do with them. I have nothing to do with the prosecution. Nothing to do with Susan Reed … or any of his people, OK? As far as I'm concerned Joe Gentz is a terrible, terrible man who killed my wife because I wouldn't loan him money. That's the son-of-a-bitch that I'm dealing with … All I want you to do is help me out because I'm an innocent man and they may charge me."

"I know, they might charge you; they might charge me for introducing him to you," Tibaudo said without emotion. "I could be charged as an accessary or something."

"Oh, fuck that! That's the biggest bunch of bullshit," protested Bashara. "That's what they say to you. They say shit, put shit like that in your head to scare you."

"These fuckin' people are all crazy," said Tibaudo. "They don't give a fuck about my business or my bills or my family."

"No they don't. They'll rattle anyone. In fact ... that's what my guy wants to know, how they threatened you and what they said to you."

"I got people coming in, I don't even know who these people are," said Tibaudo.

"I know. Well, neither do I. I'm as big of a victim here as you are – OK, bigger, 'cause I lost my wife. ... and this asshole killed her; and to get off he's trying to blame me; and they're believing him, 'cause they think he's competent. He's fruitier than a fuckin' loon ... You told me he was a little goofy, but I didn't realize how bad he was."

The conversation lasted another five minutes on a variety of topics before reverting back to the refrigerator transaction.

"I don't need anything fancy, just some shitty refrigerator," revisited Bashara. "I'll write you a check for $500 tomorrow. But I really would appreciate it if you'd talk to my guy. Nothing to do with Joe, nothing to do with the prosecution. But I could use help with this J.D."

The two made arrangements for Tibaudo to deliver a replacement refrigerator in exchange for Bashara's full payment the following day.

"Listen," said Tibaudo. "I'm sorry to hear about your wife, man."

"Oh, it's terrible, Steve, it's terrible. The fact that they're involving me. You don't understand these people. They flew down to Florida to interview a friend of mine, he's a golfing buddy of mine."

"They had guys sittin' in here for two days," ventured Tibaudo. "One of my busiest times of the year!"

"Well, here's the deal," posed Bashara. "Why don't we just meet at the property. I'll give you the fridge and the check and you bring in the new one, and then we're even."

"So you never said I'm throwing you under the bus?" Tibaudo half stated for the second time.

"No, I didn't."

"'Cause Eddie (Eddie Fahner, *Steve's Furniture* employee) turned around and said 'yeah, Bob says you're throwing him under the bus.'"

"No, bullshit! Bullshit! I never said that," protested Bashara. "All I said to him is so many people are throwing me under the bus ... not you!"

"But I introduced you to Joe, you know what I'm sayin'?" ventured Tibaudo, trying to get Bashara to bite.

"That's all you did ... Quite frankly, if I knew how bad this Joe was I never would have even brought him into my world."

Immediately after this conversation Tibaudo requested police protection and a concealed recording device. *Michigan State Police* detectives delivered a portable version that Tibaudo described as looking like a pack of cigarettes, which he would carry in a shirt pocket.

"I asked to wear the wire," Tibaudo testified. "I thought Bob was going to open up my head."

The following afternoon Tibaudo arrived at Bashara's *Lakeside Apartments* with his Red Terrier Mr. Doodles in tow to deliver the used refrigerator. Bashara met him in the rear parking lot with Thomas Ramsey, whom Tibaudo knew simply as 'the plumber guy.'

Tibaudo was ready for action with his cigarette pack-disguised recording device lodged in his front left shirt pocket, and the three of them manhandled the refrigerator down a flight of steps to the basement.

"This Gentz guy is going to throw me under the bus," Bashara said abruptly. "He came over to my house looking for money, looking for me, you know what I mean?"

"Yeah," said Tibaudo.

"I gotta get to Joe," Bashara said flatly. "If I can't get to him it's my life – are you wearing a wire?" Bashara then took a step towards Tibaudo.

"He started feelin' around to see," Tibaudo testified. "I said 'no, it's against my religion to wear a wire, I'm Sicilian.'"

"What do you have on your side?" prodded Bashara.

"It's my pistol," Tibaudo shot back.

"What kind of pistol you got?" Bashara suddenly sounded interested.

"I got a *Beretta*."

Bashara moved in closer and whispered in Tibaudo's left ear. "He wanted to know if I could kill Joe or have him killed," Tibaudo testified.

"Yeah," replied Tibaudo. "We could get to the president if the price was right."

"You arrange it," ordered Bashara.

"He wanted me to broker the deal," explained Tibaudo, "the murder of Joe Gentz."

"Work on this other thing for me," Bashara whispered as the two climbed the stairs.

The recording made on June 19 is of very low quality, although by no means worthless. For this reason, later in the day FBI Agent Hess stopped by *Steve's Furniture* and supplied Tibaudo with his second recording device, which Tibaudo described as "a smaller one, real nice. Stealthful, hold it in your hand."

Disguised as a car fob, the second device was more intricate to operate and Hess spent a few minutes giving Tibaudo instructions.

Three days later, on June 22, Bashara sauntered through the front door of *Steve's Furniture* looking for Tibaudo. Suspiciously, he eyed the security cameras as he passed. Tibaudo said he looked like a zombie. "He looked really tense, like he'd been up for days."

Bashara got up close and whispered in Tibaudo's ear. "Bob didn't want to stay in the building," recalled Tibaudo. He "wanted to go out to his (*Navigator*) and talk."

Once they reached the car Bashara again asked Tibaudo about wearing a wire as he reached over to pat him down, by now standard Bashara procedure.

"If you're wearing a wire it's my life here," warned Bashara. "Just shoot me now," he mumbled, shaking his head as they climbed into the 'Big Bob' mobile.

Bashara again wanted to know if Tibaudo could get to Joe, have him killed.

"He's incarcerated in the county jail," began Bashara, referring to the *William Dickerson Facility* in Hamtramck. Then he asked Tibaudo how he would go about the deed.

"Well, you know, we have a number of options here," Tibaudo began. "We could either put somebody in the jail with him and poison him, or we could put some glass in a salt and pepper shaker ... Or we could, if he's being moved, we could take him out with a grenade launcher."

Tibaudo has obviously seen just about every mob movie ever made and clearly has a flare for the dramatic. Bashara asked how much it would cost and Tibaudo simply said "$20,000."

"Once I pay you the money, it's a fucking conspiracy again," muttered Bashara. "OK, let's do this, sooner the better ... If Joe is found competent it would be my life." Bashara was referring to Gentz's second competency exam scheduled for July 23.

"When can you get the money?" Tibaudo asked as the two lumbered out of the *Navigator*.

"I don't know, a couple days ... I'm trusting the hell out of you man," Bashara said wirily.

"Fuck Bob, I mean, business is business, OK?"

"I'm trusting the hell out of you," Bashara repeated as they passed through the back door of *Steve's Furniture*.

"Don't worry about it. You worry too much."

"Don't you think I should?"

On his way out the front door Bashara said he'd be back on Monday (June 25) with the money. Watching him closely, Tibaudo reached over and picked up the phone and dialed. But ten minutes later Bashara was back.

"Who the fuck you on the phone with?" bellowed Bashara.

"What the fuck's wrong with you?" protested Tibaudo. "I'm making a phone call here … trying to set up a girl for the night." (Actuality he was discussing his previous conversation with prosecutors).

"Let me see the phone," Bashara roared as he snatched Tibaudo's cell phone, his face flush with anger. Scrolling through the call log he found 'Tim Matouk.'

"You're talkin' to the frickin' law," Bashara roared.

"Get your money together, then call me," deflected Tibaudo. "Then come here and start bitching me out and I'll know it's on … start bitching specifically about that refrigerator I dropped off for you and I'll know it's on, and you've got the money, OK?"

Unbelievably, Tibaudo's reassurance, if you could call it that, sufficiently, if only temporarily, kept Bashara's suspicion at bay.

As the weekend waned into Monday morning Bashara again shuffled through the front door of *Steve's Furniture*.

"He sat down across from me at the desk," remembered Tibaudo.

"I have some money for you," said Bashara as he carefully laid down $2,000 cash in twenties and hundred dollar bills, counting as he stacked them in a neat pile.

"We agreed on three thousand," insisted Tibaudo, but Bashara said two was all he could scrape up.

Incredibly, Bashara then asked for a receipt. "So I wrote him out a receipt," Tibaudo said with a shrug. "I wrote it out for $20,000 for some refrigerators and stoves, with a down payment of $2,000 and a balance of $18,000."

Laying the receipt down, Tibaudo said: "Here, sign it."

"I ain't signing that," Bashara protested, shoving the receipt back across the counter top.

"Well, you wanted a receipt, there's your receipt."

Bashara wanted the receipt to look like any other as far as the appliances go, but he wanted it to only say $2,000.

"I went to write him out a second receipt," Tibaudo testified, "but the phone kept ringing. I didn't know what to think of it ... I didn't notice that Bob had grabbed one of my cordless phones off the desk and was scrolling the caller ID."

Thinking fast, Eddie Fahner, who was on the far side of the store, used a cell phone to call the store so Bashara couldn't see the caller ID on the handset.

"He didn't want to sign the first receipt so I got up and went in my office, 'cause I had a shredder in there," explained Tibaudo. "I don't know why I shredded it, but I made him another receipt. He took a copy and I kept one."

Then Bashara abruptly declared that he needed all the appliances within three weeks. "It was the date he needed (the hit) taken care of with Joe," Tibaudo testified. "Two to three weeks. Couldn't go any longer because of his competency hearing."

"Just fucking lost," Bashara muttered, shaking his head from side to side as he slowly walked toward the front door. "Lost like a lost puppy ..." Then he climbed into his *Navigator* and drove off, heading north on Chalmers toward I-94.

With little hesitation Tibaudo quickly stashed the receipt into a drawer, reached for his cell phone and selected 'Tim Matouk' from the call list.

"A lot of people came to the store," remembered Tibaudo. "I gave them the $2,000 that Bob gave me, the receipt and the recorder."

§

A few days before his final encounter with Steve Tibaudo, Bashara again reached out to Venita Porter.

"I felt more comfortable just trying to keep things calm than to cause trouble," Porter said later, explaining why she agreed to meet Bashara. "Causing more trouble would draw more attention to myself. It was easier to just go listen than to say no. He seemed like he was getting agitated."

Porter and Bashara met in the early afternoon of June 25 near her place of work in Dearborn (just west of Detroit). Porter didn't know it (nor would it have mattered to her) but Bashara had just come from *Steve's Furniture*.

Together they drove to the nearby *Hines Park* where they found a large picnic area with a construction crew working out front. "I felt at least somebody was around there," explained Porter, clearly anxious over being alone with Bashara. "We sat on a picnic bench and I let him have his say."

Bashara told Porter about Rachel Gillette and her Personal Protection Order against him. "He said he really did love her and that she was being crazy, she had turned on him." He also talked about her cooperation with law enforcement: "He was concerned that he couldn't reach her and she was saying things that seemed to upset him."

Porter said Bashara was also aware of her contact with police: "I told him what he knew I would say, but I didn't tell him everything."

After about 40 minutes they decided to take a walk. "He pulled me into the bushes where no one could see us."

"Why did you do this to me, you turned me into a whore," Porter said flatly, adding that sex was no longer part of her life.

"He grabbed me by the neck, lifted me by the chin up on my toes and kissed me very, very thoroughly," explained Porter. "He told me he didn't want to hear me say things like that … that I wasn't a whore and I was too beautiful not to be having sex."

"I kept my hand on a box cutter in my pocket and hoped I was going to live," reflected Porter. "Then he asked me if I would come back to the house and stay with him. He said we didn't have much time, I needed to make the decision."

"Bob, that's crazy. The prosecutors know I've been telling the truth … they know how I stayed at the house before. Have you lost your mind?"

"He said he needed to feel me," Porter said.

"When we came out of the bushes there were two gentlemen that I was hoping were detectives in the park," Porter said, sounding a bit shaken. "We walked past them quickly and went to my car."

"I drove him back to his car," added Porter. "He hugged me, told me again to hurry, that we didn't have much time and then he got in his car and drove away."

§

Immediately following Bashara's departure from *Steve's Furniture* a full scale dragnet ensued. Cars were placed at several known haunches of Bashara's throughout metro Detroit. Grosse Pointe Park police placed cars at 552 Middlesex and in the alley behind the Mack Ave. rental properties.

Following his midday rendezvous with Porter Bashara headed back to Grosse Pointe, ending up at his dungeon. Before he had the chance to descend the dingy steps the police pounced: "Put your hands on the car," Bashara was ordered.

"What's this about?" protested Bashara.

"You know damn well what it's about."

Sixty seconds later Wayne County Investigator Cory Williams arrived: "Mr. Bashara, you are under arrest for solicitation to commit murder!"

Bashara was briefly held in the Grosse Pointe Park lockup before being moved downtown to the Wayne County Jail. He was immediately placed on suicide watch and his *Navigator*, the 'Big Bob' mobile, was impounded. According to media and police sources, Bashara had more than a thousand dollars in his pocket and he broke down in tears following the arrest.

Bashara was arraigned at 1 p.m. on June 27. Charged with solicitation to commit murder, he was offered a $15 Million cash bail. If the astronomical amount was posted Bashara would be required to surrender his passport, driver's license and wear an electronic tracking tether in exchange for relative freedom. A preliminary exam was set for July 24, one day after Joe Gentz's second competency hearing.

§

In the days that followed Stephanie Samuel and Nancy Bashara jointly assumed Power of Attorney over Bashara's affairs. Soon Stephanie learned of several promissory notes taken out by Bashara: "Quite a bit of money," she observed, "borrowed by the Bashara's from Nancy."

She also noticed Nancy was a co-signer on several loans and properties owned by Bashara, which quickly headed into default or receivership. Funds, approximately $9,800, were quickly withdrawn from Nancy's bank account to cover the debt.

Bashara made several calls from the Wayne County Jail in an abrupt effort to evict Thomas Ramsey. "There's too much trouble at that complex," Bashara insisted, offering scant justification for the move.

Bashara made his first call to Stephanie on the evening of June 27 and carefully shared his instructions for dealing with Ramsey.

"I'm sorry about all this," Bashara told her. "I just can't believe this is happening to me. I'm just absolutely numb." Then he told Stephanie to backdate the order to May 18, "'cause that's when I served him."

Bashara insisted Ramsey was "a loudmouth. He was no good, he didn't have a lease and he's a menace at the apartment complex." With little reason to question, Stephanie did as she was asked.

(The reason for the sudden effort to evict may be found in the fact that Thomas Ramsey, along with Steve Tibaudo, appeared on the witness list in the solicitation case against Bashara, the fact of which Stephanie was not aware).

A couple days later Stephanie made the trip down to the Wayne County Jail for her first face-to-face with Bashara:

"Steph, I was put up to this, I was set up," insisted Bashara.

"Bob, even if you were set up, and asked if you wanted a hit on someone, all you had to do is say no."

"I know, I know," Bashara whimpered, sounding like a guilty teenager.
"He looked back up," said Stephanie, and he said "It is what it is ..."

Still in denial, Stephanie was taken by surprise. "I wanted the facts," she said in testimony. In response, David Griem provided copies of the audio recording and a transcript of Bashara's exchanges with Tibaudo. Nancy read the transcripts and Stephanie spent the better part of the night listening to the recordings, diligently following along with the transcript. By morning both women realized they'd been deceived.

On July 4 Bashara and Stephanie shared another phone conversation, but this time there was significantly different tone:

"I got sucked in, what can I say?" pleaded Bashara. "And a, David (Griem) and I are meeting later in the week, and we're going to go over some stuff, so ... I'm sorry if I've let everyone down. But I done [*sic*] the best I could."

"From this point forward," chided Stephanie, "all business decisions are going to be made by us," referring to herself and Nancy.

"OK, I don't have a problem with that."

"Who is going to pay the bond should you get it?" Stephanie asked, a trace of sarcasm in her voice.

"Well, I don't know. I was hoping mom would front me the money until we sell Middlesex, but it's money that comes back to her. You don't pay it, you just put it up."

"Well, that's gonna be a decision she's going to have to make," said Stephanie, showing little sympathy.

"I know you guys are really, really disappointed and upset," said Bashara, sounding defeated. "But I want you to be able to come away from this with a nice little chunk of money for all you've been doing, so ..."

"Bob, you know what I care about? I don't care about a dime ... Do you know what my main goal is? Do you know that my main goal has shifted? Do you realize that?"

"No."

"When this all happened, who was my main focus?"

"I think me."

"Yep. Do you know who my main focus is at this point?"

"My mother?" guessed Bashara.

"Absolutely!"

"I understand, and I appreciate that Stephanie."

"It doesn't mean I don't love you. I'll never stop loving you. Your mother will never stop loving you."

"It is what it is . . ." muttered Bashara.

"No! You know what? That sounds very callous. You better think about your words and just stop talking," Stephanie boomed, becoming agitated. "We know it *is what it is* Bob, but it sounds callous, like 'oh well.'"

"That's not what I'm trying to say."

"OK, then you better think before you speak, my friend."

"Alright … but I can't change what's happened … I've been sucked in and lured in and it's terrible."

"You know, the only two people that have actually read this are your mother and I. I'm the only one who listened to it."

"I understand."

"I was up 'till four in the fucking morning! I was the one who said I need to hear it in his voice," wavered Stephanie.

"We shouldn't continue this conversation," said Bashara.

"Why Bob? It *is what it is*! Do you see how cold that sounds?"

"Yep."

"So think before you speak … From this point forward it would really behoove you to shut your mouth," lectured Stephanie, "and when you do open it, don't say anything but the truth!"

§

The following day Nancy decided it was time to retrieve Bob's items from the safe-deposit box. "I thought I better get that stuff out and mail it to Robert," she said, "because Bob was in jail, and kind of lost to me."

She drove to *Comerica Bank*, entered through the double glass front doors, then turned toward the safe-deposit room to retrieve the box. "I went in the little room and opened it up … I undid the plastic, and there were all the jewels and things that he told me about." But she also saw a hard pouch with a snap on it. "It was kind of a green and beige color."

Once it was open Nancy made a startling discovery. "I found a gun! I didn't know what to do, and I needed advice, so I put everything back." Nancy called Stephanie and asked her to meet at the bank the following day.

"Nancy didn't look mad or angry," observed Stephanie when she arrived, "she just wanted to go in."

Once they were inside the deposit box room Nancy said: "I've got to show you something," as she motioned toward the pouch. She reached inside the beige and green bag and pulled out a small .32 caliber *Smith & Wesson* revolver.

"Holy fuck!" Stephanie said in astonishment. "My eyes got big, I felt my body just drop."

"Aunt Nancy! Put that back in there and close it!" pleaded Stephanie, not knowing if it was loaded. "Have you ever seen this before?"

"Never in my life," Nancy said flatly.

Both were well aware of Bashara's vehement and constant denials of gun ownership: "I'm a pacifist," he once said. "I'm not violent. I stopped playing football because I didn't like hitting people," all voiced on *Dateline NBC*. Stephanie remembered several occasions when Bashara looked her dead in the eye, uttering the same denials, and exhibiting the same behavior with other family members.

In total silence the women returned the gun to the green bag and left the bank.

"We went directly to Middlesex and collectively decided that I would call David Griem," explained Stephanie. "Right away I put it in the dining room. There was a buffet with a hutch on top ... I put it in the buffet part."

"That was a very hard night for me to sleep in that house," remembered Stephanie. "Knowing the gun was there. It was very difficult."

Merely by coincidence, the Basharas had a previously scheduled family meeting the following day. Six family members and attorney David Griem were expected. After the meeting Stephanie and Nancy led Griem into a private room for a chat.

"I explained the story of what happened and what Nancy found," said Stephanie.

"We showed him the gun," added Nancy. "He didn't want to take it, but we didn't know what else to do."

"I saw him close his eyes and raise his hand (making a halting gesture)," recalled Stephanie. "He said, 'I've seen enough. You can close the bag. Give it to me, I'll take care of it.'"

Relieved to be rid of it, they handed the weapon over to Griem. "It was the last I saw of it," Nancy said with a sigh.

After the meeting the women assumed they were no longer subject to criminal liability until later when Stephanie made a troubling discovery: in the chaos of moving Bashara's personal belongings from Middlesex to her home in Windsor (Ontario), she had unknowingly transported ammunition for Bashara's gun across the international border.

"In his office was a filing cabinet and in one of the drawers were some office supplies, boxes of staples and such," explained Stephanie. "I put those all in a big *Rubbermaid* tub and was transporting office supplies from his home to mine."

A short time later Stephanie ran out of printer paper. "I remembered there were a couple of reams of paper (amongst Bashara's belongings) so instead of going out I went downstairs to refill my printer."

Stephanie said there were also several boxes of staples. "But I noticed one was different, and that's how I found (the box of ammunition)."

Eventually, Stephanie shared this information with Wayne County prosecutors and, in return for her cooperation was rewarded with immunity. Her assistance would also lead to the eventual recovery of Bashara's revolver from Griem's office a year later.

§

Correspondence between Bashara and former Chicago police officer Therese Griffon intensified as she became his avid confidant and errand girl. In the early summer Rachel Gillette moved to Texas and, perhaps not fully understanding the nature of their relationship, shared with Giffon her new contact information, asking specifically that it not be passed to Bashara, which (unintentionally she said) she promptly did.

Gillette's defection, exhibited by her departure and the Personal Protection Order obtained in the spring, made Bashara increasingly vengeful, voicing his frustration in multiple recorded jail phone conversations with Giffon:

"I want you to give you-know-who hell," instructed Bashara. "Because ... her attorney is coming out saying she is in hiding, she fears for her life, so let her have it."

"Thank you," Giffon said excitedly. "I can go full force now? I can be my normal charming self?

"Well, absolutely! I want you to get with J.D. and David. We're going after her."

"I did get a message from her, finally," offered Giffon. "She said, 'so you don't think I was in danger?' So that's the perfect thing, I can rip into her and tell her the truth. Well it's fuckin' bullshit. No, she was never in any danger!"

"Oh, my God, that's ridiculous!" choked Bashara.

"You stay strong. You didn't do anything fuckin' wrong and even if I can't take your calls, just know I'm here," reassured Giffon. "I won't leave, I'll fight for you."

"Thank you so much for calling," Bashara said in what sounded like a manipulative whimper.

In another jail phone exchange with Giffon, Bashara encouraged her to relocate to Detroit. Hoping to persuade her to help run his mini empire of rental properties, he made an offer she both could and would refuse.

"If you come over here (Detroit) and we work something out, I'll give you that *Cadillac*," Bashara said enticingly. "I've got an *'81 Cadillac* I'll give you free and clear. It runs like a champ!" Giffon wisely showed no interest.

Bashara spared no venom for anyone he believed had slighted him:

"My daughter's giving everyone hell," Bashara complained. "She's taken advantage of my mother and she's just, it's just unfortunate the way she's acting. She's so spoiled, it's just such a shame."

"Yeah, that's what usually happens with spoiled little girls," dismissed Giffon.

"Yep, she's just not thinking clearly … people are getting to her. The prosecution got to her, her aunt (Jane's sister Julie Rowe) is getting to her. Jane's family, Jane's friends, they're all getting to her."

"Spoiled girls," Giffon said smugly. "They're stubborn bitches."

§

Bob Bashara's attempt to have Joe Gentz killed in jail appears to have been the last straw among the family faithful, and his denials further alienated him from those who had stood by him since the beginning.

"I'm being set up here," Bashara told his son Robert in a June 27 call from the Wayne County Jail. "I've made some mistakes in my life, but – I didn't make this one here and harming your mother … I'm just gonna tell you Robert, I didn't go looking for this trouble. I got sucked in."

Now in his hour of need, Bashara was desperate for family assistance, and he even went so far as to offer up Jane's ashes as an enticement.

"I need you to listen to this real carefully," Bashara told his son. "I'm going to need your support, Jessie's support and … I even need Grandma (Lorraine Englebrecht) and Aunt Julie (Rowe), and I don't have a problem, necessarily, them having your mother's ashes."

"It's not gonna do much, you know," replied Robert, his voice echoing defeat.

"Well, I understand that. But it's very important for me."

"I'll talk to whoever you want, but it's not going to make a difference."

At this point Jane's ashes, which had seen nearly every corner of Grosse Pointe in the past five months, were in the possession of Richard Falcinelli, Bashara's new best friend from *The Lifestyle* and soon to be Power of Attorney. He was "storing them in a safe place," he said, "in a box in the basement amongst some other boxes, in a green tote bag labeled *Jane*."

"I'm not asking them to like me," Bashara continued. "I'm just asking them to be cooperative; and I want to cooperate with mom's ashes. So let them know, I'll make sure they have them."

Then Bashara tried to sweeten the deal: "There's a ring that's gonna come back, the prosecution has it right now, it was Aunt Jenny's ring, and I would like you to have it."

Robert was wholly unaware of the ring, its origins or that it had previously been in the possession of Rachel Gillette.

"Someday when you meet a girl that you want to marry," Bashara prattled on, "it's a beautiful engagement ring, a double diamond ring, and I want you to have that. OK? … This is very important to me, I mean it's gonna mean the difference between a little and a lot."

Robert's tone remained flat and unemotional. During this period he was in the midst of a move even further west, from Iowa to Texas, and his detachment from his father's travails appears to be nearly complete, further indicated by the fact that he did not seek a shred of family support for him.

§

On July 9 Joe Gentz was found competent to stand trial. A week later David Griem announced his plan to quit representation of Bob Bashara, citing that Bashara had lied to him. Chief Judge Kenneth King denied the request but on July 23 Bashara replaced Griem anyway, engaging Detroit attorney Mark Kriger.

In a July 24 preliminary hearing Bashara was bound over for trial. Steve Tibaudo and two other witnesses testified. Meanwhile, a family feud erupted at the Middlesex residence, pitting the Bashara and Englebrecht clans against one another, instigated by Stephanie Samuel's seemingly abrupt decision to change the locks. Jane's ashes and several of her personal items were at issue as the Englebrechts claimed the Basharas had conspired against them.

On August 7, Bashara pled not guilty to charges that he conspired to commit murder and nine days later Joe Gentz was scheduled for trial in January of 2013. On August 23 Bashara's trial was set for November, but on October 11 he changed his plea to guilty in exchange for a lighter sentence. In a bid for leniency, Bashara addressed Judge Bruce Morrow's court:

"I'm truly and humbly sorry for my actions," Bashara began, in a choked and muffled voice. "I apologize to this court. I apologize to Mr. Gentz. I apologize to my family and friends."

On December 10 Bashara received a sentence of 80-240 months in state prison for *Solicitation to Commit Murder* and on the 21st Joe Gentz accepted a plea-bargain to *Second Degree Murder* on the condition that he would testify in any proceedings if called to do so.

§

On January 8, 2013, Bob Bashara was moved to the *Oaks Correctional Facility* in Manistee, MI near Traverse City, and placed under Level 2 security. Oaks, originally built to house maximum security inmates, had recently been converted to offer this lower level of security and was criticized for not fully implementing it. When he arrived Bashara was already notorious among inmates, who'd followed his plight through media reports. He continued correspondence with the outside world via telephone and eMail, all of which was monitored and recorded.

On January 29, Joe Gentz was sentenced to 17-28 years in state prison for *Second Degree Murder*. On March 28, after a brief stop at the *Chippewa Correctional Facility*, Gentz was moved to his permanent residence at the *Macomb Correctional Facility* in New Haven, MI.

§

On April 17 Bob Bashara was charged with six felony offenses: *First-Degree Murder, Conspiracy to Commit Murder, Solicitation to Commit Murder, Perjury, Witness Intimidation* and *Obstruction of Justice*. As a result he was moved from the Level 2 to Level 4 security housing unit at Oaks.

(Level 4 security at Oaks essentially equates to full lockdown 22 hours per day in the cell with one hour in the yard twice daily).

§

> *"Jane's parents, siblings and children are pleased that the investigation into her murder has come to a conclusion. We want to extend our heartfelt thanks to the Grosse Pointe Park police, Detroit police, Michigan State Police, Wayne County Prosecutor's Office and all other law enforcement agencies who have worked so tirelessly and with such dedication to ensure that those responsible for Jane's murder are brought to justice."*
> - Julie Rowe, April 18, 2013

However, this ending, as it turned out, was just the beginning ...

§

On May 1 Bashara was arraigned and denied bond. Two weeks later he was moved into a cell with a man named Larry Ellington.

Ellington was a three time loser, having spent most of his adult life behind bars for various crimes including breaking and entering, criminal sexual conduct and armed bank robbery. He even escaped after his first offense. An African-American in his mid fifties, he stands about five foot seven with short black greying hair. He and Bob Bashara certainly made an odd couple.

With 22 hours every day in close proximity, the two got to know each other fairly well. They routinely passed the time talking and playing cards. Bashara had a way about him, getting mad enough to call him 'Buckwheat' after Ellington beat him at gin.

Bashara was chatty, oftentimes downright gossipy about his family. "He said his children ... don't talk to him anymore," said Ellington, "and his mom don't write him, don't take his calls." Bashara often had to use a third party just to get news of them.

"Jessica won't talk to him," added Ellington. For that Bashara blamed her Aunt Julie, who he said "poisoned her mind against him."

Bashara also told Ellington that he and Jane hadn't had sex for several years. "Jane told him 'whatever you do, don't embarrass the family.'" Bashara went on to tell Ellington that Jane's 401(k) was worth over $800 thousand dollars, and in the event of a divorce, "Jane told him not to touch it." He also said she had forced him to seek marriage counseling.

"He said he had four slaves," said Ellington, a shocking revelation to an American black man who had no idea what in the hell he was talking about. "They were women who needed more guidance in their life," explained Bashara. "He was telling me about something they called the Reformatory, where they take 'em and I guess they whip 'em. He said that sometimes they need to be spanked."

Soon the discussion turned to darker matters. In Ellington's youth he'd been a member of the *Moorish Science Temple of America*, a distant cousin to the more popular *Nation of Islam*, both of which are frequented among the black prison population in Michigan. It was widely believed, by Bashara as well, that they had ways of getting things done from the inside.

"Somebody told him I was a Moor," explained Ellington, adding that he was no longer actively involved.

"When I was playing cards with him … I told him, 'Bob, you know, you killed your fucking wife, man."

"No, I didn't kill her," Bashara said sardonically.

"Well, you had her killed. You paid Joseph Gentz to kill your wife."

"That's why I need that fucker out of the way," Ellington remembered Bashara saying. "I can't believe they're going to believe that fucking retard over me."

"He told me Gentz was at Macomb (correctional facility)," recalled Ellington. "He asked if I could reach out and touch (kill) him? I told him yes."

"Joe Gentz was the only witness," Bashara had said.

Bashara also asked about Steve Tibaudo. "He wanted him killed because he said Steve talked him into killing Joseph Gentz."

"He called him a fat fuck who carries a .38," continued Ellington. "He basically didn't have anything good to say about him (and that) he wore a wire." What Bashara didn't know was that Ellington was from the same Eastside Detroit neighborhood and already familiar with Tibaudo.

"He also mentioned a guy named Thomas Ramsey," said Ellington. "He wanted him killed because … he kept talking a lot of mess about him, starting trouble."

"I told him that would be no problem," explained Ellington. "I told him, he's in the neighborhood … I had a nephew that would go and do it … But it's gonna cost you."

"OK, how much?" asked Bashara.

"Probably $5 to $10 grand a piece … Later on he said he was having problems with his money," said Ellington. "The state was trying to take it for incarceration restitution."

So Bashara went into overtime hatching a plan. Being a landlord while in prison was even harder than doing it on the outside, and he had some property to unload, a two family flat on Guilford St. near the old *Finney High School*.

"He said it was a good investment," said Ellington. "The person who's gonna do the killin', they can get the house."

Bashara said he only owed $32 thousand on the mortgage and told Ellington it could be rented out for $600 per month. To sweeten the deal with something more immediately tangible Bashara also offered to put cash into Ellington's commissary account.

"We'd come to the agreement that he's gonna put $50 in my account a month," said Ellington. "That's all I could receive, because I owe restitution."

(Inmates have what are called 'spendables,' cash that can be spent on various items within the jail, such as food in the commissary, phone usage or for ordering reading material).

Ellington told Bashara he had an aunt who happened to be a realtor who could act as his agent. To get the transaction rolling, Bashara suggested putting her in touch with his new Power of Attorney, Rick Falcinelli.

Bashara, who routinely tore up scraps of paper with any kind of correspondence between them (lest they be used against him) handed Ellington a small four by four inch piece. "He wrote down the address and Rick's phone number at the bottom and said how my aunt could get an appraisal."

Unknown to Bashara, from the outset Ellington was merely in it for himself, a two bit hustler looking to cash in. With no intention, nor the required acumen or connections to execute such a plot, Ellington instead saw Bashara as a bargaining chip.

Hoping for a time cut in his sentence, on May 21 Ellington wrote a letter to his attorney and followed it with one similar to Wayne County Prosecutor Kym Worthy:

"I want you to know that I have some important information that I need you to know. I share a two-man room with Robert Bashara, the Gross Point [sic] Businessman that they say had his wife killed. He has been telling me a lot of things and he wants me to see if I could have two people killed. If you can, I'd like to have a conference call with you ASAP.

P.S. I sent Kym Worthy a letter. I just told her I share a room with Robert. I didn't say anything about he wants [sic] to have some people killed, but I did say he's been telling me things."

Two weeks later Ellington was visited by Wayne County investigators Tim Matouk and Cory Williams. Ellington gave them Bashara's hand written note, upon which was written: "Property on Guildford", the street address, and "MORT Balance, 30-33k."

The following day $50 was deposited into Ellington's commissary account complements of Richard Falcinelli.

But according to Ellington, Bashara wasn't through. "Bob also wanted (Wayne County Prosecutor) Lisa Lindsey killed," Ellington told the investigators. (Lindsey was the prosecutor assigned to the case from the very beginning). "He called her a black bitch."

"How much would it cost to have her killed?" Ellington recounted Bashara saying.

"It would cost a lot, but I don't know nobody [sic] would ever mess with something like that," replied Ellington, "it's gonna be hard to get somebody to go after a prosecutor."

On June 18, Wayne County Assistant Prosecuting Attorney Lisa Lindsey made the four hour trek north to the *Oaks Facility* for a face to face with Ellington. He told her he never intended to hurt anyone and never reached out to his cousin. She in turn told him, in no uncertain terms, not to expect any favorable treatment for his testimony.

Chapter 10

The People vs. Robert Bashara

As the summer of 2013 wound to a close, preliminary hearings were held in the ever expanding Bashara murder case. Presided over by Judge Kenneth J. King, it was nearly a mini-trial in itself with more than 25 witnesses called over a five day period in September.

Testimony, oftentimes uncomfortably candid and controversial from Rachel Gillette, Janet Leehman, Stephanie Samuel and Steve Tibaudo laid out a labyrinth of mystery and intrigue, sometimes confusingly elaborate, serving up a mere hint of the mountain of evidence the prosecution had amassed over the previous 18 months.

On the first day it was revealed that a handgun owned by Bob Bashara had recently been recovered. The gun had remained in the possession of Bashara's former attorney, David Griem, for more than a year. The .32 caliber *Smith & Wesson* revolver was believed to be the one referred to by Joe Gentz in his sworn statement, allegedly used by Bashara to force him to kill Jane Bashara.

Throughout the hearings Judge King admonished Bashara for exhibiting what he described as 'courtroom antics' and for making inappropriate gestures during Gillette's testimony, which he characterized as 'rubbing his heart' and 'crying tears even though his eyes were as dry as sand paper.' He even observed him "sticking his tongue out; and it wasn't a simple licking of the lips," he said. "I mean, he was going to town."

"The real shame of it all is that Mrs. Bashara probably really trusted Mr. Bashara," stated King. "A husband is supposed to protect; there's supposed to be trust in a relationship."

"Just looking at the so-called hard evidence," continued King, "the reasonable inference that can be drawn from the evidence: witnesses like ... Steven Virgona and Daryl Bradford, Patrick Webb and Larry Ellington and so fourth. Most of those witnesses ... aren't the cleanest. But when you have dealings with scum, chances are you're pretty much scum too."

"After hearing testimony the last five days about Mr. Bashara's alleged relationship with the admitted killer of Mrs. Bashara," King pressed, "the number of phone calls, the low-lifes he associated with, the false alibis, alleged murder-for-hire solicitations, it almost sounds like the defendant ... thought he was *Mafia* or something ... putting hits out on people, and not just one person but multiple people, from jail."

"We probably could have skipped the exam and gone right to trial," King surmised. "The court finds the charges were committed ... (and) there's probable cause to believe this defendant committed them."

Bashara was bound over to *Wayne County Third Circuit Court Criminal Division* and arraigned on September 20. After pleading not guilty, Bashara was remanded to the custody of the Wayne County Jail and trial was set for the following March.

§

Pretrial hearings were held in each of the first three months of 2014. The court, now Wayne County's Third Circuit, was under the jurisdiction of the Honorable Vonda R. Evans, a flamboyant and popular judge known for her sometimes over-the-top courtroom behavior and an unsuccessful attempt at landing a courtroom reality show called *Domestic Justice*.

A whirlwind of activity surrounded the Bashara defense team as Evans appointed a revolving door of attorneys including Mark Procida, Nancy Shell, David Cripps and Gabi Silver, all of whom withdrew shortly after their appointments.

On March 10, Detroit-based criminal defense attorney Lillian Diallo was named to lead the Bashara team and trial was pushed back to October. Diallo was well known in Detroit legal circles for her defense style, and she brands herself as the defender of those mistreated by the system: "Lillian will fight like a bulldog against the police and prosecutors who want to take away your freedom," reads a statement on her firm's website.

Consisting of more than 10,000 pages of documents, CDs and video to sift through in a relatively short period of time Diallo was in sorry need of help, so on April 15 Judge Evans appointed Oakland County-based defense attorney Michael McCarthy to the team. Fresh off defending Mitchell Young, a co-defendant in the Tucker Cipriano beating death of Cipriano's father (both were convicted of first degree murder), McCarthy is a 25 year veteran of both trial and appellate law.

In a mid September hearing Judge Evans dismissed a felony firearm charge against Bashara, ruling that although there was a second-hand reference to it made by Joe Gentz, there was no evidence that it had been used in the slaying of Jane Bashara. Likewise, she refused to allow testimony dealing with Gentz and Bashara's attempts to obtain insulin on the grounds that Bashara is diabetic.

On Tuesday, October 7 jury selection began, marking the official start to case number 13-8320, *The People vs. Robert Bashara*. In what would become a common daily exchange, Judge Evans addressed the defendant jovially as he entered the court: "Wow, Mr. Bashara, you lookin' good today."

For the trial Bashara traded his red prison scrubs, which he'd worn throughout the pretrial process, for a charcoal business suit and red stripped tie, cutting a vastly improved image.

The jury pool was 150 strong representing all walks of Wayne County life. Split into three groups of 50, each was given a questionnaire before direct questioning by each legal team. Questions ranged from any prior knowledge of BDSM (*The Lifestyle*) to thoughts on marital infidelity.

Ultimately three jurors were selected from Group A, which took more than a day and a half, with the balance taken from Group B (all of Group C was dismissed). After nearly three full days the jury was seated on October 9, comprised of 11 men and five women (eight black, seven white, one hispanic). Judge Evans said she expected the trial to last four to six weeks.

The Wayne County Prosecution team, which had essentially been on the case since January 25, 2012, was led by Assistant Prosecuting Attorney Lisa Lindsey, a 4 foot 10 inch bulldog with what has been described as a striking "Afro-Puff" hairdo. She was well known for her work ethic that could only be described as relentless. Assisting Lindsey was Robert Moran, Chief of Special Investigations; Patrick Muscat, Assistant Prosecuting Attorney and Assistant Prosecutor Mark Hindelang.

On October 10, in a short hearing before Judge Evans, Joe Gentz invoked his Fifth Amendment right, saying he would not testify for either side, violating his plea deal. The move exposed him to the possibility of being recharged for First Degree Murder.

§

On the morning of October 14, Judge Evens entered the courtroom just before 10:30 a.m. The defense team was assembled before her to the right and the prosecution to her left, with Grosse Pointe Park's Captain Loch and Detective Narduzzi stationed directly behind. The first day saw 25 to 30 curious citizens, law clerks and interns joining the media throng. Throughout the trial every local media outlet: print, television and radio (including two and sometimes three cameras) filled the gallery to capacity.

Judge Evans informed the jury they were not to discuss the case with anyone or each other and that there would come a time when 12 of them would be selected to deliberate and the four alternates, if still engaged, would be released. Evans announced the jury would not be sequestered before reading the charges:

Count 1: Conspiracy to Commit Murder, First Degree
Count 2: Solicitation of Murder
Count 3: First Degree Murder
Count 4: Obstruction of Justice
Count 5: Witness Intimidation
Count 6: Subornation of Perjury

Exhibiting a staggering lack of oratory skills that often betrayed her extensive command of the legal process, Lisa Lindsey methodically laid out the prosecution's case: "On January 25 in the year 2012, the police found the body of Jane Bashara, dumped in an ally in the city of Detroit like a piece of common trash." Speaking too softly to be heard, Judge Evans asked her to repeat.

"The very next day," Lindsey continued in a booming voice, "the defendant, Robert Bashara, started his public grieving at a candlelight vigil for his wife."

The prosecution was drawing from a police file bursting at the seams with more than 300 entries spread over more than 1,000 pages, several times greater than a typical murder case. The file includes all law enforcement actions including search warrants, interviews, leads and arrests. The trial was ultimately comprised of over 450 items of evidence and a potential witness list of over 300.

"An outpouring of the community came out to support him as he said at that vigil how devastated he was about what happened to his wife," proceeded Lindsey. "He continued his public grieving when he went on the airwaves to talk about what he thought about the crime, what he thought happened and how he felt, the love and affection he had for his wife."

As was common throughout the trial, Lindsey's team expanded on her message by displaying video excerpts of Bashara speaking to media from January 2012: "I have no clue," Bashara said, staring blankly away from the camera. "I have no idea what happened … I've lost my girlfriend and my partner and it's absolutely unthinkable."

Thus began the 45 minute prelude, laying out in overwhelming detail, the allegations against Bob Bashara.

The proceedings would often see excruciating delays, with court rarely commencing before 10 a.m., lunch hours sometimes stretching beyond two hours and countless unexplained hiccups and routine shuffling of the jury in and out of the courtroom. Methodically laying out their case, the prosecution demonstrated how Bashara deliberately deflected attention away from himself, illustrating his attempts to steer media and law enforcement toward the belief his wife's murder could have been connected to the *Backpage Murders*.

"He told police 'you know I don't want to narc on my poor wife, but my wife smoked marijuana, and maybe she went out to get some marijuana,' quoted Lindsey, exposing another Bashara red herring. "But he knew exactly what happened to his wife. He knew because he set the whole thing in motion behind the scenes. He told two separate people that 'this was going to be the last Christmas that I ever spend with my wife in the house on Middlesex.'"

"In the months leading up to Jane Bashara's murder, the defendant started engaging in some very strange behavior," explained Lindsey. "The defendant started approaching people, putting out feelers about finding people to do things of violence … In the late summer of 2011, at a businessman's lunch with Robert Goddard, the defendant said 'Robert, do you know anyone who could rough up a tenant for money? I need someone to put the hurt on somebody.'"

"In the fall of 2011," pressed Lindsey, "the defendant approached another person … and asked did that person know anybody who would do a hit and run for money? That person was Steve Tibaudo."

Only a week before the murder, Janet Leehman was "on the phone with the defendant, and the defendant asked her: 'Hey, do you know anybody who could rough up some tenants of mine for money?'"

"These three people don't know each other," Lindsey said matter of factly. "Never met each other a day in their life. But each person tells a remarkably similar story about the defendant seeking out a person to do violence for money in the weeks and months before his wife was murdered. The defendant was obviously looking for somebody to do violence, and he found that person in Joseph Gentz."

Painting Bashara as a master manipulator, Lindsey described how Gentz was controlled from the outset. "He knew Joe needed a place to live, he knew he was in a custody dispute and needed a place for his daughter. He also knew, from looking at the rental agreement, Joe's lack of income. All these things he knew to exploit and play on to gain Joe's trust and gratitude."

"Now, make no mistake about it," said Lindsey. "Joe did the physical act of killing Jane, and DNA will prove that. But he did it under the direction and control of the defendant."

"Joe wanted a safe place to be because there's evidence Joe was in fear for his life," continued Lindsey. "Joe would rather go to police at three in the morning and get himself locked up than be walking free on the same streets as the defendant, Robert Bashara."

"In June of 2012, as the competency hearing for Joe Gentz approaches, Bashara decides he cannot allow him to cut a deal so he propositioned Steve Tibaudo to kill him in jail," Lindsey said, pacing the length of the court. "He didn't know Tibaudo was wearing a wire and is arrested. At first he denies the charge, but ultimately takes a plea when he learns it was captured on tape."

"Now he didn't say at that point: 'I did it because I wanted to avenge the death of my wife,'" posed Lindsey. "He didn't say at that point: 'I did it because I was grief stricken' ... His simple reply was, 'it is what it is.'"

After a short recess Lillian Diallo was ready to take a swing at the prosecution's case: "This is the day, believe it or not, that Mr. Bashara has been waiting for, the day to get his side of the story out ... The evidence will show," she said sarcastically, mocking Lindsey's oft repeated line, "did not simply make it so." Then she finished up by challenging the jury to believe whatever they determined for themselves to be the truth.

"Mr. Joe Gentz ... is the confessed killer of Mrs. Jane Bashara," Diallo stated matter-of-factly. "Madame Prosecutor indicated that the police went where the evidence took them. I believe ... immediately after Mrs. Bashara is found slaughtered in her car, Mr. Bashara was named a *Person of Interest*."

"Did you go where the evidence takes you or did you take the evidence where you wanted it to go?" postulated Diallo, laying the foundation for the the primary argument of the defense, that the prosecution of Bashara was a rush to judgment, a trumped up witch hunt for which they got the wrong man.

Anticipating controversy surrounding the *The Lifestyle*, Diallo apologized before descending headfirst into the muck: "This right here (BDSM) ... is one of the prosecutor's theories, if not the main theory for this particular homicide. Salacious? Absolutely, (but) it's just not true!"

"The solicitation to commit murder on Joe Gentz," continued Diallo, "the prosecutor's theory is that it was to silence Joseph Gentz. Once again, that's not true. You will hear from their own witnesses, that when this was discussed, it wasn't ... to keep him from testifying. It was because this was the confessed murderer of his wife of 26 years."

"This was a very inevitable show, very heavy handed prosecution from day one," persisted Diallo. "Heavy handed doesn't mean guilty. Heavy handed means you just have a lot of power on their side."

§

The Bashara case was plagued from the outset by accusations of mishandling by the prosecution. Jane Bashara's clothing was not retained nor tested for DNA evidence. Tales of mistreatment of witnesses was echoed by several, particularly Gillette and Leehman. There was a serious lack of witness preparation, and in one case in particular Lisa Lindsey was asked what should be expected in cross examination to which she replied: "how should I know?"

Frances Natale, the friend of Joe Gentz who drove him all over town January 30, was now homeless and living in her van. Early in the trial she was arrested and incarcerated for two weeks until she finished testifying. In an odd twist she genuinely thanked Judge Evans as she stepped down from the stand.

A key piece of evidence that helped convict Bashara in the eyes of the public early in 2012, as reported first by *WXYZ* (ABC) and then *WDIV* (NBC) was the eyewitness account of Bashara and Gentz pulling cars from the Bashara garage the night of January 24. But, as predicted by David Griem, no such witness ever materialized.

Throughout the trial Bashara suffered multiple health issues. He was hospitalized the night before the trial began. On October 29 he collapsed while preparing for court in the *William Dickerson Detention Facility*, forcing Judge Evans to suspend proceedings for several days.

On November 10, Bashara had eye surgery, necessitating him to wear large protective sunglasses in court that he continued to wear periodically throughout the trial.

§

Testimony began in the afternoon of October 14 when Robert Goddard (a Bashara *Lifestyle* friend and businessman connected with *Lochmoor*) and Rebecca Forton (Gentz's Wayburn landlord) took the stand. The following morning an elderly gentleman from *St. Micheal's Church* named William McQueen described an exchange that occurred in the church vestry between the Bashara's two days before Jane's death.

McQueen stated that only two people were allowed in the vestry during money counting. "Bob came in, between Jane and me, and started a vitriolic conversation with her."

"A what? What does that mean," questioned Evans.

"Well, let's try acerbic," ventured McQueen.

"Well, let's try something else," Evans said in exasperation.

"It was an elevated conversation," McQueen said, finally selecting a word acceptable to the court.

McQueen's testimony itself was of little consequence, but it clearly set the tone of what was to unfold over the next nine weeks.

Perhaps the most compelling evidence came from Stan Brue of the ATF, who produced a staggering, if not completely overwhelming mass of forensic evidence connecting Bashara and Gentz by phone and text transmissions.

Between late September and the time of Jane Bashara's death on January 24 there were more than 450 connections between Bashara and Gentz (over the same period Bashara made in excess of 900 calls to Rachel Gillette and 550 to Jane).

Brue also demonstrated a pattern to the calls: In the more than 350 made between October and December, two thirds were initiated by Gentz. But in January that pattern reversed and two thirds of the more than 100 calls were placed by Bashara. The day after Jane's murder the pattern reverted, with Gentz again making two thirds of the calls to Bashara.

"The day before the murder, the defendant really wanted to get in touch with Joseph Gentz," explained Lindsey. "He calls Joseph Gentz a total of 22 times. What's interesting about this is the first call the defendant makes the day before the murder is to Joseph Gentz. The last call the defendant makes the night before the murder is to Joseph Gentz."

On the day of the murder Bashara called Gentz five times, explained Lindsey, "and once again, just like the day before, the first call the defendant makes when he gets out of bed, is to Joseph Gentz."

"But look what happens," Lindsey pressed. "The day the body is found, he stops calling Joseph Gentz. Doesn't call Gentz at all, but Gentz calls him."

"The very next day, the 26th at ten in the morning, Nancy Bashara, the defendant's mother, her cell phone contacts Joseph Gentz," said Lindsey. "This is the first time throughout their whole interaction that Gentz is contacted by another cell phone (associated with the case) and the evidence will show that it was the defendant who made the call, because Nancy Bashara will tell you, 'I don't know Joseph Gentz. I don't know Joseph Gentz's phone number. I never called Joseph Gentz.'"

"You can infer that it was the defendant who made that phone call," continued Lindsey, "because after that phone call to Joseph Gentz, the defendant goes to Joseph Gentz's job and leaves a check for him."

This was a detail not lost on the jury: "One thing that we came to a conclusion on," said Joe Fernandez, Juror #12: "When Bashara delivered the envelope the next day, it didn't just have a check for $452. That envelope had more money in there, in cash."

Much of Brue's testimony was corroborated by FBI Agent Christopher Hess, who presented data showing the location of area cell phone towers and their reception patterns (he was also instrumental in setting up Steve Tibaudo with recording equipment in June of 2012).

"We would go out on what is called a drive test," explained Hess. "In this instance, I would take a *Verizon* cell phone, attach it to a computer with some software ... and drive the entire area. As I drive through that area my cell phone is reading the signal information that is transmitted from the cell phone provider and it's captured by the software."

"At the conclusion of the drive test," continued Hess, "I take all that data, crunch it together and it gives us what the actual footprint is of the cell site."

Hess showed data of calls made through each tower and their times, thereby demonstrating relatively from where the calls were placed and received by both Basharas on January 24, 2012.

At 3:48 p.m. on the day of Jane's murder, Bob Bashara's cell phone accessed tower #994 (which provides service exclusive to the Middlesex area). Between 4:52 and 5:20 p.m. his cell phone accessed towers #144 (which provides exclusive service to the *Hard Luck Lounge* area) and #156 (which services the entire area including Middlesex and *The Hard Luck Lounge* on Mack Ave).

But most damning were connections made by Bob Bashara's cell phone through tower #994 between 6:15 and 6:26 p.m., showing that he must have been at or near Middlesex at that time. In addition, the data showed Jane Bashara's cell phone connected to towers #994 and #156 between 4:30 and 6:26 p.m. At 6:28, data shows both phones connecting to different towers, indicating they were moving in opposite directions.

Between 6:41 and 7:15 p.m. Bashara's cell phone again accessed tower #144 and #156 before returning to tower #994 and #320 (service exclusive to Middlesex area) beginning at 8:09 p.m. Meanwhile, beginning at 6:43 p.m. Jane's phone began to connect to towers heading north into Detroit.

Not only did Hess' testimony serve to place the principals at respective places at particular times, but it also helped to nail down the official timeline of events.

§

There were several family members who testified including Julie Rowe (Jane's youngest sister), Loraine Englebrecht (Jane's mother), Gwen Samuel (Bob's aunt) and Nancy Bashara (his mother). But the most compelling testimony came from Bashara's cousin Stephanie and his children, Jessica and Robert.

Stephanie Samuel, who wasn't convinced of Bashara's guilt until after she heard the solicitation recordings, testified in sheer high drama, complete with tears and tissue. She primarily recounted the tale of finding Bashara's pistol with Nancy and her unwitting storage of the ammunition at her home across the Detroit River in Windsor, Ontario.

In sharp contrast, neither Jessica nor Robert showed a trace of emotion and avoided the least bit of eye contact with their father. Their testimony was direct and to the point, recalling the events of January 24 and it's aftermath. Jessica recounted catching her father with lewd messages on his cell phone and the ins and outs of her parents troubled marriage. Robert, on the other hand, detailed the dispersement of Jane's life insurance policy and the fact that his father never really told him anything about his mother's murder.

§

Steve Tibaudo's testimony spanned several days and provided a healthy dose of drama and humor. At one point he was brought to tears while recalling the memory of his recently departed terrier Mr. Doodles, who can be heard on one of the solicitation recordings.

"I dropped my drawers and sent him a shot at the jewels," was how Tibaudo described one attempt by Bashara to search for a wire. Clearly enjoying the sound of this own voice, at one point Tibaudo was caught chuckling on the stand while listening to audio of himself singing 'The Banana Boat Song.'

"We felt like Steve Tibaudo was a crazy guy," observed Joe Fernandez (Juror #12). "We saw that he was so crooked, especially when he said that he carried two guns and a knife."

In reference to the several options laid out by Tibaudo for killing Joe Gentz, Judge Evans asked: "You were kind of making this up?"

"You kind of wing it when someone asks you to kill somebody," replied Tibaudo, sounding serious. "Channeling a little DeNiro, a little Jack Nicholson and a little Leonardo DiCaprio."

"Was Mr. Bashara buying that Leonardo DiCaprio accent you were putting on?"continued Evans.

"Oh, that wasn't Leonardo there, that was Robert DeNiro from *Goodfellas.*"

This exchange was met immediately with sniggering from the gallery. But Tibaudo's testimony wasn't all fun and games. "There were very selected parts of the Tibaudo recordings where Bob says, 'if I give you this money it's conspiracy *again*,'" stressed Bill Mohney, Juror #9. "That's the thing that got me; and also how he never mentioned that he wanted Gentz killed because he killed his wife, it was always, 'he's throwing me under the bus.'"

There was a growing consensus among several jurors that testimony from Gentz's acquaintance, Lorna Beth Riikonen, was key to the case.

Riikonen's testimony lasted just over an hour on November 5 and she displayed an uncanny, chameleon-like ability to completely remake herself following every pause in the proceedings. She spoke slowly and deliberately as she shared her incredible one night experience with Joe Gentz

The entire association between them was brief. They exchanged a few text messages and phone calls, but it was a single chance meeting, just before Christmas 2011, that the jury found so enchanting. After Gentz's surprise appearance at the airport that chilly December night, she was compelled to drive him home after he missed the last bus.

Trying to impress, Gentz started talking about someone who was planning to give him a *Cadillac* and some money to knock somebody off.

"The thing with Riikonen was she's completely unrelated, she has no ties to anybody but Gentz," observed Bill Mohney (Juror #9). "She doesn't even like him, and they were only face to face the one time. She had all this priceless inside knowledge, you just can't make this stuff up."

"We thought she was credible because she had nothing to gain from any of this," said Fernandez (Juror #12). "She said Joe told her he had a job to do and that it was hurting somebody. He also said he was coming into some money."

"Everybody else had multiple ties," continued Mohney. "They either knew Tibaudo or Virgona or Bashara or somebody else, but she only knew Gentz."

"Mr. Gentz and I were the only ones in my vehicle," Riikonen told Diallo under cross examination. "He said '*Basher, Basher,*'" that was who Gentz associated with the plot.

"And you are quite positive that's what he said," pressed Diallo.

"I am positive he said '*Bashar, Bashar.*' I will never forget that."

§

The proceedings became contentious on November 17 when Richard Falcinelli took the stand. Falcinelli was deeply devoted to *The Lifestyle* and sported the handle *Midnight Rider* in addition to his more traditional *Sir Rick*. He was apparently the only friend left in the world to Bob Bashara.

Demonstrating Falcinelli's contempt for the court (and prosecution) Lindsey quickly worked to establish him as a hostile witness, which allowed her to ask leading questions. Falcinelli made it easy by revealing he'd referred to Robert

Moran as 'Moron' and Lindsey herself as 'Fucking tele-tubby bitch,' which he seemed proud to admit.

"He called me a fucking tele-tubby your honor," Lindsey mocked to laughter throughout the court.

"No, you're Lee Lee," retorted Falcinelli with a sarcastic grin, apparently not aware of the implication.

Judge Evans wasted no time and granted Lindsey's request without delay.

§

Bashara's former friend from the *Grosse Pointe Rotary Club*, Michael Carmody, was called to the stand on November 20. He is a crotchety gentleman of about 60 who unwittingly played a significant role for Bashara.

"As regards the evening of the 24th," began Carmody, referring to his encounter with Bashara at the *Hard Luck Lounge* the night Jane Bashara was murdered, "those types of evenings were not unusual for Bob and I to have. (But) what I became aware of, and I have a strong belief in, is that I was manipulated into that meeting to form a credible alibi … for a period of time he had to account."

Carmody described the erosion of their friendship, which lasted well into the summer of 2012: "It has to do with our relationship over a period of years that ultimately was proven to be an absolute farce," Carmody explained, his voice betraying deep disillusionment. "I pretty much came to the conclusion that when Bob's mouth was moving, only lies would come out."

Also testifying on November 20 was Steve Virgona who was seen as a key player by Juror #9, Bill Mohney. "I took him as credible because his story, his timeline and what he described, was corroborated by other testimonies. If there hadn't been other similar testimonies I would not have held him as credible."

§

Testimony on November 25 was dominated by Assistant Wayne County Medical Examiner Dr. Francisco Diaz. Aided by images projected on a screen visible only to the jury, he carefully described the horror Jane Bashara experienced in the final minutes of her life.

"The body was identified on January 25, 2012," began Diaz, "and an autopsy was performed the next day." Showcasing his nearly 25 years of experience, Diaz spoke in a slow, methodical manner. His light Latino accent added unintended drama while also hinting at his vast experience.

Jury reaction to the photos was varied, but most appeared to be stunned. "It had an impact on us for sure," Bill Mohney said later. "From an objective point of view, my thought was that it was more to keep the human element in the trial, that this person, right in front of you, lost her life."

"One of the reasons those pictures were so shocking is they showed everything," recalled Joe Fernandez. "The brain is coming out, they took the top (of the skull) off and you see the blood coagulation on the back of the brain."

Jane had sustained a large bruise, or petechiae as Dr. Diaz put it in clinical terms, about five inches in length extending from her left chin to her left ear, and a contusion on the left side of her neck. In fact, Diaz pointed out that all of her injuries were confined to an area between her shoulders and head.

Diaz described the condition of Jane's head, scalp and upper body injuries as the result of multiple blunt trauma – she had been badly beaten to the head and neck, and she had a broken windpipe. "Multiple petechiae were even more prominent to the right side of the head," continued Diaz, "some on the face and inside the eye. Something was used to create that particular pattern," he added. "Jane was probably killed by a foot."

"You could see the markings of the boot," Fernandez said later, the image still vivid in his mind.

"Were these injuries consistent with trauma on the back right side of the brain?" McCarthy asked in cross examination.

"Yes. On impact the head would bounce back and fall on the concrete," Diaz confirmed. "A stamp on the neck is very consistent with the injuries."

As Diaz laid out the grizzly details, Bashara, sitting attentively at the defense table (and not in view of the screen) began to show emotion, which was clearly in view for the entire court to see.

"I thought it was very contrived," observed Bill Mohney, pointing out that Bashara hadn't shown a shred of emotion when his kids were on the stand. But he seemed to "conveniently cry at key points, and then (snaps fingers) they were off … I thought he was faking."

Reporters in court that day, who had seen this behavior many times before, were verbally skeptical. Some suggested the tears were real but perhaps not shed for Jane at all, and more likely for himself as he began to feel the noose tightening around his own neck.

"The most significant injury is on the trachea (windpipe)," continued Diaz. "It takes 33 pounds of pressure to obstruct the trachea, and more to rupture it. When the windpipe breaks it makes a cracking sound that could be audible, but it would take a significant amount of force."

"How long does strangulation take," questioned prosecutor Robert Moran.

"It's a vascular phenomenon," replied Diaz. "It would take a few minutes. She sustained a constellation of injuries. The time for her to die is not instantaneous. A few minutes pass before she loses consciousness … and after that, ultimately, death. It might take three, four minutes."

Bashara's emotional display continued, now visibly shedding tears and blowing his nose. He made a sorry sight, and frankly, for the first time, he looked completely defeated.

"Multiple instances of pressure were applied to the neck," persisted Diaz. "The mechanism of her death was strangulation. She had the classic signs, namely bleeding into the muscles of her neck, the congestion of the face, the suffusion of the face, all the petechiae."

"Is it like drowning to catch your breath?" Moran posed.

"Yes."

Leaving a lasting impression, Dr. Diaz's testimony stretched into a second, and ultimately the final day of the prosecution's case on December 1.

"You can tell there was a struggle because of the the multiple locations of trauma, from the top of her head down to her chest," explained Diaz. "There were minimal defensive injuries, the only one she sustained was where a fingernail was torn."

The fate of Jane Bashara's clothing remained a serious question during the trial and one explanation for why they were not preserved was due to the fact that the nature of the crime was never linked to sexual assault, which normally would trigger such action.

"None of the clothing was damaged?" McCarthy asked, obviously poking a sore area.

"No. The items of clothing were removed," explained Diaz. "They were placed in a bag and released to the funeral home (alongside Jane's remains) because law enforcement did not claim them from the Medical Examiners office."

Lacking a request from law enforcement this key decision was ultimately left to family members and it is believed Jane's clothing was cremated.

The final comments in the prosecution's case, delivered by Dr. Diaz, left a lasting impression: "The mechanism of Jane Bashara's death was asphyxia, as a result of strangulation and the fractured windpipe."

§

On the morning of December 2, Michael McCarthy filed for a directed verdict concerning count six, which alleged subornation of perjury. The request stemmed from the testimony of Robert Fick ('Ponytail Bob') in which he was allegedly coerced into false testimony by Bob Bashara.

(A directed verdict allows a judge to instruct the jury to return a verdict of the judge's choosing)

Robert Moran pointed out that Bashara sought from Fick his agreement to give false testimony concerning the nature of his relationship with Gillette and coupled it with the fact that Bashara repaid a $400 debt to Fick the day he testified under investigative subpoena. Further, Fick continued to avoid the truth under oath in the preliminary hearing and admitted to that fact in trial testimony.

In defense, McCarthy claimed it was merely casual conversation and that Bashara did not direct Fick to lie under oath. In fact, said McCarthy, Bashara told Fick to tell the truth.

"It seems as though this count is stronger for the obstruction of justice than witness intimidation," observed Judge Evans. "I don't believe the testimony specifically asked him to lie under oath … and I don't believe a rational trial of fact will find so." With that she ruled in favor of McCarthy'a request, essentially eliminating the sixth charge.

§

On December 3 the defense called three of four total witnesses, the second of which was Lois Valente, former wife of Bashara's civil attorney and friend Dean. She was a close friend of Jane's and testified that several conversations with Jane revealed that she removed Bob from her financial accounts following a glut of gambling debts in 2008. She also said Jane believed he was having an affair.

Valente also testified that in 2009 Jane told her Bashara was "getting into some weird sex stuff … Bob wanted to take her to a key party and Jane said she didn't want any part of that."

A shocked Valente asked Jane how she reacted. "Jane said she told him he could go do whatever he wanted … Jane talked about divorce 10 days before she died," added Valente. "She wanted to know what it would be like to be single, dating again."

"Were you fond of Bob?" queried Diallo.

After a long, slow breath Valente responded, "No."

The third witness for the defense was Grosse Pointe Park Detective Michael Narduzzi, who was aware of the initial missing person report and present at the crime scene at Annott St. He was at 552 Middlesex during both police searches. He'd made initial contact with Joe Gentz and was present for his questioning on at least two occasions.

Narduzzi was in direct contact with the prosecutor's office from the beginning and nearly a year into the case was made Co-Officer-in-Charge. No other law enforcement officer was directly involved in so many aspects of the case, and yet, because of the circumstances, he actually maintained little control over the investigation itself.

At the time of Jane Bashara's murder Narduzzi was a 16 year veteran in Grosse Pointe Park. He'd arrived shortly after the city's last homicide and admittedly had practically no experience investigating crimes of such magnitude.

Lillian Diallo began by asking about the naming of Bob Bashara as a *Person of Interest* only two days into the investigation. She also probed Narduzzi about the mysterious J.J. McKee, the friend of Joe Gentz who's name appeared on the back of the check written to him by Bashara ('JJ' was written on the back by the owner of *Art's Party Store* to easily connect Gentz to McKee, who was better known in the neighborhood).

Referring to the day Gentz was arraigned in March 2012, Diallo asked Narduzzi if he had been looking for McKee.

"J.J. was not cooperative," Narduzzi said in a businesslike tone.

"Was he subpoenaed?"

"No, ma'am."

"Did you try to take a statement?"

"It did not end well."

"Were J.J. and Joe Gentz together on critical dates?"

"Yes. I sought him out. I went and found him and talked to him. I got a partial statement. He was very uncooperative. He was a very paranoid, nervous type and he denied all knowledge."

"J.J.'s vehicle was destroyed after the murder," Diallo more stated than asked. "Any information that J.J. was involved?"

"No. At that point in time we had no other information or any other theories that J.J. was involved."

"J.J. and Gentz were together on January 24, 2012?"

"Yes."

Diallo's questioning was rather pedestrian, covering possible missteps in the case and the seeming omission or lack of followup with McKee, upon whom the defense apparently hoped to hang much of the case's reasonable doubt.

Then head prosecutor Lisa Lindsey approached for cross examination, beginning by reviewing the initial responsibility structure of the investigation: Detective Donald Olsen of the Detroit Police Department (DPD) took the lead; Captain Loch, of the Grosse Pointe Park Police (GPPP) was the Officer in Charge (OIC) who's responsibility it was to prepare the Investigator's Report. Narduzzi's initial responsibility was doing the leg work: transporting evidence, tracking down witnesses, taking statements and dealing with Joe Gentz.

The line of questioning quickly descended into a repudiation of the work Loch had produced on the Investigator's Report, which resulted in Narduzzi being named Co-Officer-In-Charge nearly a year into the case. This action effectively realigned the responsibility to finish the more than 100 page document almost solely to Narduzzi.

Lindsey pointed out that in March of 2012 the prosecutor's office was forced to intervene and request the *Michigan State Police* to assist Grosse Pointe, for which it was criticized for not fully utilizing their services. Lindsey then pointed out that Detroit Police were still in charge of the investigation when Chief Hiller (GPP) named Bashara a *Person of Interest*.

"You were in the room with Chief Hiller and Captain Loch when that decision was made," Lindsey stated as fact.

"Yes, ma'am."

"Was there any consultation with the Detroit police before you did that?"

"No, ma'am."

"And at that point it was a joint investigation between both of your departments, correct?"

"Correct."

"You knew the Detroit police had more experience with homicides than your department did, correct?"

"Yes."

"But your department chose to make a unilateral decision without the input of the Detroit police, correct?"

"Yes, ma'am."

Lindsey then verbally listed the many jurisdictions engaged to help Grosse Pointe Park: Detroit police, *Michigan State Police*, the FBI, ATF and especially, she said, the *Wayne County Prosecutor's Office*.

"We did get great assistance from the prosecutor's office," admitted Narduzzi.

"In terms of assistance, they took over, correct? The other agencies took over and did the majority of the heavy lifting, is that correct?"

"Yes."

Lindsey then abruptly shifted gears, and no one was prepared for what came next.

"There were several occasions when I asked you specifically to do things and you flat out did not do them, is that correct?" accused Lindsey.

"Yes."

"And there were several occasions when I asked you to do things that you would go and ask a male, either investigator or a male prosecutor, why was I instructing you to do those things, is that correct?"

"This is argumentative!" Diallo interjected.
"Overruled," Evans said flatly.

"Is that correct?" demanded Lindsey.

"I don't recall specifically, but yes, I probably did ask you why we were doing a few things that I didn't understand."

"OK, and did I instruct you, would I sit down and try to explain to you, what I needed done and why, and you still did not do what I requested. Is that correct?"

"Not always, ma'am."

"Not always, but a good part of the time, correct?" Lindsey insisted, agitation building in her voice.

"Yes."

"And that is why we would continually have to go to your chief," baggered Lindsey, now becoming animated, "to try to get compliance out of you, correct?"

"I don't recall you continuously going to our chief."

"You don't recall that," Lindsey said sarcastically.

"Continuously? No."

"Well, at least more than one time," Judge Evans inquired patiently. "Did she have to go to your superior about not following what she requested you to do?"

"Yes."

"Then not only did I have to go to your superior on you," pressed Lindsey, "I had to go to the superior on Captain Loch, correct?"

"Yes."

"On more than one occasion, is that correct?"

"Yes."

"And on more than one occasion," needled Lindsey, "did I indicate to you, I know you're overwhelmed, but it's time to put on your big girl panties and do the work ..."

"Oh my! ... Judge?" gasped Diallo as she gestured toward the bench, visually expressing her embarrassment.

"Excuse me?" shouted Judge Evans. "Be quiet!"

"Did I not say that both to you and to Captain Loch?" prodded Lindsey. "Put on your big girl panties and do the work!"

"I think you said big boy pants," muttered Narduzzi, visually registering his disgust.

"OK, well at any rate, did I not tell you it was time for you guys to man up and do the work?"

"Very often you said that," admitted Narduzzi, shifting uncomfortably in the witness seat.

"Now ... in terms of me being assigned to the case," continued Lindsey, "I also had my own caseload, is that correct?"

"Well, judge ...?" pleaded Diallo.

"He don't know that!" barked Judge Evans.

"He does know," insisted Lindsey, "because he – the unfair impression is, being created on this record, that I was assigned and working on day one. I was trying cases. I was there for the consultation, but I was not – so we need to get that out. That's an unfair impression ..."

"Were you aware she had other cases?" Evans pressed Narduzzi.

"I'm not aware of what her caseload was, ma'am."

"As it relates to your time as a police officer, is it fair to say that you hadn't never [*sic*] had a female superior telling you what to do," asked Evans.

"Can I object Judge?" Diallo queried.
"No!" snapped Evans.

"No," echoed Narduzzi.

Every soul in the court was riveted, every eye locked on Narduzzi and Lindsey, every ear hung on each suspenseful word, waiting for what would happen next.

"They did one hell of a job on him," Bill Mohney (juror #9) observed later. "I sincerely felt bad for him. I thought he walked into something he wasn't prepared for."

Lindsey was finished, and reaction to the proceedings was swift. It was like a bomb went off at the Grosse Pointe Park police department, tearing open for all to see just how difficult the case had been. Press and spectators alike weren't sure what they'd witnessed, but it was clearly unusual.

> *"I was very disappointed that this department was criticized by prosecutors during a trial. To state this department was incompetent is grossly unfair. Since Jan. 24, 2012, this department had one goal and that was that those responsible for the murder of Jane Bashara be brought to justice. This was an extremely complicated and complex case for all agencies involved."*
>
> -Press Statement
> Chief David Hiller
> Grosse Pointe Park Public Safety
> December 3, 2014

§

Ten minutes before 10 on the morning of December 4, the final witness took the stand in the form of Captain David Loch of the Grosse Pointe Park police. Many observers were bracing for round two of Lindsey's inquisition, but first it was Michael McCarthy's turn.

McCarthy questioned Loch for more than an hour with questions ranging from the initial crime scene, his presence at police interviews on January 26 and 27 and the handling of Joe Gentz. Of particular interest was the working agreement between departments.

"We were working it together," Loch explained. "But certainly due to their experience and knowledge, much more than we had, they naturally took the lead."

McCarthy asked Loch if he'd been aware of Bashara's involvement with BDSM prior to the interview to which he said no. Strongly implying a rush to judgement, McCarthy pushed to the subject of naming Bashara a *Person of Interest* and specifically who'd made the decision. Loch said it was Chief Hiller.

Then McCarthy broached the subject of J.J. McKee. Loch agreed with Narduzzi's assertion that McKee showed a "very limited level of cooperation … We knew they were friends. They sometimes frequented a bar on our border with Detroit."

McCarthy then asked Loch about leaf fragments found attached to Jane's sock and others outside the Bashara garage. Looking nearly identical, investigators believed them to be proof the murder occurred in the Bashara garage. In August of 2013 Loch submitted the fragments to the botany lab at *Michigan State University* for analysis and then promptly forgot about it.

In the meantime, prosecutors prepared their case partially around the leaf evidence and questioned both Detective Olsen and Sgt. Jimenez as though it proved the crime had occurred in or around the Bashara's garage.

> "I came to the conclusion that the homicide did not take place at Annott whatsoever," Jimenez said in testimony. "Because the way she was placed, how her slippers were thrown in the vehicle, *the vegetation on her foot … There was no vegetation on that side* by the driver's (door)."

"Did it ever occur to you that the leaves at Annott St. could have been analyzed (too)," McCarthy asked Loch.

"No," said Loch. "At that point when we were at the scene on the 25th, we had no idea, or any real inclination, where the homicide might have taken place."

Loch explained that it wasn't until later that detectives began to suspect the garage on Middlesex. "There was no talk at that point that we should collect the leaves in case it happened someplace else."

Further, Loch said Bashara began exhibiting suspicious behavior following the two police interviews in January and statements made by Gentz indicated the garage was the actual scene of the crime, causing the leaf samples to be overlooked for more than a year.

Loch said that at the end of October, more than two full weeks into the trial, he called MSU to find out what happened to the fragments.

"Why did it take so long before you checked back," McCarthy asked.

"Honestly, there was so much going on in the investigation, and this is my fault," admitted Loch. "I didn't make an inquiry with them until much later."

McCarthy then asked about the test results and Loch was forced to concede there wasn't a match.

Then Loch dropped a bombshell: he said he neglected to reveal the test results to the prosecution team for another 30 days.

"You sent (the results) to the *Wayne County Prosecutor's Office* during the ... mid morning hours of November 30, this past Sunday?" McCarthy asked, sounding incredulous.

"That is correct, sir."

"And that's the first time any of those folks knew about this?"

"That is absolutely the first time, and once again, there's only one person to blame for that and it's me," said Loch. "I made a terrible mistake in not turning that over to the prosecution team in a timely manner."

Loch's blindside of the prosecution team is widely believed to be the catalyst of Lisa Lindsey's tirade the previous day. But, unknown to most, she received a stern reprimand for her drubbing of Narduzzi. Fearing possible irreparable harm, from here on out Lindsey was confined to kid gloves, even in dealing with Loch, and her cross examination was relatively short, to the point and civil.

> "I wasn't expecting that at all," recalled Bill Mohney (juror #9). "I was waiting for her to rip him like the other detective ... It didn't effect the verdict. We were surprised at how ill prepared that police department was. Inside, I actually applauded the captain. When his turn came up he said it was all on me. It gave the defense nowhere to go."

§

After a relatively short lunch break Bashara rose to his feet and raised his right hand. Observers twittered as speculation mounted over whether or not he would testify.

"Do you choose to exercise your Constitutional right to testify at this time?" enquired Judge Evans.

"To not ...," Bashara hesitated.

"Do you want to take the stand," Evans asked again.

"No your honor, I do not ... I choose not to testify."

"And you've discussed this with Mrs. Diallo as well as Mr. McCarthy, is that correct?"

"I have."

"And you understand you have a Constitutional right to take that stand. Do you understand that?"

"Yes ma'am, I do."

"But at this time you're choosing not to exercise, is that correct?"

"That's correct."

"Are you doing this of your own free will?"

"Yes ma'am." Bashara sank back into his seat, symbolizing the intent of the defense to rest its case just after 2 p.m. on December 4.

With so much attention trained on J.J. McKee and the defense's assertion he was involved in the conspiracy to kill Jane Bashara, minutes later the prosecution exercised their right to call a rebuttal witness.

ATF agent Stan Brue, who previously testified regarding cellular data activity, was recalled to the stand. He stated that J.J. McKee's cell number was not used (call or text) by any numbers associated with the investigation between August 1, 2011 and June 2012, essentially draining any likelihood of McKee's involvement in the conspiracy.

Chapter 11

Last Breath

Six days later (and nine weeks after the Bashara trial began) closing arguments commenced on the morning of December 10. Each side was allotted two hours and, as the people are saddled with the burden of proof, the prosecution went first. The team, however, elected to deliver in two parts, presenting their final words after the defense.

As she had at the trial's inception, lead prosecutor Lisa Lindsey delivered the opening salvo by stressing the nature of the crime and the fact that conspiracy was behind Jane Bashara's untimely death, conceding right off the bat that Joseph Gentz had actually been the one with his hands around Jane's neck. In that vein she painted Bob Bashara as a master manipulator, a liar who built an alternate life: he created one world and was living in another. When those worlds collided, Jane ended up dead.

Lindsey explained to the jury that lies can and should be considered evidence of circumstantial guilt, illustrating the point with a quote from former Bashara confidant Michael Carmody: "I pretty much came to the conclusion that when Bob's mouth was moving, only lies would come out."

Lindsey said the nature of Bashara's lies were both of commission and omission and his alibi was constantly in flux. In his initial account of January 24, 2012, he said he was solely at his Mack Ave. property and inside the *Hard Luck Lounge*. He shared this version with the police dispatcher, Jane's friends Debbie Breen, Roxanne Flaska and Eileen Stratelak, Detective Olsen and Capt. Loch as well as Jessica and Robert.

Later, after stories surfaced of a neighbor having seen both Bashara vehicles backing down the driveway sometime after 6 p.m., his story changed to include a late afternoon trip back to Middlesex to retrieve his keys, adding that he saw her computer bag but no Jane.

In his interviews with police Bashara failed to come clean on his affair with Rachel Gillette and the impending purchase of the home on Kensington. He said he had no idea who might have murdered Jane despite threats he'd recently reported to police; and he never mentioned Janet Leehman either.

Lindsey quoted Detective Donald Olsen, who specifically asked Bashara about his use of online social media, to which he replied that he did "none of that stuff," despite the fact that records show Bashara's *alt.com* profile was deleted that same night at 10:57.

Lindsey also noted that Bashara gave conflicting statements concerning his relationship with Joe Gentz. First he said he'd only hired him to work at the rental properties, but later admitted he'd also worked at Middlesex as well. He claimed Gentz never met Jane, but later changed his tune, insisting they'd met in the backyard when Jane served them lemonade (on another occasion he said it was iced tea). Lindsey said these conflicting statements all constituted evidence of guilt.

Describing the significance of testimony by Stan Brue and Christopher Hess concerning Bashara's phone habits, Lindsey said the excessive number of calls and the odd pattern also constituted evidence of guilt. Perhaps even more damning was the fact that he began using other people's cell phones the day after Jane's murder.

Lindsey was careful to remind the jury that in the months leading up to Jane's death Bashara made overtures to three separate individuals, Patrick Webb, Steve Tibaudo and Janet Leehman, apparently attempting to find a willing accomplice to do harm to someone. All three reported hearing a similar, eerie enquiry: "Do you know anyone who could rough up a tenant?"

"Conspiracy is nothing more than the defendant and someone else agreeing to commit the crime," Lindsey counseled, explaining the significance of testimony given by Steve Virgona and Greg Barraco illustrating Gentz's attempt to draft help in killing the wife of the not so mysterious 'Bob'.

Further outlining her case for conspiracy, Lindsey also pointed out that Bashara gave Steve Tibaudo money, "with no plan in place for how it would be carried out. That speaks to the defendant's desperation. When he is desperate, he just does stuff."

"Once I pay you money it's a fucking conspiracy *again*," Lindsey quoted Bashara, adding particular emphasis on the word 'again.' "He chose the words; there's power in words."

"For solicitation all I have to show into evidence, that in word or action, that the defendant offered, promised or gave money, services or anything of value to Joe Gentz," Lindsey said before pointing out that Bashara helped Gentz find a Grosse Pointe apartment and then paid for his utilities for several months.

"He couldn't pay his own bills on time," insisted Lindsey. "Why is he assuming financial obligation for Joe Gentz, someone he just met?"

Lindsey said Joe Gentz was easy to manipulate. "Through his own words (Bashara) indicated that Gentz is slow because he calls him a retard ... The defendant has a pattern of using people," pressed Lindsey, "and when they say something against him, he wants to attack their credibility."

Lindsey also made her case for the first degree murder charge, focusing on Bashara's comment to Patrick Webb: "Sometimes I think it would be cheaper to kill the bitch."

Further demonstrating that Gentz could not have acted alone, Lindsey stressed that without Bashara he had no motive. She also noted the similarities of Gentz's statements with Jane's injuries. (Virgona testified that Gentz said Jane was laying on the floor of the garage with her neck broken and that she had been strangled. Virgona also said Gentz feared Bashara and that he believed he'd be next).

Further ruling out the possibility of Gentz acting alone, Lindsey stressed the fact that there was no sign of forced entry, no disturbance in the home and no valuables taken; and lastly, had Gentz acted alone, there was no reason for him to move Jane's body.

In conclusion Lindsey turned to the medical examiner's report, illustrating her case by hammering home the violent nature of the attack on Jane Bashara. Her injuries indicated repeated blunt force trauma to the upper portion of her body, enough to fracture her trachea.

§

Following a break for lunch, Michael McCarthy, tasked with the lion's share of the closing duties for the defense, took the floor to present his final salvo. Beginning in a voice steeped in cynicism and suspicion, the soliloquy was long winded and he barely paused for a breath over the course of 90 minutes. "Counts one, two and three," he began, "are what this trial is all about."

As he carefully laid his foundation McCarthy hammered away at what he considered the three most critical points: First: there was a rush to judgement; that law enforcement followed only evidence leading to his client to the exclusion of all other possible leads. Second: that sex and BDSM had nothing to do with the death of Jane Bashara. (In fact, McCarthy and Diallo argued that Bashara had never entertained long term plans involving Rachel Gillette or Janet Leehman). Third: accepting that Bashara's solicitation to murder Joe Gentz was particularly damning to their case, McCarthy suggested that Bashara was motivated by revenge rather than a desire to silence him, and, although counsel did not condone it, under the circumstances it was explainable.

Illustrating the first point, McCarthy said that on "the 27th day of January, 2012, the Grosse Pointe Park police department announced that Robert Bashara … was a *Person of Interest* in the death of Jane Bashara … Since that day … there's been a cloud over the head of Robert Bashara."

"Joe Gentz killed Jane Bashara," McCarthy declared; he crushed her larynx with his boot, then accepted a plea bargain to second degree murder. This, McCarthy suggested, was reason enough to believe that going after Bashara for first degree was an unwarranted obsession of the prosecution.

"He is the target. They want him; they want him bad. They want him for first degree murder, solicitation to murder, conspiracy to murder," prattled off McCarthy. "It doesn't matter who else might pop up … we want this guy, Bob Bashara!"

Then McCarthy ticked off a sizable list of prosecution witnesses he believed should have rightfully been charged including Paul Monroe (for selling cocaine and phoning in a false tip), Robert 'Ponytail Bob' Fick (the handyman who admitted to perjury) and Daryl Bradford (Monroe's friend who also phoned in a false tip).

McCarthy lamented that Therese Giffon, Nancy Bashara and Stephanie Samuel all received immunity, but then claimed the bullets Samuel transported into Canada had never belonged to Bashara in the first place.

Then McCarthy veered his attention back to Joe Gentz: "He committed a first degree murder without question. But he ends up pleading to second degree and he's only serving a sentence of 17 to 28 years!"

Moving on to the prosecution's second theory, McCarthy dismissed outright that Bashara wanted Jane dead so he could marry Rachel Gillette. "*The Lifestyle*, this whole ... BDSM ... that is a smokescreen ... It's salacious!"

McCarthy refuted the prosecution's contention that Bashara needed Jane dead so he could close the sale on the house on Kensington. "That's preposterous!" he said, adding that there wouldn't be any money coming his way soon enough anyway.

"She's the golden goose," pleaded McCarthy. Any theory suggesting Bashara killed Jane for her 401(k) didn't make sense. "It may sound a bit crass, but the fact of the matter is ... she was the bread winner. Why would he want her dead?"

Then McCarthy pivoted to the sticky issue of the solicitation of Gentz's murder, which the prosecution painted as evidence of Bashara's intent to silence him.

"Well, that's wrong!" McCarthy said sharply. "I mean, that's a theory that that happened, but the proof is there's a good reason for Bob Bashara to want to see Joe Gentz out of the way ... he knows that Joe Gentz killed Jane Bashara – he wanted revenge!"

"There's no evidence presented throughout the entire course of this trial," McCarthy insisted, again shifting his focus, "that the death of Jane Bashara occurred in the garage of that house."

Clearly the implication was directed toward Capt. Locke's ill fated ordeal of the leaf fragments sent to *Michigan State University*. "If that report had been in the hands of the prosecutor's office on the 11th of November," argued McCarthy, "you never would have had all that evidence from Melinda Jackson (*Michigan State Police* forensic scientist) about the little drop of blood found on the garage floor with luminol, and that leafy material or vegetation found six feet apart from one another."

(This issue is every bit as controversial as McCarthy implies. The leafy material, terribly mishandled by the Grosse Pointe Park police, was portrayed in testimony as proof the murder occurred in the Bashara garage and which, in turn, elicited the luminol testing that ultimately recovered DNA particles from both Joe Gentz and Jane Bashara. However, without testimony from Gentz or any other that could place the murder inside the Bashara garage, it is unlikely the luminol evidence would have been relevant at trial).

McCarthy then abruptly breached the subject of J.J. McKee, whom the defense strongly implied was involved in the plot with Gentz and was, in McCarthy's assessment, not properly dealt with by the Grosse Pointe Park police.

"Because he wasn't cooperative they didn't talk to him any more?" McCarthy questioned sarcastically. "But they find out … the reason they go see him to begin with, is because on the night of the 24th of January, the night that Jane was abducted and killed, those two (McKee and Gentz) were seen in *My Dad's Bar* together."

McCarthy's final point was directed towards the phone and cell tower records presented by Stan Brue (ATF) and Christopher Hess (FBI). Referring to Exhibit #294, which depicts the location of cell towers named in the case, McCarthy referenced an entry on page six of Hess's report:

> *"The cell sites utilized provided service in and around both locations of interest, 552 Middlesex and the location of the Mack property that the defendant owned, the Hard Luck Lounge and Dylan's Raw Bar … The antennas transmit the same frequency, therefore no determination can be made to differentiate which cellular footprint the target telephone utilized."*

"So I submit to you," McCarthy said matter-of-factly, "that call made by Bashara at 6:26 p.m. came from behind the *Hard Luck Lounge* and not from over there on Middlesex by the house."

(The passage by Christopher Hess refers to cell tower #156, the only tower providing service to both the area surrounding the Hard Luck Lounge and the Middlesex home. However, Bashara's cell phone also made contact at this time with cell tower #994, which exclusively services the area surrounding the Middlesex home).

It was Lillian Diallo who was ultimately charged with bringing it home for the defense, and she delivered in her usual firebrand-in-the-church fashion. First, she besmirched Steve Virgona for putting "Bob Bashara's name into this whole equation."

"Their sights were set on Bob," Diallo echoed McCarthy's theme. "It helped that he had all kinds of crazy, kinky sex ... So, had he told the truth about having an affair on the 27th, he wouldn't have to sit here?"

Radically shifting gears, Diallo made note of a news story involving a New York grand jury that failed to indict a police officer who placed Eric Garner (a man selling loose cigarettes outside a strip mall) into a choke hold that directly lead to his death. He was seen on police video struggling to say "I can't breathe," which quickly become a national rallying cry against police brutality.

Diallo, never one to pass on this kind of opportunity, pounced: "We have situations going on all over this country where it tells you they know their power," she said, referring to law enforcement. "I don't know what went on with this 'cause I didn't see it ... But I know what went on with 'I can't breathe!'"

Continuing Diallo's momentum, Michael McCarthy returned to deliver the final blow for the defense, summing up the case by invoking Steve Virgona's testimony by stressing that he encouraged Gentz to mention Bashara in the hopes of gaining a plea bargain.

"Joe Gentz," McCarthy said, with a shake of his head, "very easily, could frame Bob Bashara in order to make a good deal for himself."

Saddled with thoughts of the feasibility of Joe Gentz, a man with an IQ a few clicks shy of 70, as a would-be framer, and 'I can't breathe,' with it's fully charged implication of racially motivated police malfeasance firmly in the minds of the jury, court was adjourned for the day.

The next morning, just shy of 10 a.m. Robert Moran took Lillian Diallo's evocation of the Garner case head on. "This case is about the murder of Jane Bashara in Wayne County. It has nothing to do with this case of police brutality in New York."

"An innocent person does not hire someone to kill another person," declared Moran. "An innocent person does not try to hire someone to take out a witness ... or a prosecutor, because that is consciousness of guilt ... The worlds of his were colliding," Moran insisted. "The reality of his wife and his mistress were on a collision course, because he didn't want to lose Rachel."

As for the possibility of Gentz framing Bashara? "He couldn't frame a picture," Moran lamented with a heavy dose of disgust in his voice.

"Council suggested that she (Diallo) could not breathe," labored Moran. "Ladies and gentlemen, the only one who could not breathe in this case was Jane Bashara! She could not breathe as she lay on the concrete floor, in the garage gasping for breath ... because her windpipe was severed by such force that it ripped twice, horizontally and vertically."

"While the defendant watched," Moran concluded, shaking his head, "Jane's life ebbed away for three to four minutes. She was fighting for air. She's the only one in this case who could not breathe. That's what this case is about."

§

Judge Vonda Evans is a veteran of two decades on the Third Circuit Court in Wayne County, Michigan. No small feat for one barely past her fiftieth birthday. She has said her role as a judge, and her life's mission, is that of helping others. Illustrating her viewpoint, suspended directly above her bench is Brian Forbes' print *Choices*, which depicts a handgun and a large rolled wad of cash resting atop a leather bound *Bible*.

"What I do in the courtroom, I do to cure people," Evans told *The Detroit News*. "I may have to talk to them in an unconventional way ... communicate with them on a level where they are." It's doubtful anyone who has ever set foot inside her courtroom would disagree.

The 16-person Bashara jury, selected from a pool of 150 Wayne County residents, allowed for four alternates who remained undetermined throughout the trial. But before deliberations could begin four would need to be identified and released, a process accomplished by random lottery.

"I remember everyone wishing their name to be drawn, and at the same time would've been pissed having spent that amount of time for nothing," remembered Bill Mohney, Juror #9.

Juror numbers 5, 6, 7 and 10 (two black women and two white men) were selected, thanked for their service and released. Two were visibly dismayed as they rose from the seats they'd inhabited for more than two months and slowly vacated Evans' courtroom.

"It was bittersweet," remembered Mohney. "I was jealous, happy and aggravated at the same time. Aggravated because now I'm wondering, how much longer am I going to be here?"

In her pre-deliberation instructions Evans reminded the jury to keep the charges and evidence in mind rather than personal opinions. She set them free to deliberate shortly after 2:30 p.m. on December 11, but little was accomplished the first day.

"Right off the bat we let everybody vent their thoughts and opinions," said Bill Mohney, who was elected Jury Foreman.

"We went backwards," remembered Joe Fernandez, Juror #12. "We didn't start on the number one count. We started on number five, going all the way back to count one. We knew when we read all the papers that everything linked to it."

From the start it was clear that conspiracy was the most significant issue. "If we were to find him guilty, this was the one thing everything else hinged on," recalled Mohney. "Without it you don't have first degree murder because the key point is that it was premeditated."

"If we didn't find him guilty of first degree we were asked to consider second," continued Mohney. "But it wasn't, because there was zero proof he was in the room."

Apparently a few jurors were ready to convict at the outset, but others required more time to digest the mountain of evidence. "I think we were all very much ready except for one person," Mohney observed.

"I thought the witnesses painted a pretty good picture of who Mrs. Bashara was," reflected Regis Johnson, Juror #16, recognized throughout the trial for his ready sense of humor. "She was loved and it was just unfortunate she didn't recognize she was with a sociopath."

Bashara's continually evolving alibi's drew a great deal of discussion. "First it was how she probably went out to get some weed," Mohney said, shaking his head in disbelief. "Then he tried to tie it to the other murders where the women were found in the trunks of their cars. As soon as Gentz goes to the police, it's 'Gentz has been trying to intimidate him' ... The fact that the day his wife was found murdered he had to go pay this guy $452? ... So many little things that just didn't add up."

Deliberations resumed the next day with no verdict in sight. Doubt was infectious and raised voices could be heard outside the jury room. First two, then three, then four jurors became skeptical. Frustration, stemming from a single juror's request for a legal dictionary, was brought on by her uncertainty of the meaning of the words 'vitriolic' and 'exculpatory.'

"She wasn't really trying to understand the points, she was trying to assume a lot of things that were not there," explained Fernandez. "At one point she even said, 'Oh, the prosecutors ... they created these witnesses to favor them."

"The definitions were simply delays," observed Mohney.

"At one point I got so upset with her because, we were trying to help her to understand," explained Fernandez. "She would throw up her hands and say, 'I don't understand why they're doing this to him' ... she kept blaming the prosecutors."

As the hours ticked away tensions continued to mount and tempers wore thin.

"I remember towards the end we got into a big argument about something and someone started going on about the phone records and I just went off," remembered Fernandez. "We kept saying to her, you know, the defense had their case, they could have brought up a lot more witnesses."

"We were deliberating and that's the process of it," observed Johnson. "Sometimes we might have been a little bit excited."

Another hour passed before the group requested transcripts from four witnesses: Nancy Bashara, Stephanie Samuel, Bashara tenant Courtney Johns and Janet Leehman.

"You have to rely on your collective memories," instructed Judge Evans, who had also forbidden the jury from taking notes on the grounds it might cause them to miss an important point.

(Evans also explained that the Wayne County Court did not have the resources to make transcripts available for at least a full week).

Some jurors found reliance on other's memories exceedingly difficult. "Basically, it came down to two of us who were scared to make a decision," explained Mohney. "Somewhere, they wanted to read in the transcripts that Bob said he did this, Bob said he did that. I told them you're not going to find it."

The third day of deliberation began the following week on Monday, December 15. Significant interest was trained on testimony by Steve Tibaudo, particularly the recordings where Bashara can be heard saying, 'Once I pay you, its a conspiracy *again*'.

Jurors were also overwhelmed by evidence found in the testimonies of Steve Virgona and Lorna Beth Riikonen (the woman Gentz visited at the Detroit airport just weeks before Jane's murder) that solidified the jury's belief that something was in play between Bashara and Gentz.

"She really doesn't know anybody," stressed Mohney. "Gentz just spilled his guts. In my opinion he was trying to impress her. But she didn't have ties with anybody else. She was the key witness that tied it all together for most of us, as bat shit crazy as she was."

"The testimony of Lorna Beth and Steve," agreed Johnson. "Both of them had prior experiences talking to Joseph Gentz."

Around noon another question arose needing a ruling from Judge Evans. However, Bashara's notoriously poor health forced him to hospital and he was rushed to *Detroit Receiving* for an undisclosed illness. Evans sent the jury home, deciding that Bashara needed to be present for any jury questions.

Two days later deliberations resumed and Mohney made an announcement as he made his way into the jury room: "I basically said one of three things is going to happen today: hung jury, mistrial, which was briefly a very real possibility, or we come to a verdict."

"For two and half months I was looking this guy in the eye," reflected Mohney. "Whenever he looked at me, I just kept on thinking to myself, Jesus, there's actually someone out there like this, that just seems to have no – he's sorry he was busted, period."

"I think Bob Bashara's arrogance destroyed everything he had in his life," observed Fernandez. "His thinking that he could be above and beyond whatever he could get away with … He had a good life and he just screwed it up … and the lies, lying and always lying …"

"I didn't find a direct correlation between his lifestyle and his ability to commit murder," Johnson added in hindsight. "I think what's more important is that once the picture was painted of him, he came across as a narcissistic sociopath, which had nothing to do with his sexual practices."

Shortly after 2 p.m. foreman Bill Mohney submitted a note to the bailiff indicating the jury had reached verdicts on all five counts. An hour later court was hastily reconvened and quickly began to fill beyond capacity. Notables in attendance included Jane's mother Lorraine Englebrecht, younger sister Julie Rowe and Grosse Pointe Park Police Chief David Hiller, making his first and only appearance of the trial.

Security was tighter than usual as more than a dozen sheriff's deputies filled virtually every open space of the courtroom. Bashara, clad in his familiar charcoal flannel suit, red tie and off white shirt, was escorted by four deputies through the heavy wood paneled door from the detention area and without a word took his usual seat between McCarthy and Diallo.

"Before I bring the jury out, there's a couple things I want to say," began Judge Evans. "Number one, how you doin' Mr. Bashara?

"I'm OK, thank you."

"Physically?"

"Um, fair," Bashara mumbled with a slight nod of his head.

"This has been a very long process," said Evans. "From the death of Mrs. Bashara to the charging of Mr. Bashara, to ultimately the verdict."

Acknowledging the increased throng of court watchers and interested parties, Evans made it clear there would be no sign of emotion displayed in her court. "These jurors have been taken from their families and jobs, and whatever they decide, we are to respect their decision"

Emerging in single file, the jury slowly took their usual seats for the final time.

"Will the foreperson please stand," instructed the clerk.

Slowly, Juror #9 (Bill Mohney) rose to his feet and paused for further instructions before reading aloud the jury's decision on count one:

"Guilty of Conspiracy to Commit Homicide, Murder First Degree Premeditated," Mohney said, showing no emotion.

With a smirk Bashara dropped his head, slowly shaking it side to side as the sound of camera shutters permeated the room.

"As to Count Two?"

"Guilty of Solicitation of a Homicide Murder," Mohney responded; and so it went for the remaining three counts. With each one Bashara repeated the same pathetic display: a smirk and a head shake. He was guilty on all five counts.

"The jurors that were excused," observed Evans, expressing her gratitude to the jury, "I've never had an opportunity to see people who were upset because they couldn't be a part of this process."

Looking exceedingly weary, Bashara rubbed his eyes with the back of his hand, then shook his head before he methodically began rocking back and fourth in his chair, a paragon of utter disbelief.

Evans declared that sentencing would occur on January 15 before unceremoniously exiting the bench. Both defense attorneys broke in opposite directions, neither making the slightest gesture towards their client. Totally stunned and utterly friendless, Robert Bashara was slow to his feet, then turned toward the detention area door and surrendered himself to deputies.

Call him *Big Bob*, *The Mayor of Middlesex* or *Master Bob*; at this moment he was alone and destined to spend a lifetime behind bars.

§

The security line of people waiting to enter the 36th District Court was long on the morning of January 15, 2015, a crisp and cold day in Detroit. Sentencing options were few as Judge Evans' court convened for the final time in the matter of

Robert Bashara. Two of the convictions carry mandatory life imprisonment, presumably rendering the hearing to a mere formality. However, as nothing in this case proved routine, this day would be no different.

Several familiar faces appeared in the gallery, particularly Loraine Englebrecht, Julie Rowe, Steve Tibaudo and Steve Virgona.

Bashara made his customary entrance, dressed in the same charcoal flannel suit, but today he was sporting a fresh, prison length haircut. The well established and sometimes odd friendly banter with Judge Evans was noticeably absent as she greeted him with a simple, "Good morning Mr. Bashara ... Have you had an opportunity to read the pre-sentence report?"

"Your honor, I've not had the opportunity to fully read it," stammered Bashara. "It's my understanding per court rule that I have 48 hours to do so." Then he explained how he'd asked Michael McCarthy to request a court-authorized 24 hour extension but McCarthy, insisting it wouldn't make a difference, declined.

Explaining that Bashara had been brought down late the previous night from the detention facility, Lillian Diallo said there was no opportunity to make a copy available to him. "The first he's had of this pre-sentence report was this morning, so I do apologize," said Diallo, motioning toward the judge.

In response, Evans granted Bashara 60 minutes, but first Bashara asked to present prepared statements, without assistance from his lawyers, which was met with an uneasy murmur within the courtroom.

Ascending the podium as if he owned it, Bashara announced his intention to present two legal motions, but then explained that he'd been transferred back to the *Oaks Facility* within a week of his verdict and, despite making frequent attempts to contact McCarthy and Diallo, he'd failed due to limited funds or the lack of easy access to a phone.

Bashara said he asked McCarthy to file a two to three week extension so he could review the report and go over two motions on which he wanted assistance. Bashara claimed that McCarthy refused to file for the extension, saying simply that he'd be sentenced January 15. He also refused to help prepare the motions, claiming they were not relevant to the case.

Bashara's two motions were clearly intended to lay the groundwork for an appeal:

First, he wanted to preserve the official court record, specifically 'off the record' items and he requested that the court reconsider the ruling to exclude Gentz.

"He is the only one who has accused me of any involvement in my Jane's death," whined Bashara. He also pointed out that interviews and testimony from three witnesses, Virgona, Riikonen and Barraco (all friends of Gentz's) had used his words, which he believed to be hearsay, and that his counsel never had the opportunity to cross examine Gentz.

"It's unfair and prejudicial," insisted Bashara, demonstrating the vocabulary he'd acquired reading law books at the *Oak's* inmate library.

Second, Bashara said that media coverage had "unfairly compromised my right to a fair trial ... Live streaming, I feel, compromised that," Bashara said. It "most certainly affected the mindset of both witnesses and jurors."

Bashara added that live-streaming allowed witnesses to follow the testimony of others as well as comments made outside the presence of the jury. "My mother, God bless her heart, is a prime example," he said. "She indicated on the stand that she was following along the live streaming."

As a matter of fact, Bashara was misinformed. Judge Evans ordered that only opening and closing statements could be live streamed. However, live-blogging was done by at least three media outlets.

(*In testimony Nancy Bashara admitted to following the Internet blog of Fox 2's Amy Lange when she took the stand November 19*).

Third, Bashara claimed the jury was prejudiced, that most in the pool admitted belief in his guilt based on opinions they'd heard through the media, a charge vehemently refuted by foreman Bill Mohney.

Then Bashara filed an emergency motion claiming ineffective assistance of counsel, suggesting they had failed "to call witnesses I wanted called, questions I felt should have been asked, places and people for our investigators to focus on, documents and evidence to be entered into defense."

Bashara finished by saying he'd originally wanted a change of venue but was told "it would never happen." There also was the matter of an eight page community service history (in the possession of his attorneys) that he believed should have been added to the record.

"I pray that this court renders a reversal of this judgement and a mistrial," he argued as chatter began to rise in the room.

"There's no reason to grant a mistrial," decided Judge Evans, closing the door on the issue. "As to the other issues, I am going to allow them."

§

The purpose of victim impact statements is to ensure that the full repercussions of a crime are considered before sentencing, however, it seems unlikely any such effort would further what had already been covered by the trial. Still, it serves the dual purpose of closure and Julie Rowe, Jane's youngest sister, and her mother, Loraine Englebrecht, were on hand for that purpose.

"My family appreciates the monumental effort that was put forth by the court," Rowe began in a steady, almost emotional free voice. "We recognize that not every family of a murder victim receives the justice and closure that we have."

Rowe illuminated the many hardships her sister's death, lengthy investigation and trial inflicted on her family. Over the course of the three year ordeal her father, John Englebrecht, succumbed to the effects of Alzheimer's disease and the rest of the family was unable to escape tremendous emotional distress.

"Given that the crimes addressed today carry a sentence of life in prison without parol," continued Rowe, "we are especially grateful for this opportunity to speak."

"Jane would have done just about anything for Bob," Rowe continued, "except open up her 401(k); and it is this reluctance to allow him access to her life savings that ultimately led Bob to kill her ... Bob lied to all of us. Bob manipulated all of us. Bob utterly betrayed all of us."

"I miss Jane terribly, every day," began Loraine Englebrecht. "There will never, ever be closure for what he did to my daughter. Every day of my life I ask why didn't he just go and live his scummy dungeon life and leave my daughter and grandchildren alone."

"You took Jane's life," she continued, eyes trained directly on Bashara, "but I want you to live a while, because I'm not going to be here that long. But for every day I live, I want to think about you rotting in jail, and someday burning in hell."

Visibly shaken, Bashara returned to the podium and again addressed the court: "I had nothing to do with my wife's death," he insisted, adding that witnesses had lied and misstated the truth, "painting a different picture than what was true." Then he motioned directly toward Lorraine Englebrecht:

"To my mother in law …"

"Forget it!" Englebrecht spat in disgust.

"… And to all her family, who have known me for 30 years …"

Bashara launched into a seven minute tirade in which he denied killing or having any involvement in the death of his wife no less than eight times, repeatedly declaring his love for her and their children. He occasionally exhibited emotion but convinced no one.

Bashara then set his sights on the media and prosecution, admonishing them for soiling his good name and going so far as to evoke the biblical legacy of Job, to which a collective gasp of disbelief could be heard throughout the court.

"They have turned everyone away from me," Bashara pleaded. "I will admit clearly that I am nowhere as blameless as Job was before the Lord. I have done things in my life that I look back and I'm not a hundred precent proud of … I loved my Jane dearly, and have done absolutely nothing to harm her. I did not murder her. I did not conspire with anyone, especially Mr. Gentz, nor did I solicit him for this crime."

Finishing with a plea for mercy, Bashara declared he'd never stop fighting for justice and the truth, "until my hands are raw, blood comes from my eyes and I take my last breath … I will appeal this until I can appeal no more!"

But in a scathing rebuke, Judge Evans, breaking permanently from her daily niceties with Bashara, spared him no quarter, referring to him as a product of privilege, coddled by a mother who, "loved you, but she didn't know how to train you to be a man."

"There were no boundaries and no expectations," Evans lectured. "No one was off limits to you. Your mother, your family, your friends, your children and your loving wife. You are a modern day trojan horse."

"Jane ... was mentally and emotionally destroyed by you a long time ago!" declared Evans. "Not only did you orchestrate and participate in taking her life, you tried to destroy her soul long before she was murdered."

"You promised a mentally challenged man, Joe Gentz, a car and money to murder your wife. You exploited his desire to have his child, and you manipulated him to kill your wife ... I have no mercy for you!"

"Today there will be justice for Jane," Evans vented as she handed down her sentence: mandatory life for counts one and three plus an additional 21 to 55 years for counts two, four and five.

"Take him out!" Evans barked, "take him out!"

Chapter 12

A Twist of Fate

In predictable southeast Michigan fashion, spring emerged at a snail's pace, enabling the uncommonly thick surface ice covering nearby Lake St. Clair and the Detroit River to last well into April. Similar was the sense of resolution, moving past the catharsis of murder and a seemingly endless investigation, trial and conviction. But there was a glimmer of hope: *Jane's Walk*, a replica of a 13th Century French labyrinth from *Chartres Cathedral*, was dedicated as a tribute to the life of Jane Englebrecht Bashara on the grounds of *St. Michael's Church* in Grosse Pointe Woods. Built and maintained by private donation, it was conceived as a place to reflect and pray. (Jane's remains also eventually found their way to *St. Michael's* and now rest a stone's throw from the labyrinth outside the church).

Soon after Bob Bashara's sentencing on January 15, 2015, Steve Virgona, friend and occasional confidant of Joe Gentz, and Steve Tibaudo, the used appliance supplier who wore the wire that ultimately ensnared Bashara, began insinuating there was much more behind Jane's murder.

The two men conjured similar tales of dirty cops, hitmen, mafia ties and multiple accomplices. But Tibaudo pushed further, pointing to the involvement of Secret Service Agent Mark O'Reardon (who administered the polygraph test to Bashara) as evidence of a huge government conspiracy.

One theory has it that plumber/handyman Thomas Ramsey, deceased since 2013 from an apparent drug overdose, may have been involved. Both Virgona and Tibaudo at one point even fingered each other as a possible accomplice. They both entertained, although with less conviction, the possible involvement of J.J. McKee, the man seen with Gentz at *My Dad's Bar* shortly after the murder. To date none of these allegations have resulted in a shred of evidence.

For possibly the first time in his life Bob Bashara stayed true to his word. Following the March 5 appointment of Livonia-based (MI) appellate attorney Ronald Ambrose to his case, Bashara filed an appeal on March 19. As it turned out Mr. Ambrose actually filed a motion for new a trial, and a formal request was filed on August 10 on the grounds that, among other things, Bashara had fallen victim of inefficient counsel.

Hearings began on September 15 with Ambrose taking aim at Bashara's defense team, first suggesting they failed to file a *Brady Motion* (which alleges that information and evidence was not made available to the defense).

"There are witnesses Mr. Bashara wanted to be called," Ambrose argued in front of Judge Vonda Evans – reprising her role from Bashara's murder trial. "The evidence he wanted to be presented was not … It was all a character assassination. That's all it was."

Sounding suspiciously like a Monday morning quarterback, Ambrose also implied that Michael McCarthy and Lillian Diallo failed to fully vet potential character witnesses due to the fact that the defense's state funded investigators, Joseph Bruce and Henry Glaspie, were not fully compensated and therefore did not completely execute their duties.

(In fact, Bruce and Glaspie had their sights trained on J.J. McKee, who was too elusive for them to locate. Ambrose also stated, suspiciously, that McKee's automobile had been scrapped within days of Jane's murder, a possible fact that remains unsubstantiated).

Ambrose suggested the jury pool was tainted, that jurors were questioned in front of each other and that several had said they were already convinced of Bashara's guilt. He also pointed out that defense attorney's were not given access to jury questions in advance. For these reasons, claimed Ambrose, Bashara wanted a change of venue.

Ambrose also noted that the defense team failed to disclose potential health issues of Jane Bashara's that rendered an intimate relationship physically impossible, thereby bringing Bashara's extra marital affairs into context and that their agreement, that he could do whatever he wanted so long as he did not embarrass the family, was reasonable.

Changing course, Ambrose then focused on Joe Gentz, whom he characterized as having a violent history. Quoting Gentz as saying he 'hated women,' Ambrose said that Bashara's right to confront his accuser was violated when the prosecution failed to compel him to testify, a key component of Gentz's plea deal.

Then Ambrose targeted two details from Gentz's story; first, that the gun introduced into evidence was a revolver, when the one he said Gentz described was an automatic. Second, that Gentz said he entered Bashara's home at 7 p.m. the night of Jane's murder, a time accounted for in Bashara's alibi as he was at the *Hard Luck Lounge* with Michael Carmody (Bashara's friend from the *Rotary* club).

Lastly, Ambrose said Bashara wanted to testify in his own defense even though he clearly declined when asked by Judge Evans on the final day of his trial.

§

Before the new hearings could proceed Bashara was obligated to waive attorney client privilege, thereby releasing Lillian Diallo and Michael McCarthy from confidentiality restrictions. McCarthy took the witness stand first, his face displaying a heavy dose of consternation. Nearly a year had passed since the trial began and here he was, still in court dealing with Bob Bashara.

"I felt he was going to get as fair a trial as he could get," McCarthy said, concerning the possible change of venue … "They've got *Dateline* in Menominee County. I think they have televisions, I think they have newspapers," ticked off McCarthy.

"It got nationwide publicity all along," McCarthy continued, noting that a power outage during the trial was discussed on the *MSNBC* program *Morning Joe*. "When it's national publicity, where are you gonna go?"

As for Jane Bashara's health issues? "I didn't want to drag the good name of Jane Bashara through the mud by revealing some irrelevant, personal, intimate details about what might have been some sort of illness she had," labored McCarthy.

Placing Bashara on the stand was never seriously considered, and according to McCarthy, Bashara himself never expressed a desire to do so. "I don't think he would've been a good witness," McCarthy continued. "He had enough problems there that were better left alone without having him testify."

Consistent with McCarthy's demeanor, Lillian Diallo appeared as feisty as ever. "Mr. Bashara was a very active participant in his defense," she began. "Mr. Bashara did what Mr. Bashara wanted to do. If Mr. Bashara didn't want something, he had a mouth and he knew how to use it."

Diallo also stated, in no uncertain terms, that Bashara never discussed the possibility of a new venue: "Mr. Bashara didn't want to be anywhere other than in front of Judge Vonda Evans in Wayne County Circuit Court," she said matter-of-factly, adding that Bashara told her how he, "loved being there and how fairly he was being treated."

"Mr. Bashara – no offense – thinks he's the smartest person in the room – on the planet," Diallo continued, making particular note that Bashara is not an attorney. "He cannot dictate to me how something legally should go ... I was not going to be made a slave of Bob Bashara ... and I wasn't going to be pushed around by Bob Bashara!"

As for any notion that BDSM had anything to do with the case Diallo stated: "Jane Bashara was choked, strangled and brutally murdered ... Why would I waste perfectly good time finding out who wants to spank who?"

§

Over the course of six further hearings testimony was given by private investigators Henry Glaspie and Joseph Bruce, former Grosse Pointe Park Police Chief David Hiller (who had recently retired) and finally Bob Bashara himself, which necessitated the return of Assistant Prosecuting Attorney Lisa Lindsey for cross examination.

Bashara was on the witness stand for a period spanning six days over which Ronald Ambrose feebly built a case alleging that he was named a *Person of Interest* due to a personal vendetta with Grosse Pointe Park Police Chief Hiller.

"Mr. Bashara was under the impression that Chief Hiller had some sort of grudge against him," admitted McCarthy, in reference to why Hiller was not called by the defense.

"Chief Hiller was not a person we would want on the witness stand," argued McCarthy, "because that would have opened up a can of worms that had to do with an allegation brought against Mr. Bashara a number of years before that had to do with him molesting the child of one of his sisters-in-law."

"And that was unfounded, correct?" Ambrose poked.

"Well, I just know that he wasn't prosecuted," McCarthy said evenhandedly. "But I also believe that it wouldn't help the defense in the least bit to have that ... accusation brought up again in open court, in front of the jurors that had to decide whether he was involved in this murder. So absolutely not, we didn't want Chief Hiller there."

McCarthy pushed still further on the subject, indicating that the pre-sentence report in the murder case included a 'cryptic reference' made by Jane's sister, Janet Englebrecht Gottsleben: "She stated that she wished she had followed through with the prosecution at that time," recalled McCarthy, "as it would have saved her sister's life."

"Getting into character with Mr. Bashara was a very dangerous proposition," pressed McCarthy. "One of the reasons is I didn't want to open the door and have some of this business about these unsavory things, like the child molestation coming out. I didn't think character would be that good, so I didn't want to bring in character witnesses."

"He didn't get convicted because I didn't go down that road," McCarthy persisted. "I believe we got plenty of good character (testimony) into the record in spite of the fact that we had all of this seedy BDSM" (testimony).

§

Late in the afternoon of January 20, 2016, nearly four years to the day since Jane Bashara was murdered, *WDIV*, Detroit's *NBC* affiliate, reported that Ronald Ambrose dropped a bombshell: in a signed affidavit, Joseph Gentz had changed his story and now claimed he'd acted alone. Ambrose pounced and attached it to his motion for a new trial.

The revelation was further elevated by the allegation that Grosse Pointe Park police and particularly the recently departed Chief David Hiller and an unknown Sgt. Reducio (assumed to be Detective Michael Narduzzi) had coerced Gentz to perjure himself because "we have been after that motherfucker for a long time."

The affidavit, riddled with contradictions and unsubstantiated statements, is dated December 2, 2015 and was prepared by an inmate named Carlo Vartinelli, an experienced paralegal who is currently serving a life sentence for rape. Ambrose was apparently touched by Vartinelli's own hard luck story, which he characterized as 'tragic in itself'.

In the revised rendition, Gentz stated:

> "I knew Mr. Bashara was not in his house. So, I broke into his home, walked into the garage and Mrs. Jane Bashara caught me and I lost control."

> "I helped myself into Robert Bashara's home around 7:00 p.m., because I knew he generally is not home at that time. I got into the garage and began searching for something of equal or more value than the money Mr. Robert Bashara owed me.

> Mrs. Jane Bashara walked into the garage and asked me what was I doing in her home. I panicked, walked towards her and put my hands around her neck and she began struggling with me. I held her with one hand, picked [sic] an object and hit her on the head. She lost consciousness, I though [sic] she was faking so I placed both of my hands around her neck and squeezed her neck until she no longer moved.

> I then placed her body inside the rear of a black Mercedes Benz, drove to Detroit near Annoit [sic] (sort of an Alley) and left the car there with Mrs. Jane Bashara's body in the back."

Gentz went on to claim that on January 30, 2012, when he first consented to a police interview, he told police he was "mad at Mr. Robert Bashara because he refused to pay me for the two-jobs [sic] I performed," i.e. a painting project and a broken pipe in the Bashara's backyard.

"My testimonial statements against Mr. Roberth [*sic*] Bashara," the affidavit read, "was the product of coercion and subordination of perjury" by Grosse Pointe police officers. Gentz further contended that during the interview, "officers stated their bosses promised to help me out to get a lesser sentence if I cooperated with them by agreeing to their version of what happened, which is not the truth".

Officers then allegedly released Gentz to allow him to deal with personal business with the understanding that he would return. Gentz did, in fact, surrender himself in the wee hours of February 1, 2012, having been persuaded to do so by pastor Dan Fritch and Steve Virgona.

In the affidavit Gentz also claimed that during the course of three days he spent with Grosse Pointe Park police in February 2012, he was "drilled" by Chief Hiller and Sgt. 'Reducio', "about what I should testify against Mr. Bashara … At one point I asked them why when in fact I, and I alone did it."

"We're going to help you," the affidavit quoted Chief Hiller, "and you will get a lesser sentence if you help us get Robert Bashara."

Gentz went on to write that he asked both Chief Hiller and Sgt. 'Reducio' what the sentence would be and he again quoted Hiller: "I have spoken to the prosecutor and I can promised [*sic*] you a five (5) year sentence."

As for Carlo Vartinelli, Gentz wrote that for months he had requested his assistance in producing the affidavit and had been repeatedly rebuffed. "I could no longer live knowing that Mr. Robert Bashara was completely innocent," Gentz continued, adding that Bashara, "was not even in his house when I killed his wife."

The phrasing of Gentz's affidavit is eerily evocative of correspondence attributed to Bashara and echoed by Ronald Ambrose. As there is no obvious benefit for either Gentz or Vartinelli to push the issue, their actions beg the question: what was in it for them?

Perhaps the most obvious explanation is that somehow Bashara got to Gentz in prison and either threatened or offered him something of value to tempt him into revising his rendition of the murder. Or, possibly more likely, contact was made between Bashara and Vartinelli?

The revised Gentz version is remarkably similar to post conviction arguments made by Ambrose, but not so much to anything Bashara said nor was it used in his defense. Most importantly, nothing of the new rendition negates the multitude of evidence that got Bashara convicted in the first place.

Reason to be skeptical begins with Gentz's assertion that he broke into the Bashara home on January 24, 2012. However, that night Grosse Pointe Park police officer Terry Hayes searched the Bashara property inside and out for signs of forced entry and found none.

Gentz claimed in the affidavit that he was searching for 'something of equal value' to compensate for unpaid debts, but this notion is compromised by the fact that he apparently stole nothing; not a thing from the house, the items of value strewn across the front seat of Jane's *Mercedes*, nor even the *Mercedes* itself.

If Gentz killed Jane Bashara in a fit of panic, why did he calmly place her in the backseat of her car, locate the keys and drive her lifeless body eight miles to Annott St. where she was discovered? Why move the body at all? Two days later Bashara gave Gentz at least $452 dollars in a check, and evidence suggests an undisclosed amount of cash. Why would Gentz even be talking to Bashara if he had murdered his wife on his own?

§

Throughout the process to gain a new trial, Ronald Ambrose suggested that certain points of fact were omitted or ignored in Bashara's murder trial:

The gun issue: What type of gun did Bashara allegedly point at Gentz, automatic or revolver? Ambrose repeatedly refers to it as an automatic while the gun recovered in Bashara's safety deposit box was a revolver. But until Ambrose brought this matter to light no one ever questioned it was anything but a revolver, including Bashara's defense team.

The timing issue: Did Joe Gentz arrive at the Bashara home at 6 or 7 p.m.? In a recorded interview with former DPD detective Tom Berry in 2012, Gentz said Bashara called and told him to be at his home at 7 p.m. sharp. But forensic records show Jane Bashara's *Blackberry* in transit, exiting Grosse Pointe Park at 6:28 p.m. and thereafter successively connecting to cell towers located further north into Detroit.

Surveillance video recovered from the *McDonald's* located at 7 Mile Rd. and Gratiot shows Gentz entering at 7:47 p.m. Considering the distance between Annott St. and Middlesex (eight miles with a drive time of 20 minutes) and from Annott St. to the intersection of Gratiot and 7 Mile Rd. (one and a half miles with a walking time of about 30 minutes), the evidence strongly points to the simple likelihood that Gentz was mistaken and the timing was indeed 6 p.m.

There are a few notable errors of fact in the Gentz affidavit as well: Gentz's birth name is listed as John Joseph Gentz (his correct name is Joseph John Gentz). His birthdate is given as January 12, 1964 but incorrectly states his age at the time of the murder as 49. Jane Bashara's residence is listed as 552 Middlesex in Grosse Pointe Farms rather than Grosse Pointe Park.

Put in the simplest of terms, the only way to get to the bottom was to call Joseph Gentz to the witness stand, something he had thus far steadfastly rejected.

§

Suspense pulsated throughout the court when Joe Gentz indicated his desire to testify on April 12, 2016. Anticipation and anxiety intensified as he was led through the heavy wooden doors between the chamber and detention area. Escorted by two deputies, Gentz was wearing a bright yellow jumpsuit, in sharp contrast to Bashara's now familiar green drab.

Gentz was led behind the judge's bench in an effort to keep the conspirators separated before he took a spot standing next to his new attorney, John Holler. Raising his right hand Gentz swore to tell the truth before taking a seat next to the jury box, which was filled to capacity with reporters.

> "As you know, there is an affidavit in the public domain," Holler began. "He (Gentz) wishes to testify and be cross examined about how he was treated and how his testimony was shaped towards Mr. Bashara, to implicate Mr. Bashara, and how he was threatened and coaxed in the Grosse Pointe Park police station and perhaps what could be characterized as a continuation of that same type of influence in the Wayne County Prosecutor's Office. He will not testify regarding the death of Jane Bashara."

"So, contrary to what the affidavit alleges," challenged Judge Evans, "that he had gone to the location while believing Mr. Bashara was not there and rifled through the garage, and then he killed Mrs. Bashara ... He's not testifying to any of that? ... Is that what you want to do Mr. Gentz?"

"Yes, ma'am."

"Case law," Lisa Lindsey snapped as she leaped to her feet, "says you can't take the Fifth on some aspects and not on others ..."

"If you're going to testify," agreed Evans, redirecting her attention toward Gentz, "you're going to testify to everything you indicated in the affidavit ... You opened the door by making that affidavit. Now, what do you want to do? Would you like for me to give you a recess so you can make a determination? It's all or nothing."

"Yes, ma'am."

§

Following a recess of about 90 minutes over the noontime hour, Joe Gentz again stood before Judge Evans, ready to testify despite her best efforts to dissuade him. "You know it will subject you to the penalties of up to life if they reinstate this charge against you?"

"I understand that."

"And despite that fact, you want to take the stand?"

"That is correct," muttered Gentz.

Evans then ticked though a litany of possible consequences should Gentz testify, stressing each point, making certain he clearly understood. The original charge of First Degree Murder could be reinstated and/or he could be charged with perjury, both of which could carry a sentence of life imprisonment.

"I understand that," Gentz said again.

Judge Evans doubled her effort to protect Gentz from himself, questioning him over and over again, "are you sure you want to testify?" Exasperated, she finally accepted failure.

"Raise your right hand," she said with a slow shake of her head. "Do you solemnly swear affirmed testimony you're about to give in this matter is the truth, the whole truth, nothing but the truth so help you God?"

"Yes."

Almost immediately Evans put a halt to the proceedings citing the importance of Gentz's attorney, John Holler, to view video evidence deemed pertinent to Gentz's testimony that he apparently had not seen in the relatively short time he'd represented Gentz, which was limited to post conviction matters. Evans then quickly adjourned the hearings until April 21.

(The video is of Gentz being questioned during an investigative subpoena held in the prosecutor's office in December of 2012).

§

Hearings reconvened on April 21 and Evans began by again stressing the consequences facing Gentz should he testify, focusing particularly on the likelihood that a First Degree Murder charge would be reinstated and that he'd also face the new charge of Perjury, both of which could result in lifetime incarceration.

"There are two things that can happen," Evans warned Gentz. "After I view all of the testimony, I can do one of two things. I can grant a new trial for Mr. Bashara or I can deny it … If I grant it, he will get a new trial, but at the same time you still will be subjected to being sentenced up to natural life, just based on the words out of your mouth … This time there are no guarantees, I have no control over what the prosecutor's office can do. Do you understand that?"

"That's correct," said Gentz.

"And despite that, you still want to take the stand?"

"Yes ma'am."

After requesting attorneys to approach, Evans said she'd just received statements made by Gentz regarding phone conversations he'd had with his brother Steven, who happened to be present. So Evans sent the Gentz brothers and Holler into chambers before Gentz would be allowed to make his final decision. When they emerged Gentz was again asked if he wished to testify.

"You understand that if you take the stand you can be questioned on everything. Do you understand me?" Gentz gestured in the affirmative before Evans again swore him in. Not a soul in the courtroom knew what to expect next.

"Do you know of a person by the name of Carlo Vartinelli?" Ambrose began.

"I know of him, yes," replied Gentz.

"Did you ask Mr. Vartinelli to do anything for you?"

"No."

"Did you ask him to prepare any type of document for you?"

"No."

"Did you sign any document?"

"Eee-yah." Gentz's voice was trepidicious.

"Did you take that document to a notary?"

"Eee-yah, but — Yes."

"How long before you took it to the notary? Did you have it in your possession?"

"Didn't have it very long, maybe two minutes at the most."

"You made some statements in here that the police had contacted you initially with regard to the murder of Jane Bashara?"

Approaching the witness, Ambrose handed Gentz the affidavit and said: "Who prepared that document?"

"What, this?" Gentz said skeptically. "This is garbage."

"Oh wait, hold on!" scrambled Judge Evans. "Why do you say that's garbage?"

"Because this," Gentz said, thrusting the affidavit above his shoulder, "I didn't do it. All I did was give him my transcript."

"Now wait a minute, let's just hold on." Evans was incredulous. "What do you mean your transcript?"

Gentz explained that he gave Vartinelli his Pre-sentence Investigation report (PSI) and didn't know what he did with it.

"All I know is I signed this," added Gentz. "Didn't read it, didn't do nothing, and I handed it back to him."

"You didn't read it?" Evans half stated.

"Nope," Gentz said flippantly.

"Do you read good?"

"Yeah, I know how to read."

"Read it!" ordered the judge.

(Italics signify content quoted directly from the affidavit as read by Gentz. Non italics signify his immediate reaction).

Seemingly eager to comply, Gentz began reading the affidavit aloud with obvious difficulty, *"I, John Joseph Gentz ...* which is wrong!" Then Gentz abruptly paused, seemingly finished with his task.

"That's it? That's all it says," challenged Evans.

"No, there's more," Gentz whined in a voice sounding much like a grade school boy. "You want me to read the whole thing?"

"Yes!" demanded Evans, "the whole thing."

Gentz continued, reading aloud: "*I was mad at Mr. Bashara* ... I was not mad at Mr. Bashara ... You want me to read this? This whole thing is a lie!"

"What else is a lie, that you just read?" Evans asked.

"Well, the whole thing is wrong ... Jane Bashara was there, so was Bob ... *He refused to pay me for two jobs I performed* ... which is a lie. I fixed a pipe." Gentz's face was pleading as he turned toward the judge adding, "which – I couldn't fix it. It's a lie."

"*So, I broke into his house* ... which is a lie."

"You didn't break into his house?" Evans questioned, sounding annoyed.

"No, ma'am."

Lisa Lindsey made a note for the record that Gentz was not reading the words verbatim to which Gentz said: "OK, see? I told you I don't read that good ... I promised to help –".

"You [*sic*] gonna read it, and you gonna read it correctly," demanded Evans in an even voice, "and you're gonna read it out loud."

"I can't read it, I don't know all the words right," pleaded Gentz, again sounding like a stressed adolescent.

"Then say 'big word skip'," Evans instructed.

"OK. Big word skip," repeated Gentz.

"Now read it from the top."

Gentz proceeded to do as he was told, reading everything verbatim to the best of his ability. "*The truth concerning the case of Robert Bashara* ... which is false, that's a lie."

"*During the second interview I confessed to the officers that I was mad at Mr. Bashara* ... which is a lie ... *because he refused to pay me for two jobs I performed* ... *I knew Mr. Bashara was not in his house* ... which is a lie."

"*So I broke into his home, walked into the garage and Mrs. Jane Bashara caught me and I lost control* ... No, that's a lie."

"*During the interview the officers stated that their bosses promised to help me out to get a lesser sentence if I cooperate with them and agree to their vision of what happened* ... which was not the truth."

"*Chief David Hiller and Sgt. 'Redizzio' drilled me for three days, coaching me about what I should testify against Mr. Bashara, and at one point I asked them why when I, and I alone did it* ... no, I did not do it alone."

"*Chief Hiller stated: 'We're going to help you and you are going to get a lesser sentence* ... no, that's a lie. I mean they promised me stuff but ... *if you help us get Robert Bashara. Sgt. 'Dizzio' then stated: 'We want him, not you'* ... which is true, that's what they told me," he added in a slight whisper.

"*I asked them both what sentence and Chief Hiller stated: I spoke to the prosecutor and cannot promise you five years* ... *The prosecutor was aware and agreed with them. It was then that I agreed to perjure myself* ... I don't think so."

"*I again asked Sgt. Reducio why they wanted Robert Bashara and he stated: 'We have been after that mother F-er, blank blank for a long time* ... "But I don't know how true that is. I got no clue ..."

"*On January 24, 2012, I helped myself into Robert Bashara's home* ... which isn't true – which is a lie ... *Around 7 p.m.* ... that's a lie ... *because I knew he generally is not home at that time* ... which is a lie."

"*I got in the garage and I began searching for something of equal or more value* ... which is a lie."

"*Mrs. Jane Bashara walked into the garage* ... which – that's the truth. Bob was there ... *And asked me what I was doing in her home* ... "Ah, man, this whole thing is a lie," Gentz lamented, gesturing to the judge.

"I said read it!" Evans said forcefully.

"I am reading ... *walked towards her and put my hands around her neck and she began struggling with me. I had her with one hand and picked [sic] an object and hit her on the head* ... No, that's a lie ... *She lost consciousness* ...

which is a lie ... *I placed both of my hands around her neck and squeezed her neck until she no longer moved.* That's a lie."

"*I then placed her body inside the rear* ... which is a – well, I helped ... *left the car with Jane Bashara's body in the back* ... which is true. I did do that."

"*That my testimony states* [sic] *against Mr. Robert Bashara was the* ... I don't know that word (product of coercion) ... I don't know that word (subordination of) ... and I don't know that word ... *perjury by Sgt. Dizzio and Chief David Hiller.*

"Why did you sign this affidavit?" Ambrose ventured. "What made you sign this piece of paper?"

After a pause of several seconds Gentz stammered: "I'm mad."

"Why are you mad, Mr. Gentz," queried the judge.

"Number one: I was promised my safety. My safety was number one. I got assaulted four times, I got a busted hand."

"I had people putting stuff underneath my mattress, like a shank. What is my life worth?" griped Gentz, missing the irony.

"I've been called a rat," continued Gentz. "OK, what do they do with rats in prison? They kill you!"

"Why did you sign the document?" insisted Evans.

"I was mad," Gentz said again, "that's the reason."

"Well," reacted Ambrose, searching for the correct words, "the affidavit, well ... I'm not sure why, you went to any ... you asked Carlo Vartinelli ..."

Gentz explained that Carlo Vartinelli had repeatedly come to him asking for his PSI. Gentz said he had no idea what Vartinelli was getting out of it, but once he was assaulted he handed it over without question. Then Gentz shifted gears and discussed the morning of January 30, 2012, the day Detective Narduzzi knocked on his door on Wayburn before they both ended up at the station.

"We did a little interview and I walked out," Gentz said with a subtle shrug of his shoulders.

Once he left police custody that morning, Gentz said he went to stay with his friend Steve Virgona. Later that night he spilled the beans, "because they (Virgona and Daniel Fritch) are pastors. Figured I tell them what happened and they said the best thing I could do was turn myself in."

"It was about two o'clock in the morning," explained Gentz, adding that he confessed his involvement in Jane Bashara's murder.

"They had me there for four days ... They interviewed me, they took a swab, I gave them my DNA ... I was afraid for my life, if you want to know the truth ... I asked for an attorney, for four days straight ... and they didn't read me my Miranda rights ... I told them exactly what happened, I gave them everything."

"You were promised some things?" prodded Ambrose.

"At the end I was," Gentz replied before getting to the heart of the matter: "It was in the garage with Jane Bashara and Bob. After he pulled the gun and told me to kill her, he said, 'I'll give you the ring and I'll give you $8,000 and a *Cadillac*."

"Who is he?" demanded Evans.

"Bob Bashara!"

"In the garage he is saying, 'I'll give you $8,000, a ring ...'" recounted Ambrose as if ticking off items from a grocery list.

"Well, they were arguing! I mean if you want to go ... into what they were arguing ..."

"Who is they?" stressed Evans.

"Bob Bashara and Jane Bashara!"

"What were they saying?"

"Jane Bashara told Bob to get all his shit out of the garage. His signs, his golf clubs, it went to *Lochmoor*. That's what she said, she wants this shit out of – 'Bob, I want your shit out, and get it out now!'"

"I went over to move boxes," insisted Gentz. "Next thing I know he pulls a gun on me and says 'shut her up'. They were arguing still, and he says 'do it now'. So I broke her neck, yes, I, to be honest, I did do that. But meanwhile, after she was dead he walks over, her top was open, he goes over to her and he says 'I'm sorry baby. I didn't mean it' … and pulls her top back down."

Ambrose, acting as though he was blindsided by the revelation, vainly struggled to put the toothpaste back in the tube: "How long was Robert Bashara there?" he demanded.

"He was there the whole time!" Gentz spat defensively.

"So, what time did you get there?" Ambrose poked suspiciously.

"Six."

"In your interview with police you said seven, right?"

"No! Wrong! That was the wrong time. That was something else … He was there at 6 o'clock," Gentz said excitedly, "'cause he let me in the damn door!"

"Alright, so he had been there at 6 o'clock," repeated Ambrose. "He let you in, and what you're saying is he's in the garage with Jane Bashara, is that right?"

"He was there with Jane Bashara and me, yes."

"Now, you're going over there to move boxes you said?"

> "Yeah. He threatened me. I had to be there at 6 o'clock. He goes, 'I want you at my house at six exactly. I was there. He let me in … Jane Bashara was in the kitchen with Bob … He let me in the side door … There's only one way into the garage besides the garage door, but the garage door is shut … He lets me in a patio type deal, I mean it's a foyer or whatever you want to call it. I walked in, he points to the garage and he says, 'OK, I'll be right back, I gotta go get her' … He comes back with her, that's when they got in the argument … She says, 'I want you to move all these boxes.' She was just showing me certain things on the shelf and everything that was around; and then they were arguing some more about the signs."

"Signs? What are you taking about, signs?" demanded Evans.

"Some kind of … I don't know, union sign. Some kind of blue, white sign, it looks like a wheel … It was like in the front of the vehicle, and …"

"What did the sign look like?"

"It was white. It was blue. It had the white around it and it had blue and it had writing on it … It was like a wheel, like a ship wheel, that's what I can describe it as."

"With the court's indulgence," interjected Lisa Lindsey, who'd been waiting patiently for the opportunity, "we have a photograph for the court to see."

"I'd like to see that," both Evans and Gentz said in unison.

An image of the interior of the Bashara's garage, taken January 27, 2012, was projected on the screen. In the lower left corner, among a mass of various boxes, golf bags and whatnot, the image revealed a sign with 'Rotary' clearly visible.

"That's the sign she wanted out of there, and her golf clubs and some other stuff," Gentz said excitedly, adding "them boxes sitting right there too."

Gentz pointed directly to the lower left corner of the image while whispering and general chatter broke the silence in the court.

"Are you sure that's the sign you're taking about?" Evans questioned Gentz.

"Yes, ma'am."

"Your testimony is that Jane Bashara – I see the golf clubs there," stumbled Ambrose, trying to mask the discombobulation in his voice, "and who is the – next to the 'Rotary' sign is some golf clubs, is that correct?"

"That's correct," Gentz said eagerly, adding there were more golf bags that Jane wanted cleared out.

"Did Jane just want the golf clubs to go to *Lochmoor* or everything to go to *Lochmoor?*" asked Ambrose, grasping at straws.

"She wanted the golf clubs to go to *Lochmoor*, and she wanted the boxes to go to some kind of storage unit or place where he stores stuff."

"So what happened after that," continued Ambrose, "they get into an argument?"

"They got into an argument, yes, and I was in the middle. He pulls a gun on me and says 'shut her up.'"

"What kind of gun?" queried Ambrose, finally getting to his next talking point.

"How should I know what kind of gun?" Gentz shot back. "It doesn't matter! My life was the matter!"

"So he's holding the gun up to you and then what happened?" continued Ambrose.

"He pulls it. I mean, what do you want … he was standing behind the vehicle. I couldn't go nowhere."

"What kind of vehicle?" asked Evans, fishing for the obvious.

"It was a *Mercedes Benz*," Gentz insisted, getting excited again. "It was in the garage. The garage door was shut. It was only three of us in the garage, except for God!"

"And at that point," said Ambrose, "he's stating that he's going to – that Robert Bashara is going to pay you $8,000?"

"No, after she was dead. We loaded (her) in the back seat … He had the head of her and I had the feet … she was bleeding. There was blood on the garage floor … she had black slacks on too, and he had a brown jacket on, he had brown shoes. I could tell you everything … I had a brown leather jacket. I had a black pair of pants – I think I had a hoodie."

"Who is we?" asked Evans.

"Me and Bob!" stressed Gentz, showing increasingly more emotion in his voice. Recalling further details of the fateful night, Gentz said Jane was wearing a coat and slippers. After they loaded her into the vehicle, he said Bashara went back into the house and returned with Jane's purse.

"He took all the contents and everything, her wallet, and starts throwing stuff about, just threw it in the vehicle. He emptied out the purse. I mean, he just throws her credit cards and everything all over the place. Her cellphone and everything. I mean, I can tell you where the cellphone was, it was on the floorboard of the vehicle."

"Front or back?" asked Evans.

"It was in the front."

"Driver's seat or passenger seat?"

"Passenger ... Then he threatened me," Gentz said matter-of-factly. "Then he goes, 'if you ever say anything I will kill you and you will be followed,' which I was."

"And then what happened?" said Evans, shifting in her seat. "When did you leave?"

"After he shuts the door he walks out ... he got in his *Lincoln Navigator* and he goes, 'you get a ring, you get $10,000 and you get a *Cadillac.*'"

"And then he left in the *Navigator*?" probed Evans.

"Yes, ma'am ... (He) opens up the garage door and then when I was pulling out there was a silver car following me and I lost it on Jefferson ... I took some side streets and I lost it."

Gentz then methodically laid out the rest of his story, the short drive north to the alley behind Annott St. where he unceremoniously left the lifeless Jane Bashara, crumpled on the floor in the back seat of her *Mercedes*, abandoned in this long forsaken ghetto of Detroit 'like a piece of common trash.'

(Although minor details of dates, times and the amount of money promised occasionally fluctuated, according to police and Steve Virgona, the basic tenets of Joseph Gentz's unlikely tale never wavered far from the account given in court, under oath on April 21 and May 24, 2016. Powered particularly by this testimony, Judge Evans denied Bashara's appeal for a new trial on July 15, 2016).

After four and a half years, a genuine media circus, dozens of attorneys and law enforcement officers, nine weeks at trial, 72 witnesses and a protracted post trial process, there was, at long last, justice for Jane. Bob Bashara, the self-proclaimed *Mayor of Middlesex*, found himself ensnared in his own web of deceit, outmaneuvered by the one he dismissed an idiot: Joseph Gentz, the halfwit who outwitted the infamous *Master Bob Bashara*.

Appendix I: Name Index

Achatz, Russell: Gentz employer, *Achatz Burgers*, St. Clair Shores
Ambrose, Ronald: Bashara appellate attorney
Babcock, David: Detroit Police evidence tech
Baracco, Gregory: Gentz friend
Bashara, Jane: victim, wife, mother of two.
Bashara, Jessica: daughter of Jane and Bob Bashara
Bashara, Nancy: Mother of Bob Bashara
Bashara, Robert Jr.: son of Jane and Bob Bashara
Bashara, Robert Sr. (Bob): *Master Bob, The Mayor of Middlesex*, defendant
Bradford, Daryl: friend of Paul Monroe, called in false tip
Breen, Deborah (Debbie): friend of Jane Bashara
Briggs, Lori: Detroit Police CSI
Brue, Stan: ATF Cell phone records
Brusstar, John: First attorney retained by Bob Bashara
Calcaterra, Donald: *Town Mortgage*
Calloway, Laura: Grosse Pointe *St. Vincent dePaul*
Carmody, Michael: *Grosse Pointe Rotary*, Bashara friend
Diallo, Lillian: Bashara defense attorney
Diaz, Dr. Francisco: Wayne County Medical Examiner
East, Jodi: Grosse Pointe Park Police dispatcher
Elder, Doraid: Gillette attorney
Ellington, Larry: Oaks Facility cellmate of Bashara
Englebrecht, Lorraine: mother of Jane Bashara
Ennis, Sandra: friend to Jane Bashara/*DTE* employee
Evans, Vonda: judge
Fahner, Edward: *Steve's Furniture*
Falcinelli, Richard: BDSM enthusiast, Bashara Power of Attorney, *Midnight Rider*
Fernandez, Joe: juror
Fick, Robert ("Ponytail Bob"): *Lakeside Apartments* tenant/handyman
Fitzhugh, Eugene: Detroit Police CSI
Flaska, Roxanne, friend of Jane Bashara
Forton, Rebecca: Wayburn landlord to Joseph Gentz
Fritch, Daniel: friend of Gentz and Virgona, pastor, helped Gentz surrender to police
Gabel, Charles: *Lochmoor Country Club/Grosse Pointe Rotary*
Giffon, Therese: Bashara submissive, former Chicago police officer, *Across the Lake*
Gifford, J.D.: Bashara Private Investigator, formerly FBI
Gillett, Rachel: Bashara submissive/girlfriend, *Bella, B's Bella*
Gentz, Joseph: Bashara handyman
Godard, Robert: Lochmoor, BDSM enthusiast
Gottsleben (Englebrecht), Janet: Jane Bashara's sister
Gottsleben, Mark: Janet Englebrecht's husband, brother-in-law to Bob Bashara
Griem, David: Bashara attorney
Hays, Terry: Grosse Pointe Park police
Hess, Christopher: FBI phone analysis
Hiller, David: Grosse Pointe Park police chief
Hoshaw, James: Grosse Pointe Park police
Jackson, Melinda: Michigan State Police forensics
Jimenez, Moises: Detroit Police homicide detective
Johns, Courtney: Cadieux tenant of Bob Bashara
Johnson, Regis: juror
Jolly, Joy: former wife of Jim Wilson, Bashara family friend

Keller, Missy: tenant at Bashara's Mack property
Lee, McKenzie "Ralph": handyman, *Lakeside Apartments* tenant
Leehman, Janet: Bashara submissive/girlfriend form Oregon, *Slave J*
Leone, Frank: tow truck driver
Lindsey, Lisa: Lead Wayne County Prosecutor
Loch, David: Grosse Pointe Park police captain
Matthews, Patricia: closest friend to Jane Bashara
McCarthy, Michael: Bashara defense attorney
McCuish, Jim: onetime Bashara business partner
McKee, J.J.: known acquaintance of Joseph Gentz, together night of January 24, 2012.
McQueen, William: *St. Michael's Episcopal Church*
Mohney, Bill: juror
Monroe, Paul: *Lakeside Apartments* tenant/cocaine dealer
Moran, Robert: co prosecuting attorney
Moray, Mary: *Eastern Market* shop owner
Muccioli, Loraine: *Johnstone and Johnstone* realtor
Narduzzi, Michael: Grosse Pointe Park police detective
Natale, Frances: friend of Joseph Gentz
Olsen, Donald: Detroit Police homicide detective
O'Reardon, Mark: US Secret Service, polygraph
Porter, Venita: Bashara submissive
Powell, Twana: Michigan State Police, gun retrieval
Ramsey, Thomas: Bashara handyman/plumber
Riikonen, Lorna Beth: Joseph Gentz acquaintance
Rowe (Englebrecht), Julie: youngest sister to Jane Bashara
Samona, Paul, *Art's Liquor* owner
Samuel, Gwendolyn: Aunt to Bob Bashara
Samuel, Stephanie Elaine: first cousin to Bob Bashara
Sample, Kristy: bartender at the *Hard Luck Lounge*
Schatz, William: *Lakeside Apartments* tenant
Sirdenis, George: friend to Bashara family
Stratelak, Eileen: friend of Jane Bashara
Sullivan, Lance: Detroit Police video analyst
Tibaudo, Steve: *Steve's Furniture*/FBI Wire
Towar, Kimbriel: *Grosse Pointe Rotary*/*'the little blue book'* publisher
Valhall: *The Hinky Meter* publisher/editor/writer
Valente, Dean: Grosse Pointe attorney/friend of Bashara's
Valente, Lois: wife of Dean, Bashara friend
Vartinelli, Carlo: reputed author of Gentz January 2016 affidavit.
Virgona, Steve: friend and confidante of Joseph Gentz
Webb, Patrick: BDSM, *Sir Patrick*
Wilson, James: Lochmoor friend of Bashara
Wolf, Lawrence: BDSM enthusiast
Young, Andrea: Michigan State Police Bio Unit
Young, Kathy: Johnstone and Johnstone realtor

Appendix II: Timeline

2012

-Jan. 24: **-6:20 p.m.:** Jane Bashara Murdered.
-7-8 p.m.: Bashara seen at *Hard Luck Lounge* with Michael Carmody.
-8 p.m. Bob Bashara returns home.
-9 p.m. Bashara calls friends/family, reports Jane missing.
-10:36 pm.: First Bashara call to police.
-11 p.m. Police make first visit to 552 Middlesex.
-4:30 a.m.: Jane Bashara officially reported missing.

-Jan. 25: **7:30 a.m.:** Jane Bashara found murdered.
-9:30 a.m.: Bob Bashara notified of wife's death.
-7 p.m. Candlelight vigil at Grosse Pointe South High School.

-Jan. 26: Police interview #1
-Jane Bashara autopsy.

-Jan. 27: Interview #2 (polygraph)
-Bashara receives voicemail from Joe Gentz, reveals to family.
-Search warrant #1 at 552 Middlesex.
-Grosse Pointe Park Police name Bob Bashara *Person of Interest*.
-John Brusstar retained as defense attorney.

-Jan. 28: Brusstar/Bashara draft letter.
-Rachel Gillette breaks ties with Bashara.

-Jan. 29: Letter delivered to police by Brusstar.

-Jan. 30: Gentz brought in for questioning.

-Jan. 31: **2:30 a.m.** Gentz surrenders to police, confesses murder of Jane Bashara.
-10:30 a.m. Funeral
-4:30 p.m. Attorney David Griem arrives at 552 Middlesex.

-Feb. 1: **Noon:** Bashara seen leaving home with Mike Carmody.
-Bob Bashara gives front lawn press statement.

-Feb. 3: **1 p.m.** Gentz released from custody.

-Feb. 4: WDIV's (NBC) Marc Santia interviews Bob, Laura and Nancy Bashara.

-Feb. 5: Santia interview airs on WDIV.

-Feb. 6: Joe Gentz assigned public defender.

-Feb. 8: Search warrant #2 at 552 Middlesex.
-*Good Morning America* interview taped (with Bob and Jessica Bashara).

-Feb. 9: *Good Morning America* interview airs.
-*Hinky Meter* publisher ValHall interviewed on Detroit radio.

-March 2: Joe Gentz arrested at Macomb County Court.

-March 5: Joe Gentz charged with First Degree Murder.

-**March 6**: Police search Rachel Gillette's Grosse Pointe apartment.

-**April 26**: Rachel Gillette receives Personal Protection Order against Bashara.

-**May 4**: Joe Gentz preliminary exam scheduled for June.

-**May 11**: *Dateline NBC* Airs *"Secrets in the Suburbs"*.

-**June 25**: Bob Bashara arrested.

-**June 27**: Bashara charged with Solicitation to Commit Murder.

-**July 9**: Joe Gentz found competent to stand trial.

-**Oct. 11**: Bob Bashara pleads guilty to Solicitation to Commit Murder.

-**Dec. 10**: Bob Bashara sentenced to 80 months to twenty years in prison.

-**Dec. 21**: Joe Gentz pleads guilty to Second Degree Murder.

2013

-**Feb. 19**: Joe Gentz sentenced to 17-28 years for murder of Jane Bashara.

-**April 17**: Bob Bashara charged with open murder.

-**Sept. 9-13**: Preliminary hearings in Bashara murder case.

2014

-**Oct. 14, 2014**: Bashara murder trial begins.

-**Dec. 11**: Jury deliberates.

-**Dec. 18**: Verdict: Bashara guilty.

2015

-**Jan. 15**: Bob Bashara sentenced to life in prison.

-**March 5**: Ronald Ambrose appointed Bashara appellate attorney.

-**August 10**: Bob Bashara files appeal for retrial.

-**Sept. 15, 16**: Retrial preliminary hearings #1-2.

-**Oct. 14-16, 19**: Retrial preliminary hearings #3-6.

-**Nov. 13**: Retrial preliminary hearing #7.

2016

-**April 12, 21**: Retrial preliminary hearings #8-9.

-**May 24**: Retrial preliminary hearing #10

-**July 15**: Retrial preliminary hearing #11: Verdict.